NAIVE SEMANTICS FOR NATURAL
LANGUAGE UNDERSTANDING

**THE KLUWER INTERNATIONAL SERIES IN
ENGINEERING AND COMPUTER SCIENCE**

NATURAL LANGUAGE PROCESSING
AND MACHINE TRANSLATION

Consulting Editor

Jaime Carbonell

Other books in the series:

EFFICIENT PARSING FOR NATURAL LANGUAGE: A FAST
ALGORITHM FOR PRACTICAL SYSTEMS,
Masaru Tomita, ISBN 0-89838-202-5

A NATURAL LANGUAGE INTERFACE FOR COMPUTER
AIDED DESIGN,
Tariq Samad, ISBN 0-89838-222-X

INTEGRATED NATURAL LANGUAGE DIALOGUE:
A COMPUTATIONAL MODEL,
Robert E. Frederking, ISBN 0-89838-255-6

NAIVE SEMANTICS FOR NATURAL LANGUAGE UNDERSTANDING

by

Kathleen Dahlgren

IBM Corporation, Los Angeles Scientific Center

KLUWER ACADEMIC PUBLISHERS
Boston/Dordrecht/London

Distributors for North America:
Kluwer Academic Publishers
101 Philip Drive
Assinippi Park
Norwell, Massachusetts 02061, USA

Distributors for the UK and Ireland:
Kluwer Academic Publishers
Falcon House, Queen Square
Lancaster LA1 1RN, UNITED KINGDOM

Distributors for all other countries:
Kluwer Academic Publishers
Distribution Centre
Post Office Box 322
3300 AH Dordrecht, THE NETHERLANDS

Library of Congress Cataloging-in-Publication Data

Dahlgren, Kathleen, 1942-
  Naive semantics for natural language understanding / by Kathleen
Dahlgren.
    p. cm. — (Kluwer international series in engineering and
computer science ; SEC 58. Natural language processing and machine
translation)
    Bibliography: p.
    Includes index.
    ISBN 0-89838-287-4
    1. Semantics—Data processing.   2. Natural language processing
(Computer science)   3. Computational linguistics.   4. Discourse
analysis—Data processing.   I. Title.   II. Series: Kluwer
international series in engineering and computer science ; SEC 58.
III. Series: Kluwer international series in engineering and computer
science. Natural language processing and machine translation.
P325.5.D38D34   1988
410'.28'563   dc19   88-21559
                                                   CIP

Printed in the United States of America

CONTENTS

Part I. Naive Semantics   1

1. Naive Semantics   3
1.1. Using Naive Semantics to Interpret "The Programmer"   7
1.2. Compositional Semantics   10
1.3. The Classical Theory of Word Meaning   12
1.4. Word Meanings as Concepts   18
1.5. Other Decompositional Approaches   18
1.6. Computational Approaches to Word Meaning   23
1.7. Naive Semantics   28
1.8. Basis of Naive Semantics in Cognitive Psychology   29
1.9. Comparison of NS with Computational Models   36
1.10. Limitations of NS   39
1.11. Organization of the Book   43

2. Noun Representation   45
2.1. The Ontological Schema   45
2.2. Mathematical Properties of the Ontology   46
2.3. Ontological Categories   49
2.4. Nominal Terminal Nodes   52
2.5. Construction of the Ontology   55
2.6. Other Ontologies   56
2.7. Generic Knowledge   58
2.8. Word Senses   60
2.9. Feature Types   61
2.10. Conclusion   62

3. Kinds, Kind Terms and Cognitive Categories   65
3.1. The Realist Basis of NS and Kind Terms   65
3.2. Kind Types   69
3.3. Kind Types as Metasorts   75
3.4. Another Approach   76
3.5. Summary   77

4. Verb Representation 79
4.1. Ontological Representation 79
4.2. Placing Verbs in the Main Ontology 80
4.3. Sub-Classification of the TEMPORAL/
RELATIONAL Node. 82
4.4. The Vendler Verb Classification 83
4.5. Psycholinguistic Categories 90
4.6. Cross-Classification 93
4.7. Parallel Ontologies 94
4.8. Non-Categorial Features 95
4.9. Generic Representation 95
4.10. Feature Types Associated with Relational Terms 98
4.11. Conclusion 101

5. The Functioning of the Kind Types System 105
5.1. Complete and Incomplete Knowledge 107
5.2. Queries to the System 109
Inspecting the Textual Database. 109
Inspecting the Ontology. 110
Inspecting the Generic Database. 111
Inspecting Feature Types. 113
5.3. Anaphors 117
5.4. PP Attachment 118
5.5. Word Sense Disambiguation 118
5.6. Discourse Reasoning 119
5.7. Kind Types Reasoning 120
5.8. Summary of Inference Mechanism 121

6. Prepositional Phrase Disambiguation 123
6.1. Semantically Implausible Syntactic Ambiguities 123
6.2. Using Commonsense Knowledge to Disambiguate 125
6.3. Commonsense Knowledge used in the Preference Strat-
egy 128
Ontological Class of Object of the Preposition. 128
Ontological Class of The Direct Object. 129
Ontological Class of Verb. 129
Generic Information. 130
Syntax. 131

6.4. Success Rate of the Preference Strategy 132
6.5. Implementation 133
6.6. Other Approaches 135
6.7. Conclusion 138

7. Word Sense Disambiguation 141
7.1. Approaches to Word Sense Disambiguation 141
7.2. Local Combined Ambiguity Reduction 142
7.3. Test of Hypothesis 144
7.4. Noun Disambiguation 144
    Fixed and Frequent Phrases. 145
    Syntactic Tests. 146
    Commonsense Knowledge. 147
7.5. Verb Sense Disambiguation 151
    Frequent Phrases in Verb Disambiguation. 153
    Syntactic Tests in Verb Disambiguation. 153
    Commonsense in Verb Disambiguation. 154
7.6. Interaction of Ambiguous Verb and Noun 155
7.7. Feasibility of the Method 156
7.8. Syntactic and Lexical Ambiguity 157
7.9. Intersentential Reasoning 157
7.10. Disambiguation Rules 158
7.11. Efficiency and Timing 164
7.12. Problems for the Method 166
7.13. Other Approaches 167
7.14. Conclusion 169

8. Discourse Coherence 171
8.1. Background 171
    Coherence Relations. 172
    Discourse Segments. 174
    Genre-Relativity of Discourse Structure. 175
    The Commentary Genre. 177
    Compendium of Discourse Relations. 178
8.2. Modularity and Discourse 184
    Modelling the Recipient. 184
    Discourse Events. 185
    Coherence as Compositional Semantics? 188

viii

Coherence as Naive Inference. 191
Discourse Cues. 192
Parallelism. 193
Facts Explained by the Parallel, Modular Model. 194
8.3. Syntactic and Semantic Tests for Discourse Relations . 199
Main Clause. 200
Not Nominalized. 200
Active voice. 203
Tense and Aspect. 203
Transitivity Test. 203
Weak Predictions of Coherence Relations. 205
8.4. Parallelism in Coherence Exemplified 218
Using Commonsense Knowledge to Segment Discourse. 222
Empirical Study of Discourse Hierarchy. 226
8.5. Other Models 226
8.6. Conclusion 230

REFERENCES 233

Preface

This book introduces a theory, Naive Semantics (NS), a theory of the knowledge underlying natural language understanding. The basic assumption of NS is that knowing what a word means is not very different from knowing anything else, so that there is no difference in **form** of cognitive representation between lexical semantics and encyclopedic knowledge. NS represents word meanings as commonsense knowledge, and builds no special representation language (other than elements of first-order logic). The idea of teaching computers commonsense knowledge originated with McCarthy and Hayes (1969), and has been extended by a number of researchers (Hobbs and Moore, 1985, Lenat et al, 1986). Commonsense knowledge is a set of naive beliefs, at times vague and inaccurate, about the way the world is structured. Traditionally, word meanings have been viewed as criterial, as giving truth conditions for membership in the classes words name. The theory of NS, in identifying word meanings with commonsense knowledge, sees word meanings as typical descriptions of classes of objects, rather than as criterial descriptions. Therefore, reasoning with NS representations is probabilistic rather than monotonic.

This book is divided into two parts. Part I elaborates the theory of Naive Semantics. Chapter 1 illustrates and justifies the theory. Chapter 2 details the representation of nouns in the theory, and Chapter 4 the verbs, originally published as "Commonsense Reasoning with Verbs" (McDowell and Dahlgren, 1987). Chapter 3 describes *kind types*, which are naive constraints on noun representations. Part II describes the contributions of NS to computational text understanding. Chapter 5 describes the implementation of the theory in a computational text understanding system, Kind Types (KT), first described in Dahlgren and McDowell (1986a). The remaining chapters demonstrate the usefulness of NS representations in taking steps toward solving several outstanding problems in computational linguistics. Chapter 6 describes disambiguation of prepositional phrases using NS representations. This chapter was originally published as "Using Commonsense Knowledge to Disambiguate Prepositional Phrase Modifiers" by Dahlgren and McDowell, 1986b. Chapter 7 provides an algorithm for word sense disambiguation. The work was originally reported in "Using Commonsense Knowledge to Disambiguate Word Senses" (Dahlgren, 1988a). Chapter 8 proposes a model of discourse interpretation in which all modules of grammar, including naive inference, have access to each other in the process of generating a coherent picture of the meaning of a text. The proposal integrates NS with Discourse Representation Theory (Kamp, 1981, Heim, 1982, Asher, 1987). We suggest a method for extracting coherence relations using naive inference along with syntactic and semantic information.

Joyce McDowell is a co-originator of much of the work described in this book. I would like to thank Nicholas Asher, William Banks, John Bateman, Ezra Black, Tyler Burge, Joseph Emonds, Arthur Graesser, James Hurford, Leah Light, Ronald Macaulay, Eric Wehrli, Michael McCord, James Moore, Edward Stabler, Jr., Barbara Partee and anonymous reviewers for their invaluable comments and discussions of the this research. Susan Hirsh, Susan Mordechay, and Carol Lord have contributed to both the theory and the construction of the Kind Types system. The management of the IBM Los Angeles Scientific Center has been most supportive, particularly Juan Rivero, John Kepler and James Jordan. Finally, there could not have been a book without the unusual patience of my family during the course of its creation.

PART I. NAIVE SEMANTICS

1. NAIVE SEMANTICS

The reader of a text actively constructs a mental picture of the objects and events mentioned in it. The construction process uses prior knowledge and generalization about similar objects and events. In reading through "The Programmer" (below), the recipient may picture an office environment, computing machines, men in white dress shirts, and so on.

The Programmer

(1)   John is a programmer who works for a large corporation.

(2)   John entered his manager's office.

(3)   He was sitting at his desk.

(4)   John asked for a raise.

(5)   He wanted to buy a home computer for his child with the money.

(6)   John and his manager reviewed his accomplishments.

Just these few words call up a small but rich naive theory of the world, the theory associated with business, the social roles and relations within it, the field of computer programming, family relations, and so on. This stereotypical theory is shared by a significant number of people in a subculture (Cohen, 1976).

The recipient of such a text must draw upon this rich naive theory of the objects and events in it just to be able to interpret and disambiguate the text itself. The reader makes a number of inferences when reading "The Programmer" in order to understand it. First of all there are syntactic inferences which derive from non-syntactic knowledge. In sentence 5, readers infer that *for his child* modifies the verb phrase (VP). Given syntactic information alone, it could have modified the sentence as does the PP headed by *on* in (7), or the object of the verb as does the PP headed by *with* in (8).

(7)   He wanted to buy a home computer on pay day.

(8)   He wanted to buy a home computer with a printer.

Semantic inferences find the antecedents for the anaphors. In sentence 2, *his* has only one possible antecedent, given agreement, and that is *John*. In sentence 3, however, *he* could have either *John* or *manager* as its antecedent. Readers infer *manager* because they believe the person sitting at the desk in an office is usually its owner, and the previous text said that the manager owned the office. In sentence 5, *he* has the same potential antecedents as in 3. Despite a heuristic which favors the continued assignment of the same pronoun to the same antecedent in a segment of text, readers infer that in this case the antecedent switches to *John* because of an inference connecting the raise to buying a computer.

Other semantic inferences select from word senses. The noun *office* in the second sentence has 5 readings. The "place" sense of *office* is selected by the reader because the reader believes that entering involves places. Another semantic inference chooses between the collective and distributive readings for the noun phrase *John and his manager*. The collective interpretation posits one reviewing event in which both John and the manager participate. The distributive interpretation posits two reviewing events in which one or the other of them is the sole participant. In this text, the collective reading is selected because of knowledge that in the situation established by the previous sentences, a discussion is likely to have taken place.

On a higher level, the interpretation of the relations among the sentences of the text, of its coherence, requires a number of inferences. Readers infer that John went to his manager's office in order to get a raise, and that he wanted a raise because he wanted to buy a computer. In order to make these inferences, readers must know that *enter* is goal-oriented, and that the next goal-oriented event in the text is probably related to it. They must know that programmers work for a salary, and that managers give raises in salaries, so that there is an implicit indirect object *his manager* in the fourth sentence. They must know that what enables a person to buy something is having enough money to buy it, so that the cause of asking for the raise was the desire to buy the computer.

Table 1.1 Cognitive and Computer Models of Naive Inference	
Cognitive Model	**Computer Model**
John is a programmer, therefore	programmer(john) $\rightarrow$
typically John works for a salary,	$T(e_1$ work(john) & for(e_1,X) & salary(X) &
has a boss,	has(john,Y) & boss(Y) &
works for a large organization,	for(e_1,Z) & organization(Z) & large(Z) &
programs a computer.	e_2 program(john,W) & computer(W)).

The example above illustrates the pervasive use of commonsense knowledge in text interpretation. In order to interpret a text, even at the syntactic level, the recipient draws upon information not directly expressed in the text. And the recipient must engage in an active process of construction of an interpretation of the text (Bransford and Johnson, 1972, Sanford and Garrod, 1971), enabling the reader to choose from among the many possible interpretations the one most likely to have been intended by the speaker (Johnson-Laird, 1983). The theory of text understanding which we will explore in this book is that the reader constructs a cognitive picture of the text, based upon the reader's own naive theory (partially learned in his/her subculture, partially his/her own generalization from experience) of what a programmer is (a theory of "programmerhood"), what buying is, and so on, and tentatively infers much more than what the text says. Our approach to knowledge representation for text understanding follows the common-sense knowledge tradition in artificial intelligence (Hayes 1985, Hobbs and Moore, 1985, Hobbs et al, 1985, Hobbs et al, 1986, Haugeland, 1986).

Table 1.2 Cognitive and Computer Models of Naive Inference	
Cognitive Model	**Computer Model**
John buys a computer,therefore	(event(e_1 buy(john,X) & computer(X)) $\rightarrow$
typically John wants a computer,	T(want(john,X) &
has enough money for one,	has(john,Y) & money(Y) & enough(Y) &
he buys it in a store from someone,	in(e_1,Z) & store(Z) & from(e_1,R) &
later he uses it,	event(e_2 use(john,X)) &
after he buys it, he owns it, and the seller doesn't,	state(s_1 own(john,X)) & state(s_2,not(own(R,X))) &
and both John and the seller are sentients.	sentient(john) & sentient(R)).

The naive theory of "programmerhood" is not a scientific theory, but a set of related beliefs that form a construct which is employed in understanding natural language and doing other forms of reasoning, such as planning. Salter (Salter, 1983) has found that naive theories of economics are significantly related to dominant ideologies, suggesting that naive theories are not totally half-baked, but rather, that there is a continuum from solid scientific findings, through hypotheses to naive theories, with superstition on the opposite extreme. The theory of text understanding to be proposed here, Naive Semantics (NS) is designed to model the average reader's naive theory, some of which is illustrated in Table 1.1. The verbal elements of the naive theory are represented as predicates and the theory itself is represented as the implications that if John is a programmer, typically John works for a salary, for someone in a large organization, is intelligent, writes computer programs, and so on. In Table 1.2 the naive implications of verbs are illustrated with *buy*. These implications include not only the transfer of money and ownership of an object (semantic elements which appear in every theorist's representation), but also that John is enabled to do so by having money, that John intends to use what he buys, that he typically buys it in a store, and so on. The elements in both examples were drawn from psycholinguistic experiments in the prototype theory, the source of our data on naive theories (Rosch et al, 1976, Dahlgren, 1985a, Graesser and Clark, 1985a).

1.1. Using Naive Semantics to Interpret "The Programmer"

NS representations such as those above are powerful enough to drive the inferences drawn by readers of "The Programmer." The relevance of NS representations to each of these inferences will be outlined at this point. More detailed and formal solutions may be found in subsequent chapters of the book.

Reader Inferences about "The Programmer"

- In sentence 5, *for his child* modifies the VP

    NS representations of the implications of the verb *buy* includes the fact that buying can be done for a SENTIENT entity. Using this information, specific PP attachment rules based on NS can be used to attach the PP to the VP.

- In sentence 4, there is an implicit indirect object, *manager*

    This can be inferred from a generic knowledge that 1) *ask* has an optional indirect object which is a SENTIENT entity; 2) managers give salary raises; and 3) programmers work for a salary.

- In sentence 2, *his* has *John* as antecedent

This choice can be made by agreement alone, since there are only two nouns in the text so far, and only one of them is male.

- In sentence 3, *he* and *his* have *manager* as antecedent

  This can be inferred from knowledge that the manager owns the office, as directly stated in the text, from generic knowledge that offices typically have desks as contents, and from general common-sense knowledge (CK) that people who own things use them for their function.

- In sentence 5, *he* has *John* as antecedent

  The antecedent of *he* can be shifted to John here using generic knowledge that buying is enabled by having enough money and that people buy things because they want them. In addition the prior inference that John asked his manager for a /salary/ *raise, and generic knowledge that a salary raise is money, is used in the anaphora resolution for sentence 5.*

- In sentence 2, *office* has its PLACE sense

  Ontological knowledge that *enter* is a motion verb, combined with specific knowledge of sense-selecting properties of the preposition *to*, can be used to select the place sense of *office*.

- In sentence 6, *John and his manager* has the collective reading

  This can be inferred from generic knowledge of *review* that it permits a COLLECTIVE subject, and of *enter*, which has as a consequence that its subject (John) is inside its object (his manager's office).

- The event reported by sentence 2 had as goal the event reported in sentence 4

  This can be inferred from ontological (classificatory) knowledge that *enter* is a GOAL-oriented verb, as is *ask for*, and from generic knowledge that people go places with goals in mind. The latter suggests a search for a goal of entering the office.

- The event described by sentence 4 had as cause the state described in sentence 5

    Generic knowledge of *buy* includes the fact that buying is enabled by having enough money. Prior inference establishes that John asked his manager for money when he asked for the raise. Generic knowledge of *salary* and *raise* implies that if John were to receive a raise he would have more money. This knowledge indicates a causal relation between sentence 5 and sentence 4.

The intent of the above review is to show that representations of detailed naive theories in the form of ontological and generic information are sufficient to draw the inferences required to interpret "The Programmer." Using such representations, much more of the cognitive model of the interpretation can be built than in alternative representations, as the next section discusses. It is significant that the representations can be drawn from psycholinguistic experiments which are not aimed at solving problems of linguistic ambiguity, as will be established in Chapter 2. In fact, the experiments are concept-oriented. Word level cognitive models are very powerful elements in the theory of sentential and discourse level semantics. When syntactic, compositional semantic and word level semantic information are combined, a wide range of structures can be interpreted. Theories which attempt to interpret these structures without word level commonsense knowledge can account for less of the reader's interpretation of the text. Subsequent chapters of the book describe methods for representing noun (Chapter 2) and verb (Chapter 4) naive semantics. Later chapters justify and specify algorithms for deriving the types of inferences outlined above in a computational text understanding system: Chapter 6 for the PP attachment algorithm; Chapter 7 for the word sense disambiguation algorithm, and Chapter 8 for the discourse relations algorithm.

1.2. Compositional Semantics

Is it necessary to represent all of the complexity of the reader's model described above? Isn't it possible to account for much of natural language understanding with the simpler, more elegant representations of syntax and compositional semantics? This section answers these questions in the negative. We will show that naive theories are used at every level of text interpretation from parsing to word sense selection to discourse structure assignment, and that syntax and compositional semantics alone are inadequate to account for interpretation at each of these levels.

Linguistic and cognitive theory are both at the infant stage. It is not known how language is represented and processed in the mind/brain. One question is whether there are separate modules which handle syntactic and semantic processing. If there are, then separate theories, employing distinct formal languages, will be required for each of these levels of grammar. Some computational linguistic theories deny a separation between syntax and semantics (Schank, 1973, Wilks, 1975, Charniak and Wilks, 1978), and call for semantically driven parsing. We adopt the view accepted by most linguists that syntax and semantics are independent modules. This is because semantic content alone does not predict the wide range of possible syntactic structures (Marcus,1980). On the other hand it is impossible to read the semantic properties of sentences directly off of the syntax, so a separate compositional semantic theory is necessary. The determiner, for example, shows no syntactic ambiguity, but can be ambiguous between anaphoric and deictic readings. In (9), *those* can have the anaphoric reading, in which case the hearer finds some previously-mentioned men as antecedents, or it can the the deictic reading, in which the antecedent is to be found in the physical setting of the discourse.

(9)   Those men are interesting.

If syntax and semantics are separate components, we must consider how they interact, and where in the theory to account for the kind of commonsense knowledge described above.

Most semantic theories, including ours, adhere to the *principle of compositionality*, that the meanings of sentences are built up from the meanings of their component parts. In Montague grammar, for each syntactic rule there is a semantic rule which translates the syntactic structure into the corresponding intensional structure. Discourse Representation Theory (DRT) (Kamp, 1981, Heim, 1982) continues this tradition. Katz and Fodor (1963) propose projection rules to combine readings of lower-level structures to build readings for higher level structures. The principle of compositionality is required to account for the systematic effects of syntactic structures on the truth conditions of sentences. In the Montague framework, compositionality accounts for the fact that the subject of a sentence (which has as its intension (meaning) an entity), combined with an intransitive verb phrase (which has as its intension a property) results in a structure whose meaning is a truth value (a state of affairs which is either true or false in the model).

A theory of natural language understanding cannot rely solely on the syntactic and semantic modules. Although compositionality explains truth conditions arising from syntactic structure, the principle does not provide an account of word meaning which is detailed enough to explain the kinds of inferences required for the interpretation of "The Programmer" text described above. In Montague grammar, words like *programmer* and *buy* are translated as unanalyzed predicates. The goal of Montague grammar is to account for the relationship between language and the world. In the theory, the meaning of a predicate like "programmer" is identified with its extension--the set of all individuals X in the model of whom programmer(X) is true. The meaning of a sentence is a truth value. Our goal is more ambitious. We want to account for both reference and truth conditions, and for the psychological state of the recipient of a text, for whom the meaning involves both more and less than the truth conditions. It involves more because we know that the reader builds a rich cognitive picture of the situation the text describes (Rickheit and Strohner, 1985), and makes the kinds of inferences described above in the example. It involves less, because often what the recipient recovers from a text is insufficient to provide correct, unambiguous truth conditions, as we show below. Since our goal is to mimic human text understanding computationally, answer questions about a text and summarize it, we must build a model of the recipient's cognitive picture of the text.

Our research is directed towards the practical goal of text selection. We want to read large numbers of newspaper and magazine articles and select those texts which fall within the stated interests of a particular user. The goal of computationally deciding the relevance of a text requires that not only the explicitly-mentioned predicates, but the implied predicates, be recovered by the text understanding system. We would like to build a computer program which would permit a user to describe in English his domain of interest, have the program go out and read the newspapers and magazines, and provide the user with a short, extremely relevant list of references. For example, the user might be an investor in the construction industry who states that interest rates are of extreme interest to him. We want to select from among all of the texts those which state or imply an effect on interest rates. We want to exclude all texts which do not report events affecting interest rates, even those which use the phrase *interest rate*. This requires a complex cognitively based understanding of the English coming in. In contrast, if the goal were to query databases, where there is a one-to-one correspondence between words in the subset of English the query system understands and entities or relations in the database, such a cognitively-based account of text interpretation would not be necessary.

1.3. The Classical Theory of Word Meaning

If our goal is a cognitive model of meaning, the first task is to represent the meanings of words. The classical approach to this in the philosophy of language and linguistics is to decompose predicates into primitives which are truth conditional. The primitive predicates in the *intension*, the meaning of the word, determines its *extension*, the set of objects to which the word can be used to refer. The clearest example of the approach is in Katz and Fodor (1963) and Katz (1972). The noun *bachelor* is decomposed into primitives as in (10)

(10)   *bachelor* means (Human)(Adult)(Male)(Unmarried)

A sentence with *bachelor* predicated of an entity has truth conditions which include the conjunction of the primitives predicated of that entity, so *John is a bachelor* has truth conditions

(11)   Human(john) & Adult(john) & Male(john) &
         Unmarried(john)

The drawbacks of this approach have been analyzed in the linguistics, philosophy and psychology literature (Bolinger, 1965, Putnam, 1975, Dahlgren, 1976, Smith and Medin, 1981, Johnson-Laird, 1983, Jackendoff, 1983). These limitations will be reviewed here because the classical theory underlies a number of computational linguistic theories, and because the alternative theory we are proposing, naive semantics, must meet these objections.

The key problem is that people can know what a term means and use it to communicate successfully, without knowing necessary and sufficient conditions for determining its extension. Putnam (1975) shows that the classical theory cannot account for natural kind terms such as *water*. Suppose that (12) is the classical theory representation for *water*.

(12)   *water* means (Clear)(Tasteless)(Liquid)

(13)   water(X) $\Leftrightarrow$ clear(X) & tasteless(X) & liquid(X)

(12) amounts to the biconditional (13), according to the classical theory. But (13) cannot be used to determine the extension of *water*. Suppose that X is some stuff. That X has all the properties on the right-hand side of (13) does not guarantee that X is Water. The properties don't provide necessary and sufficient conditions for being water. Stuff which is vodka satisfies them. It is also possible to try replacing predicates in (13) with scientific criteria as in (14).

(14)   water(X) $\Leftrightarrow$ H_2O(X)

But then the theory of word meaning would predict that competence in a natural language presupposes the existence of correct scientific theories, and knowledge of these theories by all speakers of a language. Surely the Greeks used χρυσος to refer to gold without knowing scientific criteria for gold.

Even more importantly, Putnam argues that when we use a term such as *water*, we intend to refer to the "stuff that bears a certain similarity relation to the water *around here*". Imagine another planet, Twin Earth. On Twin Earth, each person is a counterpart to some person on real Earth. The counterparts all carry the same mental representation of *water* that we do on Earth (that is, clear, tasteless, liquid). But on Twin Earth, the chemical formula for the stuff our counterparts call *water* is XYZ, not H_2O. Upon discovering this strange circumstance, Earthians would say that *water* on Twin Earth is NOT *water*, but some other substance. Thus we use the word *water* to refer indexically to the kind Water. Speakers use a kind term with the belief that a corresponding kind exists in the actual world.

On the Putnam view, then, a kind term is used with the intention of referring to whatever entities in fact share the same internal essence as local paradigms of the kind, even if the speakers of the language cannot scientifically define what that hidden internal essence is or give reliable criteria for membership in the kind. The linguistic community as a whole relies upon the progress of science to discover the essences of the various kinds. Since the average speaker is not always able to determine whether some proposed instance falls into the extension of a natural kind term, experts are called upon to decide in unclear cases. The extension of a kind term is determined by society as a whole, not by the conceptions of individual speakers.

In summary, the realist theory as advanced by Putnam is that the meaning of a natural kind term in the mental lexicon does not in general constitute criteria for determining the extension of the term. Instead, the individual has a stereotype of the typical member of the extension which may be quite vague, and the actual extension is determined by a complex social process. Word meanings cannot be used to provide criteria for membership in extensions. This means that mental representations of words (and the sentences which contain them) are not equivalent to formulas which provide truth conditions, although sentences can be translated into truth-conditional formulas. What competent speakers know is not criteria, but a stereotype of the typical members of the extension of a word such as *water*.

The second problem with the theory is the vagueness of conceptual categories. Whether a particular object belongs in the extension of a certain terms is indeterminate, as Labov(1973) demonstrated with the terms *cup* and *bowl*. He showed subjects a range of shapes and sizes of containers, and found that while they strongly agreed that some were in the extension of *cup* or *bowl*, they disagreed on others. Winograd (1976) shows that even the application of *bachelor*, which seems to have such clear criteria, is vague. Is a priest a bachelor? How about a 17-year-old living in his own apartment?

A third problem is family resemblances. The classical theory predicts that anything which satisfies the criteria in the definition should have equal status as a member of the extension of a term. However, as Rosch and Mervis (1975) show, people conceive of membership in a number of superordinate categories as gradient. Some members are "better," more typical, instances of the category than others. *apple* and *orange* are the most typical fruits, *pickle* and *squash* the least typical. *robin* and *sparrow* are the birdiest birds, *penguin* and *bat* the least. Dahlgren (1985a) finds that *doctor* and *lawyer* are the most typical professionals, *social worker* and *librarian* the least typical. Rosch and Mervis (1975) find that high typicality correlates with the number of features a subordinate member of a category has in common with other members of the same category. Highly typical subordinate members of a category have fewer features in common with contrast categories. Thus the most typical member of a category has the greatest family resemblance to other members of that category. Dahlgren (1985a) replicates their findings for social categories.

The fourth problem which undermines the classical theory is that not all concepts lend themselves to decomposition. The problem is most clear with predicates naming perceptual properties such as *red*, *tart* and *soft*. If color concepts can be decomposed at all, the primitives are not verbal, but correspond to certain physiological features of the human visual system (Kay and McDaniel, 1978).

The fifth problem for the classical theory is exceptions. Is a one-legged man not a man, a stripeless albino tiger not a tiger? The classical theory would predict that an entity lacking one of the defining features would be excluded from the extensions of the term, but clearly we do not exclude these exceptional members.

The sixth problem besetting the classical theory has to do with truth conditions. Some terms are used descriptively. Terms such as *weed* and *junk* are used to refer to classes of objects which we stipulate as unwanted. There is no scientific or mind-independent truth to membership in these categories. Whatever plant we call a weed is one (Dahlgren, 1988b).

The final problem with the classical theory is that it cannot account for semantic shift and linguistic creativity. Dahlgren (1976) shows that word meanings shift in relation to changes in the environment in ways not predicted by the classical theory. The classical theory says that the stock of concepts from which word meanings are built consists of a set of innate primitives which totals far fewer than the words of a language. From this stock are built all of the word meanings. The Dahlgren study considers social rank terms of English in the period 690 AD through 1250 AD during which time there was a major social upheaval in Southern England as a result of the Norman Conquest. The terms considered were terms such as þeow (slave) and *ceorl* (freeman). Their meanings in 690 AD according to the primitives theory might be represented as in (15).

(15)   þeow means not(free)
          ceorl means (free)

After 1066 AD, the Normans subjugated the ceorls and made them serfs. The classical theory could represent the shift in the meaning of *ceorl* by changing (free) to not(free) in the representation. But the content of freedom and slavery differs in the two periods. In Pre-Conquest England, being a þeow did not mean being tied to the land and owned by a lord. But in Post-Conquest England being a ceorl meant being part of the property of a lord, being salable along with one's land, and being unfree to move away from the manor. So the content of the primitive (free) would have to differ in the two periods, with the result that it would not be one of a small set of primitives requisite for a simple semantic theory. Further, the primitive (free), in either of the senses relevant to early England, would not be usable to represent the modern English term *slave* in relation to American slavery of the nineteenth century. In that system a slave was tied to the plantation owner, not the land. And yet another meaning is required in relation to modern prisoners, who have many more restrictions than any of the unfree groups described thus far, and are not owned by anyone. The concept of a small universal set of innate semantic primitives is difficult to reconcile with the observed facts of semantic change over time.

The results of our research in semantic shift are related to the question of creativity in language. The theory that there is a limited stock of innate primitives predicts that people are incapable of learning fundamentally new concepts. The effect of the new social structure of Post-Conquest England on English semantics demonstrates that people do learn fundamentally new concepts. The semantics of their language adjusts accordingly, rather than imposing constraints which prevent learning.

In summary, some words do not have criterial attributes in their meaning representations. Apparently the representation of word meaning varies across the lexicon. Some words may have criterial verbal features in their representations. Obvious examples come from mathematics. A *triangle* can be defined as a "three-sided figure." Others have features which correspond to naive theories, or stereotypes of the extensions, but are used with the intention of referring to kinds, that is, to classes of objects with some sort of stable essence independent of the human view of them (*water, lemon, tiger*). Dahlgren (1988b) argues that social terms such as *knife* and *programmer* belong in this group. Still others are descriptive. Human viewpoint determines the classes (*weed, junk, witch, game*). Other words are represented in terms of visual and other perceptual features which are not readily translated into verbal predicates. Johnson-Laird (1983) adopts a similar position and concludes that "the nature of meanings differs from one word to another: intensions are not uniform" (p. 195).

1.4. Word Meanings as Concepts

We have established that word meanings cannot be accounted for by a subset of primitives which provide necessary and sufficient conditions for being in their extensions. What then are word meanings? If word meanings do not contribute to truth conditions, what is their role? The approach which we favor is to identify word meaning with concept, that is, with the cognitive representation which a person uses to recognize a category of objects or events, or a property. This approach sees no difference in form of representation between word meanings and concepts. This is the approach taken by Tarnawsky (1982), Johnson-Laird (1983) and Jackendoff (1983). Jackendoff shows that all of the phenomena which are called strictly semantic (such as class inclusion and synonymy) are needed in a theory of concept categorization. He concludes that there is no clear difference between the conceptual and semantic levels.

> *word meanings are expressions of conceptual structure . That is, there is not a form of mental representation devoted to a strictly semantic level of word meanings, distinct from the level at which linguistic and nonlinguistic information are compatible. This means that if, as is often claimed, a distinction exists between dictionary and encyclopedic lexical information, it is not a distinction of level; these kinds of information are cut from the same cloth.*

Psycholinguistic research of Marslen-Wilson and Tyler (1980) substantiates this hypothesis by showing that during sentence processing there is no distinguishable difference in timing between what have been called semantic effects and what have been called world knowledge effects.

1.5. Other Decompositional Approaches

Jackendoff and Johnson-Laird, while rejecting the view that primitives provide criterial features, both decompose word meanings into primitives, though for different reasons. Jackendoff believes that the structure of the actual world has little to do with conceptual structure. On the other hand, he believes that grammatical structure provides important constraints on conceptual structure. In the interests of simplifying the theory, Jackendoff includes in concept representations only those structures which are motivated by the grammatical structure of sentences. Another justification for the representations he offers derives from the assumption that conceptual structures are built up from elements of spatial cognition. All concepts, in Jackendoff's view, are built up from concepts that are either required to account for grammatical structure (such as THING, EVENT and ANIMATE) or can be traced to the semantics of motion or location (CAUSE, GO, FROM, TO).[1]

While clearly there must be some innate level of concept representation, as we can see with the visual system, on the level of a social term like *buy*, the Jackendovian theory is too limiting. For one thing, Jackendoff claims that all terms are represented using the same structures and primitives, but we have seen above that vocabulary probably varies in form of representation. Color terms are represented in relation to hard-wired aspects of the visual system, while other types of terms are represented more verbally. More importantly, an approach which attempts to represent the meanings of a large number of words with a single small set of primitives is unable to account for differences in meaning. Jackendoff's representations for the words *force, pressure, trick, talk into, cause to, get to, coerce into* are the same.

Secondly, the search for primitives, even a sophisticated form like Jackendoff's, leads to an intralinguistic methodology. Instead of seeing reference, that is, the relation between language and the world, as basic, Jackendoff denies its relevance to semantic theory, as he makes very clear in his first chapter. Instead, his goal is to capture the similarity in meaning among the vocabulary in various semantic fields. In Figure 1 on page 20 we see that the verbs *accept* and *buy* are represented very similarly, and differ only in that *accept* has no representation for the

---

1 To avoid a possible confusion of terminology, we emphasize that NS is intended as one component of grammar, along with *compositional* semantics, which interprets the effects of syntactic structure on sentence and discourse meaning. On the other hand, NS rejects *decompositional* semantics, a theory which represents word meanings as exhaustive decompositions into primitives.

Jackendoff's Representation in Terms of Primitives

accept
$$[LET ([X], [GO_{Poss} ([Y], [TO_{Poss} ([X])])])]$$

buy
$$[CAUSE ([X],$$

$$\left[\begin{array}{l} GO_{Poss} \ ([Y], \begin{bmatrix} FROM_{Poss} \ ([Z]) \\ TO_{Poss} \ ([X]) \end{bmatrix}) \\ GO_{Poss} \ ([W], \begin{bmatrix} FROM_{Poss} \ ([X]) \\ TO_{Poss} \ ([Z]) \end{bmatrix}) \end{array} \right])]$$

Figure 1: Jackendoff's Representations of ACCEPT and BUY

movement of money from the buyer to the seller, and uses the primitive LET instead of CAUSE to show that the verb is not a goal verb. The POSS subscript is for "possession." GO, TO and FROM are spatial primitives. This effort to capture similarity in meaning economically results in leaving out so much of the concept, that the representation is insufficient to account for the inferences we know people draw in text understanding. The *buy* representation is designed to be maximally simple, and to capture the similarity in meaning between *buy* and *accept* which both involve a change of possession of objects. This is very similar to the methodology of Katz, whose classical approach has been found inadequate by Putnam (1975) and others, as described in the previous section. Katz's representation for *buy* and *sell* are shown below.

(16)   *buy* ((((Condition)(Possesses (Physical Object)) of (Human Indirect-Object) at Time$_i$))
((Condition)(Possesses (Physical Object)) of (Human Subject) at Time$_j$), &
((((Condition)(Possesses (Sum-of-Money Second-Indirect-Object)) of (Human Indirect Object) at Time$_i$),...
((((Condition)(Possesses (Sum-of-Money Second-Indirect-

Object)) of (Human Subject) at Time$_j$),...

sell (((((Condition)(Possesses (Physical Object)) of (Human
Subject) at Time$_i$),...
((Condition)(Possesses (Physical Object)) of (Human
Indirect-Object) at Time$_j$)) &
((((Condition)(Possesses (Sum-of-Money Second-Indirect-
Object)) of (Human Indirect Object) at Time$_i$),...
((((Condition)(Possesses (Sum-of-Money Second-Indirect-
Object)) of (Human Subject) at Time$_j$),...

Comparing Katz's with Jackendoff's representation, it is clear that
the same information is represented, though the formalism differs. Neither representation indicates that money is the instrument of buying
(typically). There is nothing about the enablement condition of buying,
which is that the buyer have enough money. Nor is there mention of
a benefactee of the buying. Without this information in the representation, the inferences by recipients of "The Programmer" text cannot
be accounted for. Returning to "The Programmer" text above, recall
that in sentence (5) the recipient infers that the PP *for his child* modifies
the verb *buy* rather than the sentence or the noun *computer*. The inference that *for his child* modifies the verb phrase requires the information
that *buy* can have a sentient oblique object. The inference that John
asked for a raise because he wanted to buy a home computer requires
knowledge that buying is typically carried out with money. Similarly,
in Jackendoff's system, the representation of *ask* would not include an
implication that one asks for something because one wants something.
Nor would the representation of *enter* include the fact that it is goal-
oriented. So the information is lacking to infer that John entered the
office with the goal of asking for a raise. In general, then, the primitives
model provides insufficient information for modelling the inferences
described above for reading "The Programmer." Yet these inferences
are intuitively and uncontroversially part of an English speaker's interpretation of the text. Thus more of the reader's cognitive model must
be included to account for the facts of text interpretation.

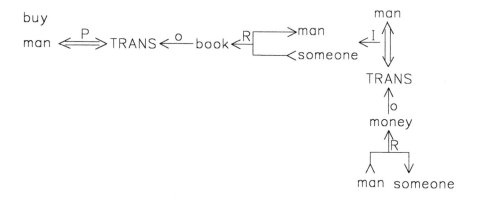

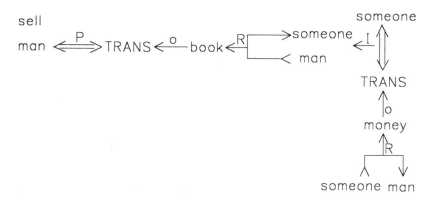

Figure 2: Conceptual Dependency Representations of *buy* and *sell*

Another aspect of text interpretation that decompositional theories cannot account for is word sense disambiguation. In decompositional theories, word senses are disambiguated by matching primitives in the representations of the words in the sentence and selecting the reading which yields the greatest number of primitives in common. However, the primitives model does not always provide enough information to make the choice. Consider the ambiguous sentence in (17).

(17)   John robbed the bank.

It is plausible to appeal to a primitive like "money" in the meaning representations for both *rob* and *bank*. But consider (18).

(18)   John drove up to the bank.

This could mean either that John drove up to a financial institution, or that John drove up to the side of a river. If the text continues as in (19), readers prefer a reading in which *bank* is interpreted as referring to a financial institution.

(19)   John drove up to the bank and into the parking lot.

If the text is as in (20), readers use knowledge of rivers to guess the side-of-the-river interpretation for *bank*.

(20)   John followed the river. He drove up to the bank.

bank has at least three readings: 1) financial institution where money is exchanged; 2) the place where such a financial institution is housed; 3) the side of a river. In (19), readers prefer the second sense of *bank* because of knowledge that the places where financial institutions are housed typically have parking lots. In (20), readers prefer the third sense of *bank* because of knowledge that the location of such banks is at the side of rivers. The reasoning in such cases draws upon detailed knowledge of financial institutions which would not be represented in the primitives model.

1.6. Computational Approaches to Word Meaning

A number of computational models of word meaning for text understanding are notational variants of the classical theory. Schank's conceptual dependencies theory posits a small stock of primitives, related by various types of arrows which correspond to case roles. Though based upon a different theory of grammar, Schank's lexical representation amounts to a Jackendovian theory. Both decompose into a set of primitives, and both make lexical representations look like sentential representations (Jackendoff's grammatical constraint). The content of the representations of *buy* in Figure 1 on page 20 and Figure 2 on page

22 are quite similar, though the notations differ. One real difference is that Schank's representation includes implied instruments, agents and benefactees, while Jackendoff's does not. Later work in the Schankian paradigm superimposes higher-level structures such as scripts upon conceptual dependency structures, but the latter remain the building blocks of the representations. Similar representations based upon case roles are found in Sowa (1984).

Another computational semantic approach is Wilks' (1975) preference semantics, which employs primitives combined with case frames and selection restrictions. Wilks' representation of *buy* and *sell*, I take it, would be as in (21).

(21)   *buy* (action) → ((*HUM SUBJ)((*PHYSOBJ OBJE)(*HUM
         FROM) (MONEY INST)((SELF OWN) CAUSE)))
         sell (action) → ((*HUM SUBJ)((*PHYSOBJ OBJE)(*HUM
         TO) (MONEY INST)((HUM OWN) CAUSE)))

This representation again uses primitives such as CAUSE, OWN and SELF, cases such as OBJE, SUBJ, GOAL, as well as selection restrictions (called classes) such as ANIMATE, HUMAN, PHYSOBJ. These word meaning representations are open to the same criticisms as any representations based upon primitives, and as can be seen they contain about the same amount of information as those of Katz, Jackendoff and Schank. An important innovation in Wilks' work is the reasoning. Wilks introduced the idea of preference strategies for word sense disambiguation. The idea is that when the reasoner cannot find an appropriate match for any sense of an ambiguous word in the representation of the verb of the sentence in which the ambiguous word occurs, it attempts an interpretation anyway. In this way it finds a interpretations of metaphors like *My car drinks gasoline*. In our theory, although we do not treat metaphor, we have incorporated the idea of preference to select the one most plausible reading of a sentence (and discourse) from among the many syntactically and semantically possible ones.

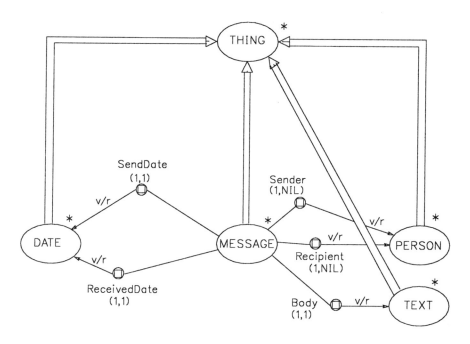

Figure 3: KL-ONE Representations of *message*

KRYPTON (Brachman, et al, 1983, 1985) is an important artificial intelligence knowledge representation language.   It has two sublanguages, one definitional, the other assertional. The details of the relationship between KRYPTON and our implementation of naive semantics will be explored in Chapter 5 after our system has been described. At this point it suffices to show that the KRYPTON definitional language, the TBox, decomposes concepts into a set of primitives which provides criteria for membership in extensions. The definitional language is expressly based upon KL-ONE (Brachman and Schmolze, 1985). Concepts are represented in a semantic network directly expressing relationships like "a WOMAN is a HUMAN." Figure 3 shows the definition of the concept MESSAGE. It illustrates the elaboration of concepts in KL-ONE. The attributes of a concept are represented as rolesets, which have value restrictions. The concept MESSAGE has a roleset *Sender* whose value must be a PERSON. Value restrictions are inherited in the semantic net. All concepts subsumed by a concept inherit its component restrictions. In the truth definition for KRYPTON, value restrictions are used to define the extensions of concepts. Truth is defined in a model, which is a set of entities in a knowledge base. The extension of a concept is the set of entities related in the model as indicated by the definition of the concept. The authors give the sample of the concept "person whose children are all doctors." Its extension "would be the elements x in the extension of PERSON such that any y such that < x,y > is in the extension of CHILD is also in the extension of DOCTOR."[2] Thus all members of the extension of a concept must satisfy its value restrictions. KRYPTON, then, is subject to the same criticism as the classical theory of word meaning.

Some approaches are not aimed at the concept level. It has been popular in recent years to capture the commonsense inferences illustrated with "The Programmer" text above by using scripts and frames (Minsky, 1975). For the "The Programmer" text above, a script would look like this (Schank and Abelson, 1977).

So far, so good. The information in Table 1.1 can be encoded. Problems arise, however. The main one is transportability. A script for one domain or experience frequently is not relevant to the next. It is desirable to build up knowledge until eventually the computer model has more and more of the knowledge people employ in reading text. If this knowledge is to be built up automatically, transportable representations are required. Another problem is script identification. When to invoke a script, and when to drop it or overlay it with another, are unsolved problems. Word-level representations in NS eliminate the problem of script identification because for every word there is the equivalent of a script (Fillmore, 1985). Finally, understandability, modifiability and changeability of the code are difficulties which have been encountered by knowledge engineers using scripts (Johnson and Lehnert, 1986).

---

2 Truth is defined in the assertional language, and connected to the TBox via a symbol table mechanism.

Business	Programmer
Isa Social Organization	Isa Social Role
Purpose - make a profit	Function - write computer programs
Location - office building	Relation - works for a manager
Roles - managers, programmers, secretaries	Dress - white shirt
	Tools - computer

A frame approach with a number of similarities to NS is Absity (Hirst, 1987). Absity shares the assumption with NS that there are independent syntactic and compositional semantic modules which both have access to lexical semantics. The meaning of each word is identified with a conceptual knowledge base represented as a frame. The frames contain slot-filler pairs, such as color = red, like the typed features in NS generic knowledge. Noun representations do not contain the large numbers of features present in NS, because Absity is not aimed at modelling the English speaker's rich naive theory. Another difference is that Absity cannot handle vagueness, while NS can. Verb and preposition representations are based upon case grammar. The Absity representation of *buy* is shown in the illustration below. In contrast, the NS representation of *buy* contains the implications of buying, including the typical location, the enabling conditions, the causes and consequences, in addition to the information Absity includes. Just as with nouns, NS representations of verbs contain more information than Absity representations. Since the reasoning in NS does not require that all instances of buying have all of its typical implications, the typical implications can be included as probabilistic features which can be overridden. Our approach shares a number of architectural decisions with Absity, but our lexical semantic theory is different.

```
[frame:       purchase
 isa:         action
 slots:       buyer (person)
              seller (person)
              bought-item
              money (negotiable-instrument)
 acts:        pay-step (give buyer money seller)
              get-item-step (give seller bought-item buyer)]
```

1.7. Naive Semantics

We propose an alternative theory of lexical representation for natural language understanding, Naive Semantics (NS). It replaces the search for linguistic or psychological primitives of meaning with the goal of modelling the detailed naive theory associated with words. NS represents psycholinguistically justified commonsense knowledge of concepts instead of minimal sets of primitives. Although the issue is controversial, what is known about cognitive psychology suggests that there is no difference in **form** of representation between concepts and memory in general. So the cognitive model must draw from the "pragmatics wastebasket" and include what was formerly considered to be encyclopedic knowledge. Recognizing that it is impossible to include all of the speaker's encyclopedic knowledge, NS hypothesizes a level which is linguistically interesting--the level shared by a subculture, and recognized as shared by members of a linguistic community. "My concept of water is that it is typically found in lakes, and other people think so, too." NS assumes that the purely linguistic aspect of this is the name of the concept, *water*. The form *water* names the concept WATER, and when text is interpreted, the cognitive representation of WATER is accessed because *water* occurs in the stream of words. In NS, the linguistic system is linked to the conceptual system via **names of concepts**.

The naive theory of WATER is the total extent of the meaning representation for *water*. In NS the cognitive representation of a word meaning is seen as being the same thing (the same representation) as the concept representation. The naive theory is shared and we know we share it. Even experts know the naive theory. A molecular physicist believes that water is a clear tasteless liquid which is found in lakes, while s/he also holds a scientific theory of the structure and properties of water. When s/he uses *water* to naive hearers, s/he expects that they will construct a model of the stuff referred to by the word *water* based upon their naive theory of WATER. The goal, then, should not be to represent the individual's concept, but the "subculture's concept" (the concept shared by a significant number of members of the subculture, and playing a significant role in linguistic communication). Knowledge of a natural language implies knowledge of a culture-specific theory of the environment. One way of learning that theory is to learn the language, which has names for the category cuts recognized in that theory. In learning the language, one learns the distinctions which are significant in the culture (Berlin, 1972, Dougherty, 1978).

1.8. Basis of Naive Semantics in Cognitive Psychology

The theory of cognitive representations which forms the basis of the generic knowledge in NS is the prototype theory (Rosch et al, 1976, Ashcraft, 1976, Mervis and Pani, 1980, Smith and Medin, 1981, Fehr and Russell, 1984, Graesser and Clark, 1985a). Rosch and others distinguish basic-level and superordinate terms. In these theories, the prototype of a superordinate term is the most typical member of the category (as measured by asking subjects to rate members of a category for typicality). At that level categories were found to have a family resemblance structure (Rosch and Mervis, 1975, Dahlgren, 1985a). For the superordinate CLOTHING the prototype is SHIRT. The prototype of a basic-level term is a description of typical instances of the category. SHIRT is described as having a collar, buttons, a front, a back, armholes, a neck opening and so on. (These data come from Ashcraft, 1976).

The basic insight of the prototype theory is intuitively understood in relation to a figure like Figure 4 on page 30. In the figure we see

Figure 4: Typical and Atypical Shirt

two shirts. The one on the left is the typical shirt (as described by subjects in Ashcraft's experiments). The one on the right is also a perfectly acceptable shirt. Upon seeing one like it, English speakers would be quite willing to call it a shirt, although it lacks a number of the features of the typical shirt. It has no collar, no buttons, no cuffs and so on. The point is, though, that when someone says (22) the understander uses knowledge of the typical shirt to construct an interpretation.

(22)   John washed his shirt. The collar was dirty.

Experiments in the prototype theory ask subjects to list features which are characteristic of objects. They are given 1.5 minutes to list whatever comes to mind on a blank piece of paper. Features mentioned by more than one out of 20 subjects turn out to be reliable indicators of a subculture's naive theory of the object. When other subjects are asked to rate those features for typicality, they rate them as highly typical of the object (Rosch, 1975, Ashcraft, 1976, Dahlgren, 1985a).

NS represents the features listed by subjects as probabilistic features of the objects. So some of the representation for *shirt* looks as follows:

(23)   shirt(Typically{haspart(button,*,X) &
          haspart(collar,1,X) &
          haspart(front,1,X) & haspart(back,1,X) &
          color(white,X) & haspart(armhole,2,X) &
          haspart(neck,1,X) & haspart(sleeve,2,X) &
          haspart(cuff,2,X) & haspart(pocket,*,X) &
          experienced_as(warm) & experienced_as(soft)},
          Inherently{(function(wear(Y,X) & person(Y)) &
          function(cover(X,Y) & person(Y)) & material(cloth) &
          construction(sew(Y,X) & person(Y)) & location(torso)}})

This can be read as, "if something is a shirt it probably has buttons, 1 collar, 1 front, 1 back, 2 armholes, 1 neck, 2 sleeves, 1 cuff, pockets, is white, is experienced as warm and soft, and inherently its function is for a person to wear it and to cover the person, and it is made out of cloth. Conversely, "if something has these features, it's probably a shirt." This captures the belief that typically shirts are dress shirts, but that a collarless shirt with no buttons and pockets, as in the atypical shirt of Figure 4 on page 30, is an acceptable shirt as well. It also reflects the fact that people associate with their concept of *shirt* other facts which are generalizations about it that look just like encyclopedic knowledge--e.g., it is made by sewing, it is made of cloth.

When a concept is represented by psycholinguistically justified CK, much more information is associated with words than in the primitives model. For example, associated with *shirt* is not only a physical description, but also many other aspects of peoples' generalizations about shirts--"shirts typically have a collar," "shirts feel warm," and so on. Other theories have denied the possibility that such open-endedness could be accounted for in a linguistic or cognitive model. Hence the search for primitives. It is instructive to contrast the representation in (23) with a representation of defining features for shirt as in (24), which has far fewer features. The point is, that while simpler and more elegant to represent, (24) has too little information to disambiguate text in which *shirt* occurs, a point also stressed by Schubert, et al, (1979). Nor is it sufficient to build a picture of a text's meaning which corresponds in any way to the human interpretation.

(24)   shirt(X) → material(cloth,X) & function(clothing) &
                haspart(openings,*,X) &
                haspart(front,1,X) & haspart(back,1,X) &
                location(torso)

The term "naive" in naive theory has great importance for the status of the representations in reasoning. "Shirts typically have a collar" is part of the naive theory of shirts. But we know that the atypical shirt in Figure 4 on page 30 is also a perfectly fine shirt. Upon reading about a shirt, we assume that it is has a collar unless other information states or implies that it doesn't. Naive semantic representations are probabilistic, and do not provide monotonic truth conditions for the sentences in which they occur.

What are the aspects of CK associated with concepts? First of all, there are two basic entity types which are named by words--objects and events.   Secondly, there are two types of knowledge about them--classificatory and generic. Generic knowledge generalizes across instances of objects and events to give probabilistic descriptions of them. Generic knowledge of objects consists of properties--"shirts typically have a collar." Included in such knowledge is the fact that typical contents of offices include desks, that typical programmers receive a salary, and that managers give out raises. Generic knowledge of events consists of implications--"a person buys something because he wants it" (Graesser and Clark, 1985a). Such knowledge incorporates the implications that buying is enabled by having enough money, and that asking implies that the subject of the asking wants something. (25) shows the naive semantic representation for *buy*. It illustrates that NS representations contain much more information than is included in other approaches to word meaning.

(25)   buy(Typically{what_enabled(can(afford(subj,obj))),
         how(with(X) & money(X)),
         where(in(Y) & store(Y)),
         what_happened_next(use(subj,obj)),
         cause(need(subj,obj))},
         Inherently{goal(own(subj,obj)),
         consequence_of_event(own(subj,obj)),
         selectional_restriction(sentient(subj)),
         implies(merchandise(obj))}).

The second type of knowledge classifies objects and events into groups which are considered similar. This follows the semantic net tradition of encoding a taxonomic hierarchy of concepts, as in KRYPTON (Brachman, et al, 1983) and NETL (Fahlman, 1979). In NS this is called ontological (rather than taxonomic) knowledge because of the realist basis of the theory. Ontological knowledge places objects and events in a broad classificatory scheme. Water is like other liquid minerals and unlike programmers, that is, WATER is a LIQUID MINERAL and PROGRAMMER is a SOCIAL ROLE. Similarly, buying is like marrying and unlike running. BUY is a GOAL-oriented SOCIAL ACHIEVEMENT and RUN is a NATURAL ACTIVITY.

The advantages of psychologically real representations are twofold. First, as cognitive psychology progresses in its understanding of human reasoning about text, the computational linguistic theory can be improved correspondingly. This will make the responses more natural and truthful as reflections of the computer user's way of thinking about the text. Secondly, the knowledge and rules which derive from empirical studies tend to be more objective than those derived from intuition, and are more likely to be reproducible. Any theories generated by purely intuitive means run the risk of being overturned by the facts. The psychological reality criterion ties the theory to empirical science.

Having established the soundness of probabilistically interpreted psycholinguistically-based representations, we turn now to the question of feasibility. How do people reason with so much complexity? The magnitude and complexity of conceptual knowledge has been dealt with in linguistic semantics chiefly by ignoring it and in computational semantics in ways which introduce other problems. Either semantic knowledge has been defined as knowledge of primitives (the classical theory) or the problem has been narrowed by domain-specificity. However, denial of the essential complexity of conceptual knowledge limits the theory unacceptably. The NS hypothesis is that for kind terms complexity is reduced by correlational constraints, called **kind types** (Dahlgren and McDowell, 1986a), which are commonsense reflections of the structure of the actual world. As Rosch (1978) pointed out, features of real-world objects do not occur independently of each other in cognitive structures. These constraints make highly unlikely the description of a concept such as "THORK, a bird with wheels." These constraints take the problem of complexity head on. Similar constraints, called **relational types**, affect conceptual knowledge associated with verbs.

People employ correlational constraints in sentence interpretation. Consider the sentence "The chicken has wheels." It can only be interpreted metaphorically, or in some way that makes the chicken unlike any real chicken. The necessary switch to metaphor, toys or pictures in interpreting such sentences empirically supports the claim that the conceptual system is encoded in such a way that it predicts feature types for certain types of objects. Kind types are types of kind terms

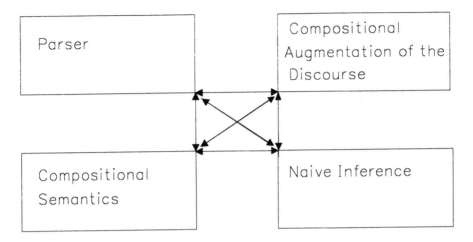

Figure 5: Components of Grammar in NS

with predictable feature types in their descriptions. These constraints predict that the set of features which can be used to describe an object or action is not all the features used to describe things, but a subset related to the ontological classification of the object. Each kind type is understood in terms of certain predictable feature types. NATURAL KINDs are conceived primarily in terms of perceptual features, while ARTIFACTs also have functional features, which NATURAL KINDs lack. SENTIENTs have internal traits, but ARTIFACTs do not, explaining why a sentence like *The machine is sad* cannot be interpreted literally. The principle that concepts in one kind type always lack feature types of concepts in another constrains the entire set of concepts. The constraints reflect the correlational structure of the actual world, though, like other aspects of conceptual knowledge, they are not truth functional. Kind Types logically are metasorts. Their logical and substantive properties are described in Chapter 3.

In summary, NS is a realist theory. It denies that meaning representations for common nouns provide criteria for membership in their extensions and that verb representations provide universally true implications of events. Instead, NS sees lexical meanings as naive theories. NS accounts for the success of natural language communication, given the vagueness and inaccuracy of word meanings, by the fact that natural language is anchored in the real world. There are some real, stable classes of objects which nouns are used to refer to, and mental representations of their characteristics are close enough to true, enough of the time, to make reference using nouns possible. Similarly, there are real classes of events which verbs report, and mental representations of their implications are approximately true. The vagueness and inaccuracy of mental representations requires nonmonotonic reasoning in drawing inferences based upon them.

NS identifies concept representation with word meaning representation, and denies a separate linguistic level of word meaning. At the same time, the autonomy of combinatorial semantics and of syntax is retained. Thus, NS also differs from approaches which use semantically-driven parsing, and instead NS assumes that parsing is a separate component from interpretation. Figure 5 on page 35 depicts the NS model. It has an autonomous syntactic component, which draws upon naive semantic information for problems such as prepositional phrase attachment and word sense disambiguation. Another autonomous component interprets the compositional semantics of sentences and discourses, as in (Kamp, 1981). Another component models naive semantics and completes the discourse representation which includes the implications of the text. All of these components operate in parallel, and have access to each other's representations whenever necessary. The workings of this model are explored in Chapter 8.

1.9. Comparison of NS with Computational Models

NS differs from approaches which employ truth-conditional, exhaustive decompositions. In those approaches, a word such as *elephant* is defined by primitives such as "has 4 legs" and "mammal." The claim is that all and any elephants have 4 legs. In contrast, NS descriptions are probabilistic. NS accepts elephants with 3 legs, though it represents the belief that elephants inherently have 4 legs. It accepts eggs which are brown, even though it also represents the belief that eggs are typically white. Further, in classical approaches, since descriptions are meant to be defining, non-defining associated information is not encoded. By contrast, NS represents a great deal of information usually associated with a concept, without the implicit claim that it applies to all instantiations of the concept. ELEPHANT can have features "not forgetful," "lumbering" and so forth, without claiming that all instances of the concept (elephants) have those features. Whereas in classical approaches, success is measured by finding a small and manageable set of primitives with which to represent all meanings, NS predicts that in principle there could be far more features in descriptions than there are words of English. In NS the content of features is seen as essentially limitless. So in naive semantics, featural descriptions associated with words have as values other words, as in Schubert, et al (1979), not primitives. It is left to a more fully developed understanding of cognition that exists at present to explain these feature values, by showing their connections with the perceptual system, their basis in judgments of category similarity.

Since NS attempts to model the English speaker's naive theory, NS representations consist of what people say when asked to write down the properties of objects and the implications of events. Rather than taking as primary someone's intuitions about the meaning relations between words in semantic fields, NS takes evidence of cognitive representations as basic. In NS semantic field relationships can be deduced, because the information which makes members of a semantic field similar is encoded, but such relationships are not the basis of the methodology. As Schubert, et al (1979) point out, inference-sharing among similar words need not be directly encoded. In NS, the content of word representations is derived from empirical data about the cognitive structure of the categories named by the words. Thus NS differs from other approaches in that it is psycholinguistically based. Clearly NS represents only part of the cognitive representation. We know that there is more to naive theories than what subjects write down in 1.5 minutes. However, what subjects say does reflect some of the richness of naive theories, if incompletely. NS differs as well in using standard first-order logic rather than a special representation language. Because NS targets the word level, to a large extent the results are transportable to any domain. The word level is useful throughout a linguistic community.

The NS approach bears a number of similarities to the approach being taken in the Tacitus Project (Hobbs, et al, 1986), which had its origins in efforts by researchers in Artificial Intelligence to encode large amounts of commonsense knowledge with the aim of controlling robots. Subsequently, commonsense knowledge research was integrated with research in text understanding. The goal of the Tacitus Project is to understand text about machine failures using CK. In orientation, the approaches are quite similar. The difference is the methodology. The Tacitus Project builds a complete naive theory of "commonsense metaphysics" and uses elements of this model as primitives in word meaning representations. The representations of naive physics are first order formulas (like our ontology). The domains of interest in naive metaphysics are scalar notions, granularity, time, space, material, physical objects, causality, functionality, force and shape. Meanings of lexical items are represented in term of these core theories. The word "wear down" is defined in terms of "abrasive event," which is defined in terms of "remove" and "particle." "Remove" is defined in terms of a "change" from "attached" to "not attached." Words meanings are refined down to the level of naive metaphysical concepts such as space, time and surface. There is also the goal of having naive inferences "provable" within the system. So, from "high usage" the system should be able to infer "likelihood of wear."

> Usage is a set of using events, and the verticality requirement on "high" forces us to coerce the phrase into "a high or large number of using events." Combining this with an axiom that says that the use of a mechanical device involves the likelihood of abrasive events...and with the definition of "wear" in terms of abrasive events, we should be able to conclude likelihood of wear.

There are several methodological differences here. NS does not attempt to make a coherent system of axioms out of naive theories. The feature types and kind types are relatively gross constraints on concepts. We ask subjects what features they think are characteristic of objects, and what implications events have. The resulting set of features could in principle be inconsistent, although they usually are not. There is no attempt to connect naive theories with naive physics. The Tacitus project was originally concerned with robot control, where the naive theory has to connect with physical operations and spatial layouts, while our goal has been to infer the relevance of text to a reader's stated interests. Our goal does not require contact with extensions, as robot control does. As a result of the less stringent constraints on our naive theories, we have been able to represent hundreds of words (as will be detailed in Chapters 2 and 4), and use these representations to address several outstanding problems in computational linguistics. In contrast, the Tacitus project has represented a few words, but in ways which completely work out the logic of a naive theory.

1.10. Limitations of NS

One limitation of NS is that we know that some concepts are represented in non-verbal ways (such as color and other perceptual terms). Even portions of natural kind terms are represented perceptually. For example, the concept ORANGE probably includes a memory of taste. Rosch (1978) has shown that cognitive representations of a number of concrete categories involve motor movements. The representation of CHAIR includes memory of the motion of sitting down in one.

Another problem is that while word level CK is useful, it is insufficient to provide all of the inferencing power people use in interpreting text. Practically anything people know can, in certain discourse contexts, be used in interpreting the discourse. Between two individuals, common knowledge unknown to anyone else can be used to make discourse coherent. So NS can go only so far. Until massive computer databases of general knowledge exist (as for example, that of Lenat, 1986), computational text understanding will reflect only a small part of human text interpretation.

In NS, some features are unanalyzed predicates. At the lowest level in the system (feature values), the system doesn't really understand. Until these features can be translated into operational or visually-based representations, they will remain mere symbols.

Another drawback of word level representations for a dialect is that word meanings vary in situations (that is, the physical and social settings in which language is used). Dialect representations are incorrect in certain situations. For example, in one office the term *secretary* may refer to persons who type, file and answer telephones, and in another, persons who format word processing texts for printing. If all speakers involved speak a single dialect, such as California undergraduate English, their use and understanding of English will nevertheless differ in the office context. To be useful, such a lexical representation must be localized, reflecting slight changes in usage for particular domains.

Though context is a problem, word level representations are actually the most productive starting point, and should lay the basis for a theory of contextualization. The most useful computational models of text understanding will be those which model a dialect closely, rather than those which provide a representation scheme and no words, on the grounds that word meanings are context dependent. Given the limited capabilities of text understanding systems in the short term, the most useful program of research is lexical representation of the dialect. Users of a system which modeled their dialect closely would not need to be knowledge engineers. From a base of several thousand words, they could localize the system to the desired contexts, encoding only the differences between the local use of certain words and their general use in the dialect. In the long term, research targeting word meaning in a language should lay the basis for research into automatic contextualization.

Another problem is the lack of a well-developed nonmonotonic logic for NS. The effect of "Typically" and "Inherently" in the generic representations is to predict that people are willing to override descriptions in cognitive representations. For example, a text which described water as muddy should be understandable. This is a very problematical area which has received a lot of attention in the artificial intelligence literature (McCarthy and Hayes, 1969, Reiter, 1980, Halpern, 1986, Asher, 1984, Dunin-Keplicz, 1986).

As a first approach to nonmonotonic reasoning, NS makes the simplifying assumption that the text contains no metaphor and can be taken as literal (the "literal text" assumption). In the literature on computational models of belief (Halpern, 1986), a major problem is autoepistemic reasoning. Given one of the speaker's beliefs, which additional beliefs can be ascribed to the speaker? If it is assumed that the text is literal, the problem is simplified, because only the revisability of the reader's beliefs need be modeled. The statements of the text can be assumed true (intended as true by the writer). In other words, the text obeys Gricean conversational maxims. (Other work will have to take into account falsity in the text, and beliefs of actors in the text, an especially important issue in narrative). The beliefs of a reader with respect to a theory of the world are incorrect and inconsistent. NS assumes essentially probabilistic representations, e.g., mechanics typically fix cars, where "typically" is interpreted as a probability. We need a corresponding theory of naive inference, of what counts as "true" for the reader (where "true" is warranted belief). Presumably the reason for reading literal text is to learn about the world, so the theory of naive inference would account nonmonotonically for how to get from the understanding of the text to a new set of beliefs, and how these beliefs are likely to be reflected in the actual world (or in databases).

One aspect of nonmonotonic logic concerns the interpretation of pronouns as in (26) and (27).

(26)   John has a brother who is a mechanic.

(27)   He helped him fix his pickup.

Though the text is ambiguous, the preferred interpretation is that "he" in sentence (27) refers to the same individual as "a brother" in (26). (On the less plausible reading, "he" refers to the same individual as "John"). People infer that "he" is the brother because mechanics typically fix cars. But they know that the inference is only tentative and could be proven invalid by subsequent text, such as "John was angry that he had to help his brother." This reasoning is nonmonotonic because the anaphoric inference which identifies the brother with "he" does not have the same validity as information unambiguously asserted by the text as such. If sentence (26) is represented as (28), the inference represented as (29) is only tentative.

(28)   has(john,Y1) & brother(john,Y1) & mechanic(Y1)

(29)   P(help(past,Y2,Y3)) & P((Y3 = john) & (Y2 = Y1))

A second aspect of nonmonotonic reasoning has to do with discourse relations. Consider the text in (30).

(30)   John entered his manager's office. He asked for a raise.

So far the text is the same as "The Programmer" and readers infer that John entered the office with the goal of asking for a raise. But if the next sentence is (31), that inference must be withdrawn and be replaced with the inference that entering the office only enabled, but did not have as goal, the asking.

(31)   He hadn't intended to, but he couldn't control himself.

This example illustrates two problems in nonmonotonic reasoning. One is that inferences need to be given some kind of strength measures. The goal inference above should be weaker than the inference that directly after entering the office, John is in the office. Secondly, it illustrates the classic problem of incomplete knowledge. Without some heuristics, the potential that new information will weaken or override previous inferences implies inherently exponential growth in the amount of reasoning required as more text is read.

A third aspect of nonmonotonic reasoning in text understanding reflects typicality in generic descriptions. Suppose that a text says:

John's shirt was the same color as the apple he was eating.
It was a lovely pale yellow.

After the first sentence it can be inferred that both the shirt and the apple are "red," because apples are typically red. After the second sentence, the reader knows that the text claims that the shirt was yellow, not red. The ability to infer red(X) only tentatively, and to override it in light of new evidence must be modelled. Some kind of modal operators on the inferences are required.

apple(X) $\rightarrow$ P(red(X))

A most promising approach to this is (Asher, 1984). Asher proposes an interpretation of P as a "speaker content function" based upon conditional probability. The formalism must also take into account possible feature values, so that turquoise is not a possible value of the feature type color for APPLE. In other words, there is a closed-world assumption for certain feature/kind pairs. It also assigns probabilities to each feature value in the range of possible values for each feature type. A portion of the generic description of *apple* illustrates the formalism. The example states that with regard to the feature type COLOR, APPLE can have values red, green, yellow and no others, with subjective probabilities .5, .3 and .2, respectively. For the feature type SIZE, APPLE can only have the value handleable.

apple {color((red,.5),(green,.3),(yellow,.2)),(size(handleable, 1.))}

1.11. Organization of the Book

Chapters 2-4 describe NS lexical representations. Chapter 2 presents and justifies the approach to nouns in NS. Chapter 3 explains the derivation of kind types from noun representations. Chapter 4 explains the basis of verb representations. In the remaining chapters, the NS approach is brought to bear upon a number of outstanding problems in computational linguistics which have seemed unsolvable because they involve world knowledge. Chapter 5 describes the functioning of the Kind Types system, a text understanding system embodying NS solutions to these problems. Chapter 6 delineates the NS solution to prepositional phrase attachment ambiguities. Chapter 7 treats word sense disambiguation. Finally, Chapter 8 explores a method of extracting coherence relations from discourse, using syntactic, compositional semantic and naive semantic information in parallel.

2. NOUN REPRESENTATION

2.1. The Ontological Schema

The NS representation of nouns has two aspects, classification and generic knowledge. The NS classification scheme is an ontology which sorts objects and events into major categories (e.g., REAL vs ABSTRACT). The basis of the scheme derives from psycholinguistic evidence of the way people view the major category cuts of the environment, linguistic evidence like selectional restrictions, and philosophic concerns. Generic knowledge consists of features considered common to objects in the naive view of the world. The features in NS representations are taken from psycholinguistic studies in the prototype theory. Each feature is typed appropriately (e.g., COLOR, SIZE). The generic knowledge is constrained by *kind types*, which reflect correlational constraints among feature types in descriptions of objects subordinate to nodes in the ontology. Kind types are presented in Chapter 3.

Some of the NS ontology appears in Table 2.1. It is intended to reflect naive belief concerning the structure of the actual world and the significant "joints" in that structure. It encodes the major category cuts of the environment recognized by the dialect of English it models. The term "taxonomy" is also used for a similar classificatory scheme in other theories. We call it an ontology rather than a taxonomy, because of the underlying philosophical stance which sees a complex causal relation between the structure of the actual world and the commonsense view of the world's structure. The goal is to encode an ontology which is consistent with an empirically verifiable cognitive model. As much evidence as possible was derived from linguistic and psycholinguistic research. The schema was originally developed to handle the predicates, both nouns and verbs, found in 4100 words of geography text drawn from textbooks.

Table 2.1 The Ontological Schema

ENTITY	→	(ABSTRACT V REAL) & (INDIVIDUAL V COLLECTIVE)
ABSTRACT	→	IDEAL V PROPOSITIONAL V QUANTITY V IRREAL
QUANTITY	→	NUMERICAL V MEASURE
REAL	→	(PHYSICAL V TEMPORAL V SENTIENT) & (NATURAL V SOCIAL)
PHYSICAL	→	(STATIONARY V NONSTATIONARY) & (LIVING V NONLIVING)
NONSTATIONARY	→	(SELFMOVING V NONSELFMOVING)
COLLECTIVE	→	MASS V SET V STRUCTURE
TEMPORAL	→	RELATIONAL V NONRELATIONAL
RELATIONAL	→	(EVENT V STATE) & (MENTAL V EMOTIONAL V NONMENTAL)
EVENT	→	(GOAL V NONGOAL) & (ACTIVITY V ACCOMPLISHMENT V ACHIEVEMENT)

At this writing, 1500 nouns and 600 verbs have been classified in terms of the ontology (and represented generically as well).

2.2. Mathematical Properties of the Ontology

Despite the complexity of constructing a computer model of the ontology, two commonly-used simplifications, binary trees and n-ary trees, were rejected. First, though binary trees, such as Figure 6 on page 47 (adapted from Keil (1979), have simplifying mathematical properties, they are not likely to be psychologically real. People easily think in terms of more than two branches, such as FISH vs BIRD vs MAMMAL, and so on, off of the VERTEBRATE node. Secondly, most representations assume that the ontology is a tree and that at each node a single choice is made, so that the resulting structure is planar. But cross-classification is needed since commonsense reasoning uses it. People understand, for example, that entities cross-classify as either individuals or collectives and as either real or abstract. This means that at each node, more than one plane might be needed for

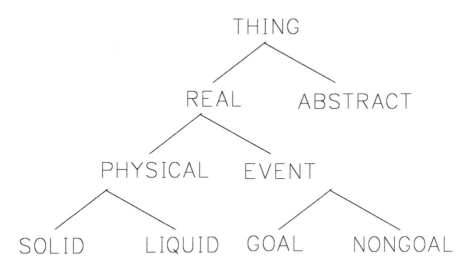

Figure 6: Binary Ontology

branching. We use a cross-classification hierarchy that permits each node to be cross-classified in *n* ways. For example, in the top level rule of Table 2.1 ENTITY cross-classifies as either ABSTRACT or REAL, and as either INDIVIDUAL or COLLECTIVE. This corresponds to the claim that cognitively there are essentially parallel ontological schemas for individuals and collectives. For example, people know that a cow is an animal, real and concrete, and a herd consists of animals, also real and concrete. Thus we have the parallel ontology fragments in Figure 7 on page 48. Table 2.2 illustrates the assignment of the words *cow, herd, idea* and *book* under ENTITY. The coding of the cross-classification is handled as in (McCord, 1985).

The ontology also assumes instantiations may be multiply attached to nodes. Thus the representation is actually a lattice rather than a tree. For example, an entity, John, is a HUMAN with the physical properties of a MAMMAL, and is also a PERSON who thinks, under SENTIENT. Similarly, a clinic is both an INSTITUTION and a PLACE. There are a number of semantic and syntactic effects of this duality. Because a clinic is an institution, *clinic* can be the subject of mental verbs such as *announce* and *schedule*, as in *The clinic announced new services*. Because *clinic* is a place it can figure in locational prep-

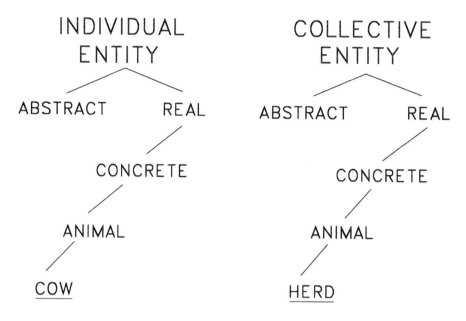

Figure 7: Parallel Portions of the Ontology

ositional phrases, as in *John drove to the clinic.* To capture this duality in the ontological schema, *clinic* is attached to both PLACE and IN-STITUTION. Multiple attachment was justified by an examination of the texts. It was found that references to human beings in text deal with them either as persons (SENTIENTs) or as ANIMALs (physiological beings), but rarely as both at the same time.

	INDIVIDUAL	COLLECTIVE
REAL	*cow*	*herd*
ABSTRACT	*idea*	*book*
Table 2.2 *Entity Node Cross Classification*		

2.3. Ontological Categories

The INDIVIDUAL/COLLECTIVE cut had to be made at the level of ENTITY (the highest level) at the same place as the ABSTRACT/REAL cut. We found that the INDIVIDUAL/COLLECTIVE distinction pervades the lexicon and must be a primary cut in the ontology. Our term COLLECTIVE applies to all collections of entities. There are three subgroups. Sets are collectives in which each member of the set is identical to all the others (*herd, mob, crowd, fleet*). Masses are collections whose members are referred to only in terms of measurable units (*sand, water*). Finally, there are structures where the members have specified relations, such as in institutions (*school, company, village*). Some properties work differently for the collectives than for individuals. Because *cow* is attached under ANIMAL, "cow is a kind of animal" is true. In contrast, *herd* attaches to ANIMAL, but "a herd is a kind of animal" is not true. A herd consists of animals. We have found that though there are gaps among the collectives, a surprising number of types of entities have collective names in English. For example, propositions come in collectives (*discourse, theme, book*). Animals come in collectives (*school, swarm, gaggle, herd*). The distinction is reflected in the selectional properties of verbs as well as nouns. Many verbs select only INDIVIDUAL (*mingle*) or only COLLECTIVE (*stampede*) subjects or objects.

REAL entities sort themselves among the categories PHYSICAL, TEMPORAL, and SENTIENT. This distinguishes thinking beings, which includes persons, roles and institutions, from all other objects and events. At this same choice point, real entities also cross-classify as NATURAL and SOCIAL. Table 2.3 illustrates the assignment of example words under the REAL cross-classification.

The SENTIENT/PHYSICAL distinction is placed high because in commonsense reasoning, the properties of people and things are very different. SENTIENT is often placed as a subordinate of LIVING (Keil, 1979). Instead of loading all of that complexity into a single HUMAN node under ANIMAL, we make the SENTIENT/NON-SENTIENT distinction high up in the hierarchy. There is ample

	INDIVIDUAL		COLLECTIVE	
	NATURAL	SOCIAL	NATURAL	SOCIAL
PHYSICAL	rock	knife	sand	fleet
SENTIENT	man	programmer	mob	clinic
TEMPORAL	earthquake	party	winter	epoch

Table 2.3 *Attachment of Nouns under REAL*

support in the philosophical and psychological literature for the fundamental nature of the distinction. Strawson argues that the most fundamental distinction in epistemology (human knowledge) is that between thinking and non-thinking beings (Strawson, 1953). In cognitive psychological research, Gelman and Spelke (1981) show that newborns can distinguish humans from all other objects, and that they rapidly develop a deeper and more complex understanding of humans than of other objects (Gelman and Spelke, 1981). Another reason for placing SENTIENT high up in the ontology is that it captures the linguistic fact that a number of verbs select for persons, roles and institutions as subjects or objects. *John, secretary* and *college* may all serve as subject of mental verbs such as *sue* and *argue*. Thus the SENTIENT distinction captures the similarity between persons and institutions or roles. A final reason for the distinction is word sense ambiguity facts. For example, a large number of nouns in English have an ambiguity between a locational and institutional reading, which can be accounted for by the SENTIENT distinction. In (32) below, *office* has the PLACE reading, and in (33) the SENTIENT reading.

(32)   John's office is on Main Street.

(33)   John's office called Harry.

Also, a number of verbs are disambiguated according to whether they have SENTIENT subjects. The verb *support* in (34) is likely to have the financial sense because the subject is SENTIENT, whereas the verb *support* in (35) has the physical reading.

(34)   The investors supported the bank.

(35)   The sandbags supported the bank.

The NATURAL/SOCIAL distinction was also placed high in the hierarchy. Entities (or events) which come into being (or take place) naturally must be distinguished from those which arise through some sort of social intervention. Entities which are products of society, and thereby have a social function, are viewed as fundamentally different from natural entities in the commonsense conceptual scheme. The distinction is a basic one psychologically (Miller, 1978, Gelman and Spelke, 1981). SOCIAL entities are those which come into being only in a social or institutional setting, with "institution" being understood in the broadest sense, for instance family, government, education, warfare, organized religion, etc. Social entities are always functional. Although natural objects are sometimes used functionally, as when a rock is used as a weapon, social objects such as a knife can only come into being socially, and never naturally. This is the basic distinction between SOCIAL and NATURAL entities in the ontology.

Dahlgren (1988b) justifies the NATURAL/SOCIAL distinction philosophically, and argues that it reflects a difference in kinds, because social terms refer to kinds just as natural kind terms do. Kinds are classes or real world objects such as Water and Lemon which have an explanatory internal similarity among them. The communicative effect of such terms in a natural language crucially depends upon the existence of at least some real classes of objects corresponding to the terms. The claim is that there are also real classes of social objects such as Knife and Secretary, and that the similarity of objects in these classes is not merely perceived.

The NATURAL/SOCIAL distinction applies to SENTIENT just as it does to PHYSICAL. A NATURAL, SENTIENT entity is a PERSON, that is a *man, woman, boy,* whereas a SOCIAL, SENTIENT entity is a ROLE, *secretary, miner, president.* A collection of PERSONs is a BODY, *crowd, mob.* A collection of ROLEs is an INSTITUTION, *hospital, school.* The distinction affects all nodes under REAL. EVENTs are either NATURAL (*earthquake*) or SOCIAL(*party*). The distinction applies to verbs (RELATIONALs) as well as nouns (see Chapter 4). An example is *run* vs *jog.* Multiple attachment interacts with this distinction. John is NATURAL as a HUMAN, SENTIENT and SOCIAL as a PROGRAMMER, and SENTIENT and NATURAL as a PERSON. Again, there is the possibility of multiple attachment. We reserved the term ARTIFACT for NON-LIVING SOCIAL objects to distinguish them from natural non-living objects.

2.4. Nominal Terminal Nodes

Every path through the ontology results in a terminal node which is named and which represents a unique class defined by its attachments up the hierarchy. The higher node names have theoretical importance, but the terminal node names are for convenience only. Terminal node names distinguish the individuals from the collectives. For instance, the collective node corresponding to PLANT is FLORA. The individual node corresponding to DISCOURSE is PROPOSITION. Similarly, STUFF is the collective of MINERAL, INSTITUTION is the collective of ROLE, and BODY is the collective of PERSON, etc. Table 2.4 gives a list of the terminal nodes in the schema, along with examples of nouns which attach to them, and the path from the higher-level nodes to the terminal nodes.

Table 2.4 Nominal Terminal Nodes

justice	**IDEAL_THING**	←	INDIVIDUAL & IDEAL
sentence	**PROPOSITION**	←	INDIVIDUAL & PROPOSITIONAL
one	**NUMERICAL**	←	INDIVIDUAL & QUANTITY
inch	**MEASURE**	←	INDIVIDUAL & QUANTITY
unicorn	**IMAGINARY**	←	INDIVIDUAL & IRREAL
man	**PERSON**	←	INDIVIDUAL & SENTIENT & NATU-RAL
nurse	**ROLE**	←	INDIVIDUAL & SENTIENT & SOCIAL
hurricane	**ACT_OF_GOD**	←	INDIVIDUAL & NATURAL & EVENT
party	**SOCIAL_EVENT**	←	INDIVIDUAL & SOCIAL & EVENT
heat	**NATURAL_STATE**	←	INDIVIDUAL & NATURAL & STATE
love	**SOCIAL_STATE**	←	INDIVIDUAL & SOCIAL & STATE
tree	**PLANT**	←	INDIVIDUAL & NATURAL & STATIONARY & LIVING
mountain	**NATURAL_PLACE**	←	INDIVIDUAL & NATURAL & STATIONARY & NONLIVING
elephant	**ANIMAL**	←	INDIVIDUAL & NATURAL & SELFMOVING & LIVING
spore	**LOWER_ORDER**	←	INDIVIDUAL & NATURAL & NONSELFMOVING & LIVING
river	**FLOW**	←	INDIVIDUAL & NATURAL & SELFMOVING & NONLIVING
rock	**MINERAL**	←	INDIVIDUAL & NATURAL & NONSELFMOVING & NONLIVING
building	**SOCIAL_PLACE**	←	INDIVIDUAL & SOCIAL & STATIONARY & NONLIVING
wheat	**DOMESTIC_ PLANT**	←	INDIVIDUAL & SOCIAL & STATIONARY & LIVING
steer	**DOMESTIC_ ANIMAL**	←	INDIVIDUAL & SOCIAL & SELFMOVING & LIVING
e. coli	**CULTURE**	←	INDIVIDUAL & SOCIAL & NONSELFMOVING & LIVING
truck	**VEHICLE**	←	INDIVIDUAL & SOCIAL & SELFMOVING & NONLIVING
knife	**MANMADEOBJ**	←	INDIVIDUAL & SOCIAL & NONSELFMOVING & NONLIVING
	PLACE	←	INDIVIDUAL & NONLIVING & STATIONARY

Table 2.4 (Cont.) Nominal Terminal Nodes

	ARTIFACT	←	INDIVIDUAL & SOCIAL & NONLIVING
	DOMESTIC_ VERTEBRATE	←	DOMESTIC_ANIMAL
chicken	**DOMESTIC_BIRD**	←	DOMESTIC_VERTEBRATE
bird	**VERTEBRATE**	←	ANIMAL
sparrow	**BIRD**	←	VERTEBRATE
trout	**FISH**	←	VERTEBRATE
bovine	**MAMMAL**	←	VERTEBRATE
moose	**BOVINE**	←	MAMMAL
monkey	**PRIMATE**	←	MAMMAL
John	**HUMAN**	←	PRIMATE
law	**IDEAL_GROUP**	←	COLLECTIVE & IDEAL
novel	**DISCOURSE**	←	COLLECTIVE & PROPOSITIONAL
host	**IRREAL_GROUP**	←	COLLECTIVE & IRREAL
crowd	**BODY**	←	COLLECTIVE & SENTIENT & NATURAL
clinic	**INSTITUTION**	←	COLLECTIVE & SENTIENT & SOCIAL
monsoon	**ACT_OF_GOD_ GROUP**	←	COLLECTIVE & NATURAL & EVENT
winter	**NATURAL_STATE GROUP**	←	COLLECTIVE & NATURAL & STATE
forest	**FLORA**	←	COLLECTIVE & NATURAL & STATIONARY & LIVING
range	**REGION**	←	COLLECTIVE & NATURAL & STATIONARY & NONLIVING
pod	**FAUNA**	←	COLLECTIVE & NATURAL & SELFMOVING & LIVING
mold	**LOWER_ORDER GROUP**	←	COLLECTIVE & NATURAL & NONSELFMOVING & LIVING
river sys-tem	**FLOW_GROUP**	←	COLLECTIVE & NATURAL & SELFMOVING & NONLIVING
gold	**STUFF**	←	COLLECTIVE & NATURAL & NONSELFMOVING & NONLIVING

Table 2.4 (cont.) Nominal Terminal Nodes

renaissance	**HISTORICAL_ EPOCH**	←	COLLECTIVE & SOCIAL & EVENT
marriage	**SOCIAL_STATE_ GROUP**	←	COLLECTIVE & SOCIAL & STATE
wheat	**CROP**	←	COLLECTIVE & SOCIAL & STATION-ARY & LIVING
shopping mall	**COMPLEX**	←	COLLECTIVE & SOCIAL & STATION-ARY & NONLIVING
drove	**HERD**	←	COLLECTIVE & SOCIAL & SELFMOVING & LIVING
penicillin	**CULTURE_ GROUP**	←	COLLECTIVE & SOCIAL & NONSELFMOVING & LIVING
armada	**FLEET**	←	COLLECTIVE & SOCIAL & SELFMOVING & NONLIVING
assemblage	**COLLECTION**	←	COLLECTIVE & SOCIAL & NONSELFMOVING & NONLIVING
	PRODUCT	←	COLLECTIVE & SOCIAL & NONLIV-ING
	AREA	←	COLLECTIVE & NONLIVING & STA-TIONARY

2.5. Construction of the Ontology

The ontological schema was developed in two steps. First, the verbs from the corpus of geography texts were classified according to selectional restrictions (SRs) on subjects and objects. Second, the minimal categories needed to accommodate these SRs were arranged in a hierarchical schema. Certain SRs, such as HUMAN, LIVING, CONCRETE, were expected. Others were surprises. Some verbs required complements that were marked for PLACE, and others required either subjects or objects to have certain moveability features. These are:

STATIONARY: normally immobile, attached to the earth, moved only at great effort (*tree, building*).
SELFMOVING: normally in motion or designed for motion, in some cases with no apparent initial source (*dog, truck*).

NONSELFMOVING: normally immobile but can be moved with slight effort (*brick, rock*). A source for the motion is expected, usually something SELFMOVING.

Once the set of categories was established, the next stage was fitting them into an ISA hierarchy. There were several constraints guiding this process. First, we wanted the ontology to reflect findings from recent work in cognitive psychology on conceptualization (Keil, 1979, Miller, 1978, Gelman and Spelke, 1981), as well as linguistic facts such as selectional restrictions. Second, the ontology had to be as compact as possible. Third, we wished to minimize empty terminal nodes to which no nouns attached. During this process it was also necessary to decide which of the SRs represented category cuts in an ontological schema and which were merely features on individual lexical items. The guiding principle here was that if the distinction under examination (e.g. LIVING/NON-LIVING) pervaded some subhierarchy, then it was assigned to a branching point. But if some distinction appeared only in isolated parts of the hierarchy, then it was represented as a feature. Properties which were assigned feature status were items like SIZE and FUNCTION.

2.6. Other Ontologies

Because the ontology is based on findings in cognitive psychology, linguistic selectional restrictions, and philosophical concerns, we predict that it should be easily transportable to new domains. The ontology, if valid, should be useful everywhere and readily expandable to take into account detailed classifications in specific domains.

Adding a new domain should involve growing the ontology at the leaves, not changing the higher-level nodes. This prediction has proven true thus far. We have been successful in adding the domain of business, finance, and international trade to the original geography vocabulary.

There are a number of steps in the process of adding a domain. Each node in the ontology is a set of category labels which defines a class of terms. Attached to most nodes, but not all, is a set of feature types which serves as a template for generic information for any word attached at that node. The first step in adding a new word to the ontology is to try to attach it to one of these terminal nodes. This process has one of three results: (1) In the case of a match, the new word is subsumed under the kind type associated with the terminal node and is attached to the terminal node, inheriting all the feature types attached along the path. (2) In one kind of non-match the terminal node is too finely specified and the set of category labels includes some that do not apply. In this case, the word is attached higher up in the ontology. This is usually the case for generic and superordinate terms. (3) In the other kind of non-match the terminal node is underspecified for the word. In this case the ontology must be grown out from the terminal node. Such a situation will arise in parts of the ontology which at present are shallow and under-developed or when a new domain is encountered. Adding cross-classifications at terminal nodes results in growing the ontology "downward" to create new paths and new terminal nodes, with the old terminal nodes now becoming higher-level nodes. For instance, the node ANIMAL could be cross-classified very finely with the taxonomic classes of the science of zoology, if necessary, or with a more commonsense cross- classification on the order of PETS vs. DOMESTIC vs. WILD, combined with 4-LEGGED vs. FLYING vs. CRAWLING vs. SWIMMING, for instance. Occasionally terms will be encountered that cannot be handled in any of these ways. In these cases, it may be necessary to introduce a new cross-classification at a higher level node. For instance, in adding the words needed to read the *Wall Street Journal*, we encounter a class of terms which refer to financial instruments (*stock, bond, letter of credit, voucher, check, coupon*, etc.). While these terms all have a physical manifestation (some piece of paper), in general when referred to they are intangible (*IBM's stock went up one point yesterday*). Care must be taken when adding cross-classifications at a higher node, however, to avoid proliferating empty terminal nodes. This is a sure sign that the proposed cross-classification is spurious. That is, it is likely that a TANGIBLE/INTANGIBLE distinction is genuine for certain SOCIAL entities only.

On the other hand it is known that the commonsense view of the world includes a number of different points of view in which the same objects are classified in different ways (Cantor and Mischel, 1979). For example, in developing the ontology, we attempted to include FOOD. But people do not classify foods as ANIMAL vs PLANT, but rather according to their function in meals, or the way they are arranged in grocery stores. Further, any object has a different set of properties as a FOOD than it has as a LIVING thing. FOODs have flavor and method of cooking, while LIVING things have habitat and behavior. Thus there are a number of possible ontologies in CK, but we know that the one described in this chapter is employed in all domains.

2.7. Generic Knowledge

A corpus of 4100 words of geography text was used as the starting point of the analysis, because geographies have wide ontological coverage in the vocabulary they employ. The texts in the corpus describe lifestyle and industry in various countries. A good first approximation of cognitive structures are the features which come from psycholinguistic studies in which subjects are asked to freelist characteristics common to objects in categories such as DOG, LEMON and SECRETARY. Generic descriptions of the nouns in the text were drawn from such psycholinguistic data to the extent possible. The features were those listed by subjects as "characteristic" of objects in psycholinguistic experiments in the prototype theory (Rosch et al, 1976, Ashcraft, 1976, Fehr and Russell, 1984, Dahlgren, 1985a). The generic information represented for nouns are features which one-fifth of the subjects free-listed when asked to list characteristics or descriptions of objects named by the nouns. The number of subjects ranged from 20 to 75. Turning the experiment around, and asking other subjects to rate these features, they rate them as highly typical. In other words, subjects whose task is rating agree with the freelisters. Any feature which is produced in a freelisting experiment by several subjects is thus likely to be shared in the relevant subpopulation (Dahlgren, 1985a). The number of features shared for a term in this way averaged 15. The source of descriptions of social roles was data collected by Dahlgren (1985a). For physical objects we used generic descriptions from Ashcraft (Ashcraft, 1976), including raw data generously supplied by the author. For those nouns where no data existed, generic descriptions were constructed in conformance with the types of information generated by subjects for similar nouns.

NS representations of this psycholinguistic information consist of two lists which are associated with each noun. The first is a list of typical features and the second is a list of inherent features. A typical feature is one which subjects believe applies to typical instances of the concept. Most concepts have more typical features than inherent features. A programmer is typically "intelligent"; a company typically has "employees," a "president" and "secretaries," and so on. Inherent features are those which seem to form part of the essential nature of the kind or class of objects referred to by a term. Thus, a man is inherently "male," a wife is inherently "married," a knife inherently "cuts." From our sample, a programmer inherently "programs a computer" and is "trained," a company inherently "engages in business." The typical/ inherent distinction is important in reasoning. We are much more willing to override a feature like "intelligent" for programmer than we are a feature like "programs a computer." The decision to place features in the typical list or the inherent list for a sort or predicate was decided by two judges.

These representations are illustrated by PROGRAMMER in (36). PROGRAMMER is attached to the terminal node ROLE and thereby inherits SENTIENT, SOCIAL, REAL, INDIVIDUAL, and ENTITY from the ontology. The generic information is shown as two lists enclosed in braces, the typical list followed by the inherent list. The entire representation is a two-place ground clause in VM/PROLOG. All features are categorized into types such as COLOR, SIZE, and so on. This becomes important in reasoning, as will become clearer in Chapter 5.

(36)   programmer ({income(high), relation(work(subj, for(Z)) & salary(Z)),
         relation(work(subj,in(Y)) & organization(Y) & large(Y)),
         relation(employee),internal-trait(shy),internal-trait(mathematical),
         internal-trait(intelligent),internal-trait(organized),
         internal-trait(self-contained), appearance(wear(subj,X) &

glasses(X))},
{(function(program(subj,W) & computer(W)),
education(trained),
status(high), tool(computer)}).

2.8. Word Senses

Many nouns have multiple senses. Although there are often met-aphorical relations between word senses, they are not predictable. Rather than compute relations between word senses, the senses are listed as separately indexed elements under a form (noun or verb). Very often the different senses have different ontological attachments. Five senses of *office* are listed in (37), corresponding to uses as below:

1. The office called John.
2. Mary went to the office.
3. John ran for office.
4. John contributed his good offices.
5. The U.S. Patent Office made a decision.

(37)   office({1,INSTITUTION,{hierarchy({management,staff}),
          roles({management(manager), staff(secretary),staff(clerk)})}},
          {function(business)}},

          {2,PLACE,{haspart(*,chairs),haspart(*,desks),
          haspart(*,telephones),haspart(*,typewriters),
          location(downtown)},{haspart(*,doors),
          haspart(*,windows),location(building)}}},

          {3,ROLEINITSELF,{function(legislative),

          function(executive),function(judicial),
          status(high)},{relation(elected),
          function(government)}}},
          {4,TEMPORAL,{},{function(service)}}},

          {5,INSTITUTION,{hierarchy({head,staff}),

roles({head(official),staff(researcher),
staff(clerk)})},{function(government),
rank(executive)}}).

2.9. Feature Types

The typical features are represented by the same set of predicates used to represent the inherent features, thus achieving some economy in the rules. Nevertheless, the number of features needed to encode generic knowledge is theoretically limitless. Fortunately, a small and manageable set of 54 feature types encodes all of the features encountered in the 1500 nouns described thus far. Table 2.5 lists all 54 feature types. The number of feature types should expand as more nouns are described, but not by much. When asked to list typical features of various concrete objects, subjects tend to name features which fall into a small number of types such as SIZE, COLOR, SHAPE, and FUNCTION (Rochester, 1976, Ashcraft, 1976). Similarly, in studies of social terms of English, subjects listed features which fell into just nine feature types, such as STATUS, SEX, INTERNAL TRAIT and RELATION (Dahlgren, 1985a). The protocols involved thousands of features. (These types are the basis of the kind types to be described in Chapter 3.)

Notice that a feature type such as SIZE or COLOR may be inherent for one noun but only typical for another. For instance, while blood inherently has COLOR "red," a brick is only typically "red." While a brick inherently has SHAPE "rectangular parallelopiped," bread is only typically "loaf-shaped." In some cases, a sort has both inherent and typical values for a single feature type. For example, a doctor has the inherent FUNCTION "treats sick people" and the typical FUNCTION "consoles sick people."

Table 2.5 Feature Types for Nouns		
age	appearance	association
associated entity	author	behavior
color	construction	content
direction	duration	education
exemplar	experienced as	in extension of
frequency	function	habitat
haspart	hasrole	hierarchy
internal trait	legal requirement	length
level	location	manner
material	name	object
odor	operation	owner
partof	physiology	processing
propagation	prototype	relation
requirement	rolein	roles
sex	shape	size
source	speed	state
status	strength	structure
taste	texture	time

2.10. Conclusion

The ontology in NS is similar to taxonomies in other systems. The difference is that nodes were included based upon findings in cognitive psychological research, linguistics and philosophy. The generic knowledge in NS is more of a departure from other lexical semantic theories. The representations are not seen as definitional, but as probabilistic, stereotypical pictures of the objects of reference. Further, representations are seen as open-ended. Only part of the competent speaker's naive theory is represented. However, this results in far richer, more inclusive representations than found in other frameworks. Features are not limited to a small subset of concepts. In principle, there could be as many or more features as English words. These rich representations must be constrained in some way. Chapter 3 describes the NS approach to constraints on generic knowledge.

3. KINDS, KIND TERMS AND COGNITIVE CATEGORIES

Naive Semantics is a realist theory which assumes that the stability of the actual objects and classes of objects (kinds) themselves explains the communicative power of natural language which logically is only probabilistic (Boyd, 1986). Some believe that actual objects are irrelevant to semantics because the cognitive model intervenes between language and the world. (Others believe that actual objects are irrelevant to cognitive psychology as well, because of distortions introduced by perception (e.g., Jackendoff, 1983)). The realist basis of NS is what makes it consistent with the commonsense knowledge tradition in artificial intelligence, which computationally models the relationship between humanlike reasoners (robots) and the actual world. NS hypothesizes that the reader's naive theory works because both the author and the reader use words with the intention of referring to real entities, real classes of entities (kinds) and real events and they succeed in referring enough of the time to make language a useful tool of communication (Kripke, 1972, Winograd, 1972, Putnam, 1975, Dahlgren, 1988b).

3.1. The Realist Basis of NS and Kind Terms

Fundamental to the realist basis of NS is the notion of kind terms, a subset of the common nouns (Quine, 1969, Carlson, 1977). Kind terms name collections of entities with an explanatory essential similarity among them. As Putnam (1973) puts it:

*An important class, philosophically as well as linguistically, is the class of general names associated with **natural kinds** -- that is, with classes of things that we regard as of explanatory importance; classes whose normal distinguishing characteristics are 'held together' or even explained by deep-lying mechanisms. **Gold, lemon, tiger, acid** are examples of such nouns.*

Recent work on kinds broadens the notion. Boyd (Boyd, 1986) suggests that any homeostatic cluster of properties which is stable and causally important can be named by a kind term. Dahlgren (Dahlgren, 1988b) argues that social terms like *knife* and *secretary* name kinds just as natural kind terms do. Cognitively, kinds are often reflected as concepts, though there are cases in which a kind is not a salient collection of entities for a culture, and is therefore not recognized by that culture. Examples of natural kind terms then, are *water, gold, lemon,* and *tiger,* artifact kind terms, *knife, pickup,* and *house,* and social kind terms, *miner, nurse,* and *secretary.* Non-kind terms are *triangle, junk* and *weed.* Kind terms correspond to conceptual categories (*lemon* names the concept LEMON), and refer to kinds (*lemon* refers to Lemon, a class of objects in the actual world). (These will be the typographical conventions of this book). The technical term "refer" is used here as in (Putnam, 1975) and (Kripke, 1972).

The argument that social terms such as *President* are kind terms turns on the question of whether or not semantic analysis can uncover the criteria for membership in their extensions. If it can, then social terms are not kind terms, but are nominal. That is, their extensions satisfy criterial definitions. The classical example of a nominal term is *triangle.* In Dahlgren (1988b), we argue that social terms are kind terms. Recall from Chapter 1 that we cannot claim that meaning representations are truth conditional, because some speakers of a language, or all of the speakers, may not know what the essence of a natural kind term is (criteria). Natural kinds are mind-independently real, and some have hidden internal essences, that is, the properties which define the kind may not be known to some or even all speakers of the language. The argument that social terms are kind terms establishes that social kinds are mind-independently real, as well. Social policy and human functioning in social roles determine which objects are members of social kinds. The difference between social kind terms and natural kind terms is that the essence of some social kinds, such as President of the U.S., cannot be hidden to everyone. That is because they are *constitutive,* which means that their existence depends upon social rules decided upon by some person or social group. Unless some person(s), such as policy-makers or personnel directors, know the criteria for belonging to these social kinds, they cannot come into existence. Often persons functioning in social roles are consciously aware of the essence of the role (but not always). So these kinds don't seem mind-independently real, because their essences have to be in the minds of at least some people, i.e., those who create the kind, and those who are function in it. However, these social kinds are mind-independently real, though they have constitutive origins. Other social kinds, (such as Middle Class), have hidden essences and were not created in acts of conscious verbal decision. These social kinds are not constitutive. However, in cases of constitutive social kinds where some members of society know the essence, does not guarantee that all speakers know criteria. In terms of the semantics, not all users of a social kind term know the essence, and their successful reference using the term is explained by a causal chain to the originators of the social term, and by the real existence of the kind, not by their knowledge of criteria for membership in the kind. Thus the semantics of social kind terms works exactly the same way as the semantics of natural kind terms. Successful communication is guaranteed by the existence of real, stable classes of objects, not by speakers' knowledge of criteria which determine the classes.

Kind terms have a complex relationship to the actual world. First, the use of a kind term with the intention of referring to a kind does not imply that a corresponding kind exists. The conception of the kind *lily* does not correspond to an actual botanical classification. As commonly used in English the term *lily* is not intended to include onions, but the botanical class does include onions (Dupre, 1981). Second, some natural kinds are not named by a particular language. For example, English lacked *proton, neutron* and other terms for atomic structures prior to their discovery. Finally, theoretical terms are used to refer to kinds which are only hypothetical (cf. *atom*, before the atomic theory was proven). NS is concerned with putative kinds (kinds identified and named by a subculture) which may or may not correspond to actual kinds. This point may seem to contradict the claim above that reference to kinds is made possible by the existence of real, stable classes of objects, but it does not. Our claim is both that, in general, real, stable classes explain successful reference to kinds, and that, given the weak epistemological position of humankind, there can be a mismatch between the use of kind terms, and the existence of kinds in the world.

A theory of word meaning for common nouns faces several unresolved questions in philosophy and psychology. What are kinds? What are kind terms? How do kind terms relate to concepts (cognitive categories)? Is there linguistic meaning separate from concept? The working hypotheses adopted in NS are:

1. Kinds are classes of real objects whose superficial characteristics are symptomatic of a shared essence or homeostatic cluster of properties with explanatory importance.

2. Kind terms are linked to concepts (cognitive categories) as well as to classes of real objects. This implies that representations of practical knowledge and representations of lexical knowledge (of meaning) have the same form.

3. The existence of kinds does not depend upon human perspective. Water would be water whether humans ever recognized the kind or gave it a name. The kind POSSLQ (significant other) exists as a census category, but English speakers have not given it a name as yet.

4. The view that kinds exist in the actual world is fundamental to explaining the way language works given that mental representations do not provide truth conditions.

How do people communicate and learn things from each other when the mental representations invoked are vague, inaccurate and inconsistent? In the NS view, language works because kind terms refer to real classes of real objects. (The classes are stable enough to ensure that when people use their truth-conditionally inadequate representations, they manage to communicate with each other.) Their inferences (about the way the world is) are confirmed or denied by experience with actual objects and events. Mental representations are close enough to correct to make relatively reliable inferences about the objects of reference, and as long as real objects are sometimes present, these inferences make language a useful tool of communication. Real objects (and actions) anchor language to the world and make linguistic communication possible. Abstract vocabulary, such as *unicorn* and *three*, is not basic to the theory of natural language semantics. This view accords with that of Johnson-Laird (1983) who takes reference as the basic phenomenon to be explained in semantic theory. Theories which try to exclude reality (Jackendoff, 1983) build semantic representations using an intralinguistic methodology. They compare the meanings of words in semantic fields like *buy, sell, accept, receive*. Elements which are similar (or different) justify semantic primitives in the meaning representations of the words in the semantic field. As was argued in Chapter One, this methodology is unworkable and fails to reflect mental representations of word meanings (Smith and Medin, 1981). There is no principled way of distinguishing knowledge of word meaning from knowledge in general, including non-verbal knowledge (Miller, 1978, Marslen-Wilson, 1980, Tarnawsky, 1982, Green, 1983, Jackendoff, 1983, Johnson-Laird, 1983, Fillmore, 1985).

3.2. Kind Types

In Chapter 1 we introduced NS representations of kind terms, and argued that they should include as much of the competent speaker's naive theory of a kind as possible. These representations introduce large numbers of features in each description. In principle, there could be as many or more features as English words. Such representations appear hopelessly complex. The magnitude and complexity of conceptual knowledge has been dealt with in linguistic semantics chiefly by ignoring it. In computational semantics either semantic knowledge has been defined as knowledge of primitives (the classical theory) or the problem has been narrowed by domain-specificity. However, denial of the essential complexity of conceptual knowledge limits the theory unacceptably. The NS hypothesis is that for kind terms cognitive complexity is reduced by correlational constraints, called **kind types** (Dahlgren and McDowell, 1986a), which are commonsen reflections of the structure of the actual world. As Rosch (1978) pointed out, features of real-world objects do not occur independently of each other in cognitive structures. These constraints prevent the description of a concept such as "THORK, a bird with wheels." These constraints take the problem of complexity head on. Similar constraints, called **relational types**, affect conceptual knowledge associated with verbs. Ironically, though competent speakers of a natural language do not know enough to specify truth conditions for kind terms, they know limitations on possible descriptions of kinds.

People employ correlational constraints in sentence interpretation. Consider the sentence "The chicken has wheels." It can only be interpreted metaphorically, or in some way that makes the chicken unlike any real chicken. The necessary switch to metaphor, toys or pictures in interpreting such sentences empirically supports the claim that the conceptual system is encoded in such a way that it predicts feature types for certain types of objects. Kind types are types of kind terms with predictable feature types in their descriptions. These constraints predict that the set of features which can be used to describe an object or action is not all the features used to describe things, but a subset related to the ontological classification of the object. Each kind type is understood in terms of certain predictable feature types. NATURAL KINDs are conceived primarily in terms of perceptual features, while ARTIFACTs also have functional features, which NATURAL KINDs lack. SENTIENTs have internal traits, but ARTIFACTs do not, explaining why a sentence like *The machine is sad* cannot be interpreted literally. The fact that concepts in one kind type always lack feature types of concepts in another constrains the entire set of concepts. The constraints reflect the correlational structure of the actual world.

Because most word meaning representations (including semantic nets) are based upon a calculus of primitives, and as such are not realist in their basic assumptions, they permit, and therefore predict, any combination of the features in descriptions. If it is assumed that there is a limited stock of primitive concepts from which all other concepts are built, and that they are built by conjunction (or netting, which is essentially the same thing), then it is predicted as a corollary that all combinations of the stock of primitives are permissible concepts. But we know this is not the case. In the realist theory, there could be no communication unless there were some real objects which were stable and existed independently of human perception. Since language is based in reality, and its function is to communicate about reality, the cognitive structures built for interpreting language reflect constraints on the actual world. This is not to deny the role of imagination and

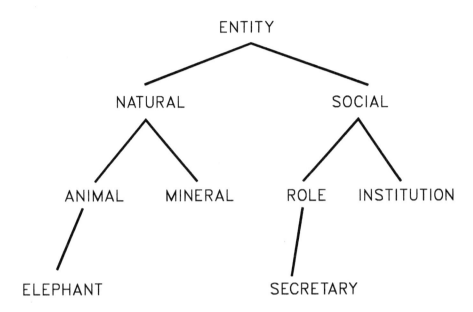

Figure 8: Ontological Attachment of ELEPHANT and SECRETARY

creativity, only to explain the limitations which make reasoning with language possible.

The feature types described in the previous chapter figure importantly in kind types, which are types of kind terms with predictable feature types in their generic descriptions. Kind types correspond to superordinate terms in the NS ontology which make significant conceptual distinctions---PLANT vs ANIMAL, PERSON vs OBJECT, NATURAL VS ARTIFACTUAL. Such distinctions are substantiated in cognitive psychological research (Keil, 1979). Kind types capture the patterns of features which subjects list when asked to describe kinds in various kind types. The observed patterns of features correspond to real-world correlational constraints. Figure 8 shows the placement of *elephant* and *secretary* in the ontology. The kind type ANIMAL predicts that *elephant* will have certain types of properties, such as habitat, which *secretary* lacks, and that *secretary* will have certain types of properties which *elephant* lacks. So kind types are a mapping from the ontology to the generic information. Consider Tables 3.1 and 3.2.

Table 3.1 lists the generic description of *elephant* in the right-hand column, and Table 3.2 the generic description of *secretary*. The middle column in each table lists the feature types corresponding to the features in the descriptions. The left-hand column shows which nodes in the ontology those feature types are predicted by. The point is that it is completely predictable from the fact that *elephant* is a LIVING entity that its description includes habitat (and not income), and that *secretary* as a ROLE has relation and income in its description, and not habitat. (An individual in that ROLE, viewed in terms of his/her attachment to the HUMAN node, would be described with the same feature types as *elephant*.

It is an empirical fact that feature types are correlated with ontological classifications. The kind types were extracted empirically

Table 3.1 Animal Kind Type		
Node in Ontology	Feature types associated with the node	Feature values for *elephant*
ENTITY	haspart haspart partof	trunk 4 legs herd
PHYSICAL	color size texture	grey vehiclesized rough
LIVING	propagation habitat	live births jungle
ANIMAL	sex behavior behavior	male or female lumbers eats grass

from the generic data after all the features were typed, by inspection of types of features associated with the concepts at each node of the ontology. Associated with each node in the ontology is a kind type which is a constraint upon the types of features permissible in the generic descriptions of concepts under that node. Entities may be described by features falling into some or all of these feature types, and no others. Features at lower nodes inherit feature type constraints from the nodes above them in the ontology. For instance, any node under SOCIAL may have certain feature types, and any node under ROLE may have those feature types inherited from SOCIAL, as well as further feature types, as below:

SOCIAL   - Function, Requirement, Processing
ROLE   - {SENTIENT},{SOCIAL}, Relation, Income

At each node, only certain feature types are applicable. Conversely, each feature is classified by type as a COLOR, SIZE, FUNCTION, INTERNAL TRAIT or other.

Table 3.2 Social Role Kind Type		
Node in Ontology	Feature types associated with the node	Feature values for *secretary*
SOCIAL	function	types
	function	files
	function	answers phones
	requirement	can type
SENTIENT	internaltrait	friendly
	internaltrait	helpful
ROLE	relation	works for someone
	income	low pay

Table 3.3 Nominal Kind Types			
ENTITY	INEXT(in extension)	SOCIAL	FUNCTION
	HASPART		REQUIREMENT
	PARTOF		PROCESSING
	EXP(experienced as)	ROLE	(SENTIENT)
	PROTOTYPE		(SOCIAL)
	SOURCE		RELATION
	ASSOCIATED WITH		INCOME
SENTIENT	INTERNAL TRAIT	PERSON	(SENTIENT)
	GOAL		HASROLE)
LIVING	(PHYSICAL)		RELATION
	PROPAGATION		STATUS
	HABITAT		NAME
	PHYSIOLOGY		
	AGE	PROPOSI-	CONTENT
ANIMAL	(LIVING)	TIONAL	AUTHOR
	SEX		HASPART
	BEHAVIOR		GOAL
PHYSICAL	SHAPE		FUNCTION
	SIZE		
	COLOR	ARTIFACT	(PHYSICAL)
	MATERIAL		(SOCIAL)
	TEXTURE		OPERATION
	ODOR		CONSTRUCTION
	TASTE		OWNER
	LOCATION	INSTI-	(SENTIENT)
	STRENGTH	TUTION	(SOCIAL)
	STATE		STRUCTURE

The theory of kind types makes predictions about feature types as in Table 3.1. For ELEPHANT, the theory of kind types predicts that as a ANIMAL, it has sex and behavior ("lumbers") type features, as LIVING, it has propagation ("live births") and habitat ("jungle") type features, as PHYSICAL, it has color, size and so forth, and as ENTITY, it has parts ("trunk") and part of ("herd") type features. Feature types above ANIMAL are inherited from higher nodes in the ontology. Similarly for SECRETARY, the theory of kind types predicts that as ROLE, SECRETARY will have certain types of features. Inherited from the SENTIENT kind type are feature types INTERNAL TRAIT

("friendly"). Inherited from the SOCIAL kind type are feature types
FUNCTION ("answers phones") and REQUIREMENT ("can type").
In addition, RELATION ("works for someone") and INCOME ("low
pay") type features are predicted with a ROLE. Table 3.3 provides a
complete list of the nominal kind types which we have observed thus
far in the psycholinguistic data in which these patterns of correlational
constraints are manifest.

3.3. Kind Types as Metasorts

Formally, kind types are metasorts (Cohn, 1985). The terminal
nodes in the ontology are sorts, and the kind types are metasorts which
constrain the possible *types* of sorts recognized by the system. (38)
summarizes their formal properties. If F is the set of all the features
which occur in all generic descriptions of concepts named by common
nouns, then we can partition them with FT, a set of feature types, such
that every f in F belongs to one ft in FT. This is a simplification,
because there are examples of features which fall under different types
in the different descriptions. KT is the set of all kind types kt. For
every kt in KT, where kt is associated with a node in the ontology such
as ANIMAL, there is some FT_{kt} which is a set of feature types in FT.
FT_{kt} consists of the specific feature types (such as sex and behavior for
ANIMAL) associated with the kt node in the ontology, unified with
the union of all the feature types of all the kind types of the nodes
which dominate the kt node in the ontology. (For ANIMAL, this is
the union of all the feature types in the kind types for LIVING, PHYS-
ICAL and ENTITY). What this kind type predicts is that the features
in the generic description of any noun attached at the kt node in the
ontology will be drawn from among the feature types in FT_{kt}.

(38)   **Kind Types as Metasorts**

$$F = \{\, f \mid f \text{ is a feature} \}$$

$$FT = \{\, ft \mid ft \text{ is a feature type} \} \quad (FT \text{ is a partition of } F)$$

$$KT = \{\, kt \mid kt \text{ is a kind type} \}$$

$$\forall \mathbf{kt} \in \mathbf{KT} \quad \exists \mathbf{FT_{kt}} \qquad (\mathbf{FT_{kt}} \subseteq \mathbf{FT})$$

$$\mathbf{FT_{kt}} = \{ft_1, ft_2, ...\} \cup \bigcup_i \{\mathbf{FT_{kt_i}}\}$$

where $\mathbf{kt_i}$ are immediately

dominating nodes in the ontology

N common noun

C commonsense knowledge function

N $\in$ **kt**

where $\mathbf{kt} \in \mathbf{KT}$

$$\mathbf{C(N)} = \{ f \mid \exists \mathbf{ft} \in \mathbf{FT_{kt}} \quad s.t. \ f \in \mathbf{ft} \}$$

3.4. Another Approach

Schubert, Goebel and Cercone (1979) develop a refinement of the inheritance hierarchy in their system which is similar in spirit, though not content, to kind types. In order to facilitate search through a complex, rich semantic net, which like our generic knowledge is not based upon primitives, they type concepts as "appearance," "color," "location," "size." Then they build an inheritance hierarchy among feature types. For example a "color" ISA "appearance" ISA "external-quality" ISA "physical-quality." They can then easily answer questions like "What is Clyde's appearance?." This is a refinement of the idea of feature types, but does not capture the same information as kind types. Kind types restrict the feature types which a concept can have based upon it's position in the ontology. The topical organization of feature types in Schubert, et al (1979) imposes no such constraints.

3.5. Summary

In summary, NS is a realist theory. It denies that meaning representations for common nouns provide criteria for membership in their
extensions and that verb representations provide universally true implications of events. Instead, NS sees lexical meanings as naive theories.
NS accounts for the success of natural language communication, given
the vagueness and inaccuracy of word meanings, by the fact that natural
language is anchored in the real world. There are some real, stable
classes of objects which nouns are used to refer to, and mental representations of their characteristics are close enough to true, enough of
the time, to make reference using nouns possible. Similarly, there are
real classes of events which verbs report, and mental representations of
their implications are approximately true. The vagueness and inaccuracy
of mental representations requires nonmonotonic reasoning in drawing
inferences based upon them.

4. VERB REPRESENTATION

4.1. Ontological Representation

In NS, the representation of verbs, like nouns, involves both an ontology and generic knowledge.[3] The verb ontology derives from both the Vendler (1967) classification scheme, which is concerned with linguistic properties of verbs, and the results of cognitive studies which identify distinctions that are important in human reasoning about events. The generic knowledge for verbs consists of typical and inherent implications of events. Psycholinguistic studies of verbal categorization find that implications, rather than semantic fields, are significant in human reasoning with verbs.

This section describes and justifies the TEMPORAL Ontology shown in Table 4.1. Examples of lexical attachments are shown in Figure 9 on page 81.

TEMPORAL   →   RELATIONAL ∨ NONRELATIONAL
RELATIONAL →   (EVENT ∨ STATIVE) &
                          (MENTAL ∨ EMOTIONAL ∨ NONMENTAL)
EVENT   →   (GOAL ∨ NONGOAL) &
                          (ACTIVITY ∨ ACCOMPLISHMENT
                          ∨ ACHIEVEMENT)

Table 4.1 *The Temporal Sub-Ontology*

---

3 The research reported in this Chapter was originally published in McDowell and Dahlgren (1987).

4.2. Placing Verbs in the Main Ontology

In NS verbs are attached to the main ontology at the node TEM-PORAL for two reasons. First, tense morphology attaches to verbs, so that any information concerning the temporality of situations will be encoded on the verb. Second, the relations indicated by verbs must be interpreted with respect to their location in time in order for the discourse structure of a text to be properly understood. There are two implications of this attachment with respect to a theory of how the average person commonsensically views the world. One, the events and actions indicated by verbs are viewed as real entities. Two, the difference between parallel sentences like *John fought with Bill* and *There was a fight between John and Bill* is seen as linguistic and not conceptual. Conceptually, the noun *fight* the noun andthe verb *fight* are found under the same ontological node. We believe this accords well with the facts.

Attachment of verbs at the TEMPORAL node does not imply, however, that we view nouns and verbs as essentially the same sort of linguistic object. Implicit in our work with nouns is the assumption that nouns in utterances refer to real-world entities and that lexical nouns name classes of entities, some of which are kinds and some of which are not. This is compatible with the view of compositional se-mantics (model theoretic or Montague semantics (Dowty, 1981) in which nouns are viewed as one-place predicates. That is, they are argument-taking functions which take individuals into truth values. Verbs are viewed as n-place predicates, functions which take n-tuples into truth values. The (extensional) meaning of any sentence is then composed by recursively combining functional terms with quantifiers, operators, and logical connectives.

It is an interesting question whether verbs also name classes--classes of events or actions. Formally, one-place verbs (*run, sleep*) are indis-tinguishable from nouns. As functional terms they take individuals into truth values. However, the majority of verbs are n-place predicates where $n > 1$. Moreover, the arguments to verbs are nouns. That is, the verbal function has as its domain n sets of individuals each of which is defined by some nominal predicate.

	NATURAL			SOCIAL		
	MENTAL	EMOTIONAL	NONMENTAL	MENTAL	EMOTIONAL	NONMENTAL
NONGOAL ACHIEVEMENT	forget	startle	die	confess	fall in love	forfeit
NONGOAL ACTIVITY	dream	suffer	float	babble	grieve	drift
GOAL ACHIEVEMENT	spot	surprise	kill	announce	arouse	marry
GOAL ACCOMPLISHMENT	memorize	calm down	consume	teach	entertain	build
GOAL ACTIVITY	think	torment	run	study	gloat	jog
STATIVE	know	fear	be	advocate	mourn	own

Assignment of Verbs to Ontological Classes

Figure 9

So there are some formidable obstacles to viewing nouns and verbs as objects of the same extensional type. Informally, it may seem attractive to view a verb, such as *hit*, as naming a class of events, hitting-events, which would all have some associated family resemblance, just as the kind Dog has its associated generic description (see "Generic Information." on page 130). But this notion is directly contradicted by the psycholinguistic evidence. In particular, Huttenlocher and Lui (1979) have shown, and Graesser and Hopkinson (1987) have confirmed, that the cognitive organization of verbs centers around goal-orientation and argument types and is uncorrelated with the semantic fields to which they belong. That is, whatever is common to all events of hitting is not a set of typical features (as for nouns) but the kinds of things which can participate in an event of hitting. Furthermore, as we will see below, the generic descriptions associated with verbs differ radically from those for nouns and cluster around the implications of the event or action indicated by the verb, i.e. they are given in terms of other events and actions. Finally, there is the consideration that in using verbs, speakers refer to real-world situations (Barwise and Perry, 1983). A full description of a situation includes a time, a place, and the fully-specified relation (verb plus arguments). So it is clear that in this respect as well that verbs and nouns require separate treatment. In Chapter 8 we describe a theory of discourse which takes events placed in space and time as real entities.

Therefore, we make a primary category cut at the node TEMPORAL between nouns, which name classes of entities, in this case temporal entities like *party, hurricane,* and *winter,* and verbs, which indicate relations between members of these nominal classes, like *hit, love, remember.* We attach verbs to the TEMPORAL/RELATIONAL node and temporal nouns to the TEMPORAL/NONRELATIONAL node.

4.3. Sub-Classification of the TEMPORAL/RELATIONAL Node.

Following on our method for developing the noun ontology, we considered both linguistic and psycholinguistic studies in developing the ontology of verbal concepts. While there is a large and growing body of studies on the psychology of events and event concepts, the findings of these studies have not hitherto been used to construct a classification scheme for lexical verbs which indicate events and event concepts, as far as we know.

4.4. The Vendler Verb Classification

Nearly all linguistic work on verbs follows the Vendler (1967) classification scheme to some extent. The focus of the Vendler scheme is the behavior of various verbs with respect to their tense morphology and temporal relations in a discourse. This system with a few examples of each type is shown below in Table 4.2. Explanation of the table follows.

The Vendler (1967) system is reflected in the TEMPORAL/ RELATIONAL Ontology (Table 4.1) where RELATIONAL divides into EVENT or STATIVE and EVENT divides into ACTIVITY, ACHIEVEMENT, or ACCOMPLISHMENT.

	Ac-tivity	Accomplish-ment	Achievement	State
	run, think	*build a house, read a novel*	*recognize, find*	*have, want*
Possesses Progressive Tenses	+	+	-	-
Terminus	-	+	+	-
Change of State	-	Gradual	Punctual	-
Subinterval Property	+	-	-	+

Table 4.2. *The Vendler Verb Classification Scheme*

The first cut (STATIVE/EVENT) turns on a standard syntactic test and is straightforward. STATIVE verbs may not appear in the progressive, but may appear in the simple present. This is illustrated in (39) for *know, love,* and *be.*

(39)   *John is knowing French.
         *John is loving Sally.
         *John is being in Paris.

         John knows French.
         John loves Sally.
         John lives in Paris.

EVENT verbs may appear in the progressive. They may also appear in the simple present, but if they do, then they are interpreted as describing habitual or characteristic states. This is illustrated in (40) for *drive, snore,* and *sleep.*

(40)   John is driving a truck.
         John is snoring.
         John is sleeping.

         John drives a truck.
         John snores a lot.
         John sleeps late on Sunday.

A second parameter is whether or not the situation described by the verb has a change of state associated with an identifiable terminus. Both ACCOMPLISHMENTs and ACHIEVEMENTs entail a change of state associated with a terminus. For instance, for the predicate *build a house* the change of state occurs when the house is finished. Before the terminus there was no house (or only a partially-built house). After the terminus there is a completed house. Similarly, for the predicate *reach the summit,* the terminus occurs at the moment the summit is reached. Before the terminus the climber is heading for the summit. After the terminus the climber has reached the summit. By contrast, STATE predicates such as *know* and *love* have no associated change of state inherent in the meaning of the predicate. ACTIVITYs also have no inherent terminus associated with a change of state. They may simply end, or they may be culminated by an ACCOMPLISHMENT or an ACHIEVEMENT.

A third parameter is whether the change of state associated with the terminus is gradual or punctual (abrupt). An example of a gradual change of state (ACCOMPLISHMENT) is *build a house*, where the ongoing activity of building results in a more and more completed house until the actual completion. With ACHIEVEMENTs, like *reach the summit*, there is no cumulative activity. Before he reaches the summit, the climber is climbing, or riding a funicular, or such. Reaching the summit is a punctual event of a different category than the activity which led up to it.

Finally, the verbs are divided between those which have what has come to be known as the subinterval property (Bennett and Partee, 1978) and those which don't. STATEs and ACTIVITYs have it, ACHIEVEMENTs and ACCOMPLISHMENTs don't. A verb which has the subinterval property is *sleep* and one which does not is *find*. If John slept for an hour, he was sleeping at any point in time, no matter how finely the time is subdivided, during that hour. But if John found his wallet in an hour, then it is not true that he was finding his wallet at any point in time during that hour.

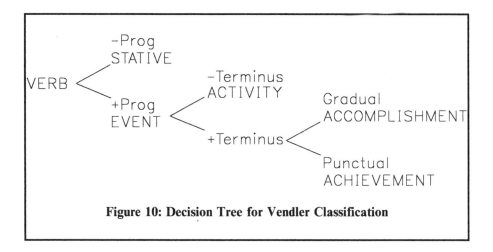

Figure 10: Decision Tree for Vendler Classification

A decision tree which captures these distinctions is displayed in Figure 10 on page 85. We use this system to classify verbs as ACTIVITYs, ACCOMPLISHMENTs, ACHIEVEMENTs, and STATEs. Figure 11 illustrates the Vendler (1967) classes with respect to an interval of time bounded by two time points, t_1 and t_2. If we say *John loved Mary* with reference to this interval of time, we do not imply that John ceased to love Mary as of t_2. If we say *John built a house* with respect to this interval of time, then we do imply that the house was completed as of t_2 and that *John was building a house* is an appropriate description of John's activities between t_1 and t_2. We can also say *John flew* or *John was flying* with respect to this interval of time without implying that t_2 marked the end of the flight. But if we say *John arrived in Paris*, we do imply that this event occurred punctually at t_2 and that it is not appropriate to say, with respect to the interval, *John was arriving in Paris*. Table 4.2 illustrates these distinctions in relation to verb classification.

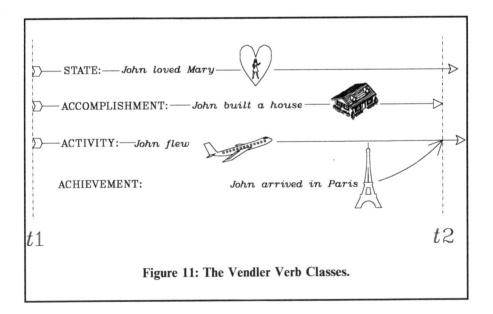

Figure 11: The Vendler Verb Classes.

There are several standard tests for the Vendler (1967) system which can be found in Dowty (1979) and others. We have employed three

such tests which pairwise distinguish ACTIVITY from ACCOMPLISH-
MENT   from   ACHIEVEMENT.   The   first   is   the   *stop/*
finish + complement test. An ACTIVITY verb can appear as the complement of *stop* but not of *finish*.

(41)   John stopped running.
          *John finished running.

The second is the *in/for-an-hour* test. An ACHIEVEMENT predicate
can appear with phrases like *in an hour* but not with phrases like *for
an hour* and vice versa for ACTIVITY verbs.

(42)   John reached the summit in an hour.
          *John reached the summit for an hour.
          *John ran in an hour.
          John ran for an hour.

Finally, ACCOMPLISHMENT verbs can appear as complements of
both *stop* and *finish*, and with phrases like *in an hour* and marginally
with phrases like *for an hour*.

(43)   John stopped building the house.
          John finished building the house.
          John built the house in a month.
          ?John built the house for a month.

Example (44) shows how these tests work with predicates from the
three different EVENT categories.

(44)   ACTIVITY

               John stopped running.
               *John finished running.
               *John ran in an hour.
               John ran for an hour.

          ACCOMPLISHMENT

John stopped building the house.
John finished building the house.
John built the house in a week.
?John built the house for a week.

ACHIEVEMENT

*John stopped reaching the summit.
*John finished reaching the summit.
John reached the summit in an hour.
*John reached the summit for an hour.

There is one serious problem with using the Vendler (1967) system which has been noted by Steedman (1977), Dowty (1979), and Moens and Steedman (1987), and others. Namely, the system seems more appropriate for classifying predicates than individual verbs. Take *build* as an example. We can easily conceive of an ACTIVITY of building which cumulatively results in the ACCOMPLISHMENT of building a house. So how should *build* be classified? For another example, take *push*. We can imagine an ACTIVITY of pushing a cart, which results in an ACCOMPLISHMENT if we succeed in pushing a cart to Rome, for example.

This is actually more an apparent problem than a real one. It is a severe problem if one is trying to classify verbs without recognizing that there may be several senses of any verb and that any verb may have several subcategorization frames. To turn this around, it is impossible to classify verbs according to the Vendler system in such a way as to cover all senses and subcategorization frames in a single assignment. Instead, any verb can be relatively easily classified for any pair of sense and subcategorization frame. Consider *build*. Transitive *build* requires a direct object. One sense of *build* is to construct a concrete artifact. Examples of this sense/frame pair are *build a house, build a wall, build a model*. This sense/frame pair is clearly ACCOMPLISH-MENT and if we designate this sense of *build* as *build1* then *build1* is attached to ACCOMPLISHMENT. Next, consider *run*. This verb has two subcategorization frames: it is both transitive and intransitive. In its transitive use it has several senses: *run a mile, run a company, run a*

program, etc. These sense/frame pairs for *run* and assignments are
shown in Table 4.3 (although we do not mean to imply that this is an
exhaustive list). This table gives the subcategorization frames for *run*
in terms of specific lexical items which may appear as the direct object
of transitive *run.* We generalize this in the representation, however, by
assigning sense indices to verbs in terms of the ontological category of
the direct object.

Frame	Sense	Index	Assignment
Intrans.		1	ACTIVITY
Trans.	*a mile*	2	ACCOMPLISH-MENT
Trans.	*a company*	3	ACTIVITY
Trans.	*a program*	4	ACCOMPLISH-MENT
Table 4.3. Frames, Senses, and Attachments for *run*			

Thus *run2* is a transitive verb with direct object of the category MEA-
SURE; *run3* is a transitive verb with direct object of the category IN-
STITUTION; and *run4* is a transitive verb with direct object of the
category PROPOSITIONAL.

By limiting consideration to the elements which are strictly
subcategorized by a verb, we also avoid a familiar problem which has
seemed to limit the usefulness of the Vendler (1967) system. For example, consider *push* in the two phrases *push a cart* and *push a cart to
Rome.* In the first phrase the predicate is an ACTIVITY, but in the
second it is an ACCOMPLISHMENT. It is the prepositional phrase
to Rome which converts the ACTIVITY *push a cart* into an ACCOM-
PLISHMENT. However, since the prepositional phrase is not strictly
subcategorized by *push,* we ignore it for the purposes of classification.
In the case of a verb like *put,* however the prepositional phrase is strictly
subcategorized and would not be ignored in classification. The assignment for *push* can then be overridden during processing if more than
the minimal frame is present, perhaps using the sort of network proposed by Moens and Steedman (1987).

As Table 4.3 and the preceding discussion imply, in order to correctly assign a verb sense to an an ontological category, we need to know the subcategorization information for the verb in question and the ontological class of the nouns which are potential fillers for the argument slots. This accords with Huttenlocher and Lui's (1979) findings. Nouns in NS system are attached to ontological nodes (as explained in "2.1. The Ontological Schema" on page 45). Subcategorization information is included in the grammatical dictionary along with morphological information. Selectional restrictions (category restrictions on the arguments of verbs) are encoded in the generic descriptions (see below) for each verb sense. Thus, the information needed for assignment of verbs to ontological categories can be found in the lexical representations, and no additional coding is required. We claim then that the classification problem for verbs is manageable if word senses and subcategorization frames are considered together.

4.5. Psycholinguistic Categories

We introduce two category distinctions on the RELATIONAL node to reflect psycholinguistic findings. The MENTAL/ NONMENTAL/EMOTIONAL distinction is made at the highest level and was motivated by the same considerations which led us to place SENTIENT at a high level in the main ontology (i.e., as a choice point on the REAL node). As we showed above, people divide the objects in the world into those which are like themselves (the sentients) and those which are not (Gelman and Spelke, 1981, Strawson, 1953). Similarly, we felt that it would prove useful to distinguish in some way the locus of the event or action indicated by a verb, as taking place in the mind of the agent, the emotions of the agent or in the world outside of the agent. At the very least this will constrain the types of arguments allowed. That is, the agent/experiencer of a MENTAL verb must be SENTIENT and this does not need to be stated as a separate selectional restriction on every MENTAL verb. The assignment of verbs to the categories MENTAL, EMOTIONAL, and NONMENTAL has been unproblematic.

A second psycholinguistically-based category is GOAL/ NONGOAL. All non-states are cross-classified as GOAL-oriented or not by this distinction. This is supported by virtually every experimental study on the way people view situations, i.e., GOAL-orientation is the most salient property of events and actions. For example, Trabasso and Sperry (1985) find that events are best recalled which feature goal states and consequences of goals and the salient features of events are goals, antecedents, consequences, implications, enablement, causality, motivation and temporal succession and coexistence. This view is further supported by Abbott, Black and Smith (1985) and Graesser and Clark (1985a).

As a working hypothesis, we have two tests for the category GOAL/ NONGOAL. If a verb can appear felicitously in the frames in (45), (substituting for VERBED or VERBING, with semantically and pragmatically appropriate continuations for . . .) then it is GOAL-oriented. If not, then it is nonGOAL-oriented.

(45)   John VERBED in order to . . .
         John tried to . . . by VERBING

For instance, the GOAL verb *dig* is illustrated in (46) and the NONGOAL verb *find* is illustrated in (47)

(46)   John dug a hole in order to bury the cat.
         John tried to reach China by digging a hole.

(47)   *John found his keys in order to be on time for his appointment.
         *John tried to impress Mary by finding her keys.

There are some points to be made with regard to GOAL-orientation. The first concerns the relationship between goal-orientation and intentionality. Every intentional action has a goal, if only the action itself. Furthermore, there can be a chain of goals pursued by a conscious agent. For instance, John might look for Mary's keys with the immediate goal of finding them and the further goal of impressing Mary. In this case, however, the goal of impressing Mary is a general goal which

John holds and which he attempts to achieve by carrying out all sorts of actions. Simply looking for Mary's keys is designed to impress her. Finding them is icing on the cake. In other words, John can't ensure that he will find Mary's keys in anything like the way that he can ensure he will have a big enough hole to bury the cat if he digs long enough. On the other hand, John might serendipitously find Mary's keys and make a big show of returning them to her, in order to impress her. We claim that there is no way John can intentionally find Mary's keys and that therefore he cannot have any goal in finding them. Finding the keys, however, may well be the goal of searching. Furthermore, when we consider what the possible goals of an event or action might be, we must restrict ourselves to well defined immediate goals (i.e., *finding* is the goal of *searching*, but *impressing Mary* is not).

Second, we have found that [NONGOAL, ACCOMPLISHMENT] is a null category. This results from the nature of ACCOMPLISH-MENT verbs which have as their GOAL the change of state associated with the terminus. You can't build a house without holding the GOAL of building the house. That is, ACCOMPLISHMENTS are inherently GOAL-oriented. On the other hand, curiously enough, [NONGOAL, ACHIEVEMENT] is not a null category. That is because the activity leading up to an achievement is always totally distinct from the achieve-ment itself. For instance, if my goal is to build a house then I engage in the activity of building a house and accomplish my goal when the house is finished. But if my goal is to reach the summit, then I engage, not in the activity of reaching the summit, but in the activity of climbing and my goal is achieved only when I am physically located on the summit as a result of climbing. But there are many achievements (punc-tual events resulting in some change of state) which occur serendipitously (such as John's finding Mary's keys) or in the course of some totally unrelated activity. These are the clearly [NONGOAL,ACHIEVEMENT] verbs like *forget, lose, die,* and *find.*

Third, [SOCIAL,NONGOAL,ACTIVITY] is a sparse category, and in fact we have had great difficulty finding suitable examples. The examples given in Figure 9 just barely qualify according to our tests. This simply reflects the fact that nearly all SOCIAL ACTIVITY is intentional and GOAL-oriented.

4.6. Cross-Classification

There are thus two kinds of cross-classifications on the node RE-LATIONAL: those inherited from TEMPORAL and those resulting from the sub-classification on RELATIONAL. (See Table 2.1). The latter have just been discussed: RELATIONAL divides into MENTAL, EMOTIONAL, or NONMENTAL as well as into EVENT or STATIVE. EVENT divides into GOAL or NONGOAL as well as into ACTIVITY, ACHIEVEMENT, or ACCOMPLISHMENT. The inherited cross-classifications are SOCIAL/NATURAL and INDIVIDUAL/COLLECTIVE. A verb describes a SOCIAL relation iff the relation has reality only within the domain of a social institution.

It may at first glance appear that the ontological category of the arguments of a verb (SOCIAL vs. NATURAL, for example) might determine whether the verb should be classified as SOCIAL or NATURAL. However, this doesn't work. For instance, we can say *John forgave Mary* and *The doctor forgave the nurse.* The verb *forgive* in the first sentence is NATURAL, and it doesn't seem essentially more SOCIAL in the second sentence than in the first. However in *The man sentenced the woman* and *The judge sentenced the defendant*, the verb *sentence* is essentially SOCIAL no matter whether the arguments are NATURAL, as in the first sentence, or SOCIAL as in the second. SOCIAL verbs are classified in the same manner as ROLEs.

The question remains whether the INDIVIDUAL/COLLECTIVE distinction is valid for verbs. For the time being we have set aside this issue in building our system, but we address it briefly here. A COLLECTIVE noun names a set, mass, or structure which has component members that have some class similarity. In the case of sets, like *herd*, each member of the set is the same kind as every other member. In the case of masses, like *water* or *sand*, even the smallest amount is of the same material nature as the collective term (a drop of water is still water). In the case of structures, like *company*, each member (*president, secretary, janitor*) is of the same kind type as every other (i.e., ROLE). It seems that it is at least cognitively possible to extend this concept of COLLECTIVE to verbs, even though the English lexicon might not contain very many COLLECTIVE verbs. Accordingly, a COLLEC-

TIVE verb would be an event or action which can be similarly subdivided. The problem is that since all events and actions exist over an interval of time, any event or action can be so subdivided into a set of shorter events or actions. But it will usually not be possible to say that all of the subevents are each an X, in the same way that all members of a herd of cows is a cow. For instance, an event of running can be subdivided into events of raising the legs, lowering the legs, pushing off from the ground, etc. These subevents do not have class similarity. But verbs which have the subinterval property (STATEs and ACTIVITYs) resemble masses. That is, whether I am raising my legs, lowering my legs, pushing off, etc., I am still running. In this respect subinterval verbs like *bounce*, where there is some sort of repetitive quality, are more like sets. Steedman (1977), in fact, noticed this point and proposed an addition to the Vendler (1967) classes, which he labeled "actions," based on words like *bounce*. Clearly further work is needed to determine whether the INDIVIDUAL/COLLECTIVE distinction is in fact relevant to verbs.

4.7. Parallel Ontologies

There are other parallel ontologies for verbs, just as for nouns. An example is the OCCUPATIONAL ontology. For our original corpus (geography texts), we have found it necessary to identify the occupational categories AGRICULTURAL, MININGMANU (mining and manufacturing), TRADE, SERVICE, and EDUCATION, because many of the texts concern industrial activity, importing and exporting of goods, and other economic matters. It is easy to see why this classification differs from a cross-classification such as GOAL/NONGOAL. A cross-classification is an exhaustive classification of all attachments at a particular node. This is true of GOAL/NONGOAL. A subontology available for optional multiple attachment does not exhaustively classify the attachments. For instance, all EVENTs are either GOAL-oriented or not. But it is not true that all GOAL-oriented verbs can be divided among the OCCUPATIONAL categories listed above.

4.8. Non-Categorial Features

Many linguistic studies of verb classification emphasize categories such as motion and possession/exchange (cf. Miller and Johnson-Laird, 1976) and categories reflecting other semantic fields. For instance *take* and *receive* are both verbs relating to possession and exchange. Experimental studies have shown, however, that distinctions like GOAL/ NONGOAL were far more salient for conceptual categorization than concepts like MOTION and POSSESSION. In particular, Huttenlocher and Lui (1979), have shown that cognitive organization of verbs is tighter around exhaustive categories like GOAL-orientation and argument types and looser around categories like motion or possession where one verb might potentially sort into more than one category. However, verbs of exchange, for instance, are apparent in many parts of the ontology. There are states: *have, own*, achievements: *win, lose*, accomplishments: *acquire, buy*, and activities: *exchange*. These concepts are useful in much commonsense reasoning. Motion verbs imply change of location for some argument; possession verbs have implications for ownership and transfer of ownership. Indeed these often show up as primitives in systems which employ primitives (cf. EXCHANGE in Miller and Johnson-Laird, 1976 and PTRANS, MTRANS in Schank and Riesbeck, 1981). We have included such knowledge as generic information (see next section) coded on the individual verbs in lexical entries and not as part of the ontology.

4.9. Generic Representation

In developing generic descriptions associated with verbs, we relied heavily on work done by Graesser and Clark (1985a), who examined hundreds of responses of subjects to simple narratives, both answers to questions and freely-generated responses. Our work does not directly encode the representation system for narrative situations worked out by (Graesser and Clark, 1985a) but instead we have adapted their findings to construct generic descriptions associated with verbs. In Graesser and Clark (1985a)'s data, there was wide agreement among subjects on the implications of the relation described by a verb. We have adapted these as feature types associated with verbs. These feature types are accessible in the KT system via the following set of questions which KT can answer with respect to the verbs in the lexicon. The set of answers to these questions for any verb constitutes a generic description of the relation described by the verb, where X is some EVENT or STATE.

(48)   *What caused X?*
            What enabled X?
            What was the goal of X?
            What happened next (after X)?
            What was the consequence of X?
            What does X imply?
            When did X happen?
            Where did X happen?
            How did X happen?

This point of view is supported by the findings of several researchers. In addition to the work of Graesser and Clark (1985a) from which these questions were drawn, Trabasso and Sperry (1985) find that events are best recalled which feature goal states and consequences of goals, and that events categorize around settings, initiating events, internal responses, attempts, consequences, and reactions. Trabasso and Sperry (1985) find that the salient features of events are goals, antecedents, consequences, implications, enablement, causality, motivation and temporal succession and coexistence.

   As with the nouns, this information is divided into two lists associated with each verb in the lexicon. One list encodes typical features of events and the other inherent features of events. In addition, many verbs "select" certain types of arguments. For instance, *think* selects a sentient subject and *build* selects an artifactual object. These are selectional restrictions on the verbs. If a verb's arguments violate these restrictions, then the verb is used metaphorically or bizarrely as in *The tree thought* or *John built a new girlfriend*. Selectional restrictions on the arguments of the verb are encoded for each sense of a verb along with the generic information. The generic description for *buy* is shown in (49).[4]

(49)   buy({what_enables(can(afford(subj,obj)))),
          how(with(X) & money(X)),
          where(in(Y) & store(Y)),
          what_happens_next(use(subj,obj))},
          cause(need(subj,obj)))},
          {goal(own(subj,obj)),
          consequence_of_event(own(subj,obj)),
          selectional_restriction(sentient(subj)),
          implies(merchandise(obj))}).

The richest such description for a particular verb would include a full set of answers which describe typical features and another full set which describe inherent features.

This representational scheme differs substantially from one which would employ semantic primitives. In such a scheme, the meaning of any lexical item is held to be decomposable into a finite set of primitive semantic concepts, atomic, indivisible meaning chunks. For instance, *buy* is a verb of exchange and such verbs are schematized in Jackendoff (1983) as in Figure 1 on page 20. In such a scheme, each item in capital letters represents one semantic primitive. Other verb categories could use none, some, or all of these primitives together with others in order to capture all the information needed for understanding the concept. Our system rejects the use of primitives and instead encodes the conceptual implications of events associated with words in terms of other words. Thus, in the example given above for *buy*, **how, where, what_happens_next, cause, goal, consequence_of_event, selectional_restriction,** and **implies** are predicates encoding verbal generic features in NS, but *money, store, use, need, own, human,* and *merchandise* are simply words. Whatever information is encoded for the concepts associated with each

---

4 In these entries *subj* refers to the logical subject in deep structure, rather than the surface subject, and *obj* refers to the logical direct object of the verb. *obliq* refers to the second object, which can be an indirect object or prepositional phrase attached to the VP. Mention of subject, object and oblique arguments of the verb makes possible predications on those arguments, such as human(subj).

of these words will be available via the generic feature predicates that contain them. Neither the generic feature predicates nor the words are viewed as primitive building blocks of meaning.

The generic feature types for verbs can be used for probabilistic reasoning about events and states indicated by verbs in texts. For instance, on the basis of the entry for *buy* (49), if the text includes the sentence *John bought a book*, the system could infer that John probably bought the book in a store and paid for it with money. It should be obvious, however, that the system cannot infer that John bought the book because he wanted to be educated. This is because *buy* can have a variety of objects, such as *truck, pineapple, dog,* etc. John does not buy a pineapple or a dog in order to get educated. All that can be inferred as being generically associated with *buy* are the implications which could apply to any object. Deeper inferences are possible, for instance that people buy things for the sake of their functions, that the function of a book is to be read and to provide information, and therefore John bought the book to read it and get information from it. However, such inferences are only possible under severely constrained circumstances.

4.10. Feature Types Associated with Relational Terms

The feature types associated with the relational classes are shown in Table 4.4.[5] Recall that generic features for nouns fall into a finite number of types. Associated with each node in the ontology there is a predictable cluster of feature types, e.g., associated with PHYSICAL are Size, Color, and Texture and associated with SOCIAL is Function.

----

5 Items in braces are dominating nodes and indicate that any features attached to these nodes are inherited by the nodes they dominate in the verb ontology in Table 4.1.

RELATIONAL	→	LOCATION	(where(...))
		TIME	(when(...))
		CAUSE	(cause(...))
		ENABLEMENT	(what_enables(...))
		CONSEQUENCE	(consequence_of_event(...))
		SEQUEL	(what_happens_next(...))
STATIVE	→	{RELATIONAL}	
EVENT	→	{RELATIONAL}	
		MANNER	(how(...))
MENTAL	→	{EVENT}	
NONMENTAL	→	{EVENT}	
EMOTIONAL	→	{EVENT}	
GOAL	→	PURPOSE	(goal(...))

Table 4.4. *Feature Types on Relational Terms*

Any nominal entity which is both PHYSICAL and SOCIAL is expected to have features for Size, Color, Texture, and Function. A [PHYSICAL,NATURAL] entity will have features for Size, Color, and Texture, but not for Function. The case is somewhat different for verbs. As can be seen from the table, the majority of features which encode the information necessary to answer the questions motivated by the work of Graesser and Clark (1985a) are associated with the RELATIONAL node itself. Only two such features are predictably limited to cross-classifications on RELATIONAL: **goal** is associated with GOAL and *how* is associated with EVENT. Of course, not every feature will necessarily be relevant for a given verb; eg., the features LOCATION and TIME would not be relevant in the entry for *claim*.

Two other generic features types encode information about the arguments of verbs. The first is **selectional_restriction** which provides the ontological class of the arguments of the verb. Two examples are:

catch	selectional_restriction(animal(subj) & physical(obj))
claim	selectional_restriction(sentient(subj) & proposition (sbar))[6]

Huttenlocher and Lui (1979) have reported that there is an asymmetry between the mental representations of verbs and nouns and that classification of verbs depends as much on the typical arguments of verbs as on hierarchical organization of the semantic fields to which they belong. This finding predicts that verbs which share selectional restrictions should have ontological similarity. This prediction is borne out by inspection of NS verb representations. Of the verbs encoded to date, those which share the selectional restriction (sentient(subj) & proposition(sbar)) are *claim, note, notice,* and *realize.* These are all classified as [MENTAL]. Verbs which share the selectional restriction (animal(subj) & physical(obj)) are *catch, draw, lift, press, pull,* and *shake.* These are [NATURAL,GOAL,NONMENTAL]. This result is especially significant because initially representations for the KT system were constructed by different people. The ontological classifications were not consulted when the generic descriptions are developed, nor were generic descriptions consulted when the ontological assignments are made. (Presently we use ontological classification to guide the construction of lexical entries, as described in Chapter 5). When a larger number of verbs is encoded, it may be possible to associate particular selectional restriction specifications with particular RELATIONAL nodes. These would correspond to generic feature types for nouns.

The other generic feature which encodes information about the arguments of verbs is the predicate **implies** which provides word-level information implied about the arguments of the verb. Some examples follow.

accept	implies(gift(obj) $\lor$ award(obj))
bear	implies(child(obj) $\lor$ fruit(obj))
employ	implies(tool(obj) & useful(obj))

This information is highly specific to the individual verbs encoded and we would not expect that any feature value would be predictably attached at certain ontological nodes. Nevertheless, the **implies** predicate is one we have derived from the work of Graesser and Clark (1985a). That is, subjects consistently named the implications of events as highly salient features along with goals, consequences, etc.

---

6 The symbols **subj, obj**, and **sbar** stand for the NP subject, object, and S′ complement identified during parsing.

4.11. Conclusion

The verb representations in NS depart significantly from those in other theories. Most other lexical representations of verbs use case primitives (Schank, 1973, Wilks, 1975, Miller and Johnson-Laird 1976, Sowa, 1983, Hirst, 1987) or other primitives (Katz, 1972, Jackendoff, 1983), as Chapter 1 details. The generic knowledge in NS includes all of the information these others include, and more. The feature types in NS which correspond to the lexical information in other approaches are the selection restrictions, which are stated in terms of the syntactic subject, object and oblique NPs, rather than in terms of deep cases. In addition, NS includes information excluded in alternative theories, concerning the other events surrounding the event referred to by the verb. The events which enable, cause, and result from the event referred to by the verb are all included. This means that rather than primarily viewing verbs in terms of the types of nouns they can take as arguments, NS views them in terms of typical implications.

PART II. THE KIND TYPES SYSTEM

5. THE FUNCTIONING OF THE KIND TYPES SYSTEM

The Kind Types system (KT) presently uses the naive semantic representations described in Chapters 2 through 4 and the disambiguation methods to be described in Chapters 6 and 7 to read text and show its understanding of the text by answering questions. In future development of the system, this understanding will help determine the relevance of text to a user's stated interest. When KT reads English text, it employs a parser and logic translator by Stabler and Tarnawsky (1986) to create a PROLOG database containing all of the assertions in the text. In addition, it uses NS representations to understand some of the implications of the text. The Naive Semantic Lexicon is divided into the following databases:

a) Ontological Schema
b) Generic Information
c) Typing Information
d) Kind types

Separate databases are used for different types of CK because they each require specific types of reasoning, as we discuss in the next section. The components of the Kind Types System are shown in Figure 12 on page 106.[7] The system takes text and queries as input. Input is parsed by the "Syntax" component and the output of the parser is a labelled bracketing which may contain word-sense and syntactic ambiguities. These are resolved in the next step, "Disambiguation." This is the point at which the system uses semantic information to guide parsing. Only one parse is generated by the parser. The PP-attachment

---

7 At this writing we are converting KT to use McCord's Modular Logic Grammar (McCord, 1987) for parsing and Discourse Representation Theory (Wada and Asher, 1986) for semantic translation. In the new architecture, anaphora resolution takes place in the Discourse Representation module. The functionality of the system remains as described in this Chapter.

and word sense disambiguation algorithms make the final choice of structure and word sense based upon naive semantic preference strategies. The anaphor resolution algorithm applies at this point as well. Then the semantic translation component, "Sentential Translation" converts the labeled bracketing into first order logic formulas represented as as PROLOG clauses. If the input is text, that is, a sentence in the indicative, the PROLOG clause is placed in a textual database, which completes processing. If the input is a query, that is, a sentence in the

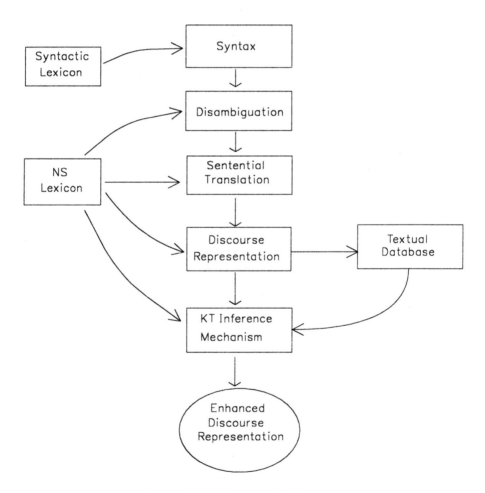

Figure 12: KT System Architecture

interrogative, it is translated to a PROLOG clause with uninstantiated variables. This is input to the "KT Inference Mechanism," which matches the query clause to textual database or to the NS databases depending upon the type of query. The inference mechanism first checks whether a query is ontological. If so, it looks for the answer in the ontological database using a problem solver for inheritance. Ontological queries are based on the closed world assumption, which we explain below. If the query is generic, the inference mechanism looks first in the text for the answer, and then in the generic database. If the query is neither ontological nor generic, then it is treated as a query of the text, and the inference mechanism uses the problem solver to see whether the answer is to be found in the text. Both generic and textual queries are answered according to the open world assumption.

5.1. Complete and Incomplete Knowledge

At present, KT employs default logic (Reiter, 1980). In reasoning, KT deals with two kinds of knowledge, complete and definitive, on the one hand, and incomplete and probabilistic, on the other. We assume that classification is definitive, in the commonsense view. Thus, any valid inference which can be derived ontologically is definitive. Given the ontological fact *programmer(mary)* and the rule (50), KT knows for certain that *human(mary)* is true.

(50) $\forall$ X programmer(X) $\rightarrow$ human(X)

It also knows that if something is HUMAN it is not ABSTRACT, because these are mutually exclusive attachments to the ontological lattice. If the system is asked, "Is the programmer abstract," it answers, "No." This is Reiter's closed world assumption, which means that if the system cannot prove a clause which states a proposed ontological fact, such as *abstract(mary)* or *(woman(X) & abstract(X)*, then the clause, and its associated proposed ontological fact, must be false. Thus, the system effectively handles the exclusivity of sets called for by Hendrix (1979) and Tenenbaum (1985).

On the other hand, the system knows which knowledge is incomplete. With respect to generic descriptions, KT knows that it has knowledge only at the probabilistic level. If asked, "Is Mary intelligent?" it responds, "Probably so." This reflects the fact that most English speakers share a prototype of programmers as intelligent. With generic questions, KT makes the open world assumption, which means that if the system finds no match for a clause like $(happy(X)$ & $dog(X))$, in the generic database, this could be due to incomplete generic knowledge, rather than to an incongruity between typical dogs and happiness. Answers to generic questions are qualified as either typical or inherent. If no answer to a generic question can be derived, KT responds, "I don't know." These are qualitatively different answers from the definitive (yes/no) answers to ontological questions. This ability to reason about incomplete definitions is similar to Levesque's proposal for incomplete databases (Levesque, 1984).

Generic information is handled differently from ontological information. First, it is tentatively inferred, and checked against the current knowledge base of information built up from reading the text. If anything in the textual database conflicts with a generic inference, the latter is overridden. KT takes the text as the authority, and if the text says that an entity has a feature contradicting those in its commonsense knowledge of the entity, the text's claim comes first. For example, suppose a text says that a programmer is not intelligent, which contradicts the typical feature of "intelligent" for programmers. KT then overrides the generic knowledge with textual knowledge, as in (51).

(51)   Is the programmer intelligent? No, the text says not intelligent.

The cancellation takes place simply by matching to the textual database first. Similarly, if a text said that an elephant had three legs, the KT system would know that it had three legs, and not the inherent four that elephants have. By overriding inherent features, KT gets around the cancellation problem which arises when features are viewed as logically necessary. If "has four legs" is taken to be a logically necessary feature, any three-legged elephant forces a contradiction, or special processing for exceptions. The KT system accepts both facts as true, with no contradiction. This particular elephant has three legs, and elephants inherently have four legs.

5.2. Queries to the System

In this section we illustrate the answering of queries to KT, describing the knowledge bases which are accessed, and the order in which they are accessed. "The Programmer," repeated here, exemplifies the type of text KT understands.

The Programmer

(52)   John is a programmer who works for a large corporation.

(53)   John entered his manager's office.

(54)   He was sitting at his desk.

(55)   John asked for a raise.

(56)   He wanted to buy a home computer for his child with the money.

(57)   John and his manager reviewed his accomplishments.

Inspecting the Textual Database. When the text is read, it is parsed and translated. The translation is saved in the Textual Database. The logic translation of the first two sentences of "The Programmer" is shown in (58). This is stored in the textual database.

(58)   programmer(john)
            corporation(corporation21) &
            large(corporation21) &
            work(event1,pres,john) & for(event1,corporation21) &
            enter(event2,past,john,office23) &
            office(office23) &
            manager(manager24) &

poss(manager24,office23) &
poss(john,manager24).

The KT inference mechanism first tries to answer a query by solving
to the Textual Database. A query such as *Is John a programmer?* is
translated into the PROLOG goal

←programmer(john).

Built into the natural language component by Stabler and Tarnawsky
is a metainterpreter which solves queries of all axioms active in the
system. This permits us to query ontological and generic information
as well as textual information. The possibility of infinite recursion
arises. This is true in principle for the human reasoner, as well. KT
prevents infinite recursion by limiting inferences to a depth of 5. The
problem solver derives the answers to queries, matching logic translations of the queries, which are in the form of PROLOG goals, to the
textual database. The problem solver solves to the Textual Database
with this goal. It matches the logic translations of the query to the
database, with results as below:

Q: Is John a programmer?
A: Yes.
Q: Does John work for a corporation?
A: Yes.

Inspecting the Ontology. If the query cannot be answered from the
Textual Database, which is considered the ultimate source of knowledge,
the KT inference mechanism check whether the question is ontological.
Ontological knowledge is coded as PROLOG axioms like

role(X) ← programmer(X).

From this axiom PROGRAMMER inherits SENTIENT, SOCIAL,
REAL, INDIVIDUAL and ENTITY from the ontology. The problem
solver attempts to solve the query in the ontological hierarchy. It finds
all nodes in the hierarchy above the queried node. The following examples illustrate ontological knowledge.

Q: What is a programmer?
A: A programmer is a role, sentient, social,
   individual and an entity.

If an entity has dual attachment, for example as a HUMAN and as a
ROLE, then KT explains inheritance relations along both paths of the
ontology as follows:

Q: What is John?
A: John is an individual natural, animate, animal, human
and also a programmer, individual, social, sentient, role.

Direct ontological questions are also answered:

Q: Is programmer a role?
A: Yes.
Q: Is John human?
A: Yes.

Verb ontological attachment is encoded in PROLOG axioms such
as:

```
goal(X) ← program(X).
activity(X) ← program(X).
social(X) ‹ program(X).
mental(X) ← program(X).
```

This knowledge is used to answer the following type of query:

Q: What is programming?
A: A goal-oriented, social, mental, real, temporal activity

Inspecting the Generic Database. If the query is not ontological, the
KT inference mechanism attempts to answer it with generic knowledge.
Recall that the generic representation of PROGRAMMER contains
lists of typical and inherent features, as below:

programmer ({income(high),relation(work(event1,subj) &

for(event1,Y) &
manager(Y) & for(event1,Z) & organization(Z) & large(Z)),
relation(work(event1,subj) & for(event1,W), & salary(W)),
relation(employee),
internaltrait(shy),internaltrait(mathematical)
internaltrait(intelligent),internaltrait(organized),
internaltrait(self-contained),
appearance(wear(subj,X) & glasses(X)),
location(office)},
{(function(program(subj,R) & computer(R)),
education(trained),
status(high),
tool(computer)}}).

The present system does-not as yet encode the ranges of possible feature values and the probabilities called for in section "1.10. Limitations of NS" on page 39 above. Notice that some features, such as work(event1,subj) & for(event1,Y) & manager(Y) are in the form of PROLOG expressions. This makes it possible to use the whole complex feature as input to the English grammar in order to formulate an English response to a question such as "What does the programmer do?," or "Does the programmer wear glasses?."

The following examples illustrate queries of generic knowledge. The form of the answer depends upon whether the feature is typical or inherent. Any feature type in a noun or verb representation can be queried. The first two queries have different form, but the same meaning, and the same answer.

Q: What does a programmer do?
A: Inherently, a programmer programs a computer.
Q: What function does a programmer have?
A: Inherently, a programmer programs a computer.
Q: What tools does a programmer use?
A: Inherently, a programmer uses a computer.
Q: What appearance does a programmer have?
A: Typically, wears glasses.
Q: What internal traits does a programmer have?
A: Typically, shy, mathematical, self-contained, intelligent,
   and organized.

Feature values can be queried directly, as well as by type, as in the
following examples. The first query inspects the TOOL feature in the
generic knowledge, while the query "What does a programmer do?"
inspects the FUNCTION feature.

Q: Does John use a computer?
A: Inherently so.
Q: Who built the computer?
A: Inherently, people.
Q: Does John wear glasses?
A: Probably so.
Q: Does John program in an office?
A: Probably so.
Q: Is John happy?
A: I don't know.

If no information is found in either the text or the CK concerning a
generic feature question, the system responds that it doesn't know, the
open world assumption.

   Inspecting Feature Types. The feature typing database classifies features as follows:

income(high).
income(middle).
income(low).
relation(work(event1,subj) & for(event1,Y) & manager(Y)).
relation(work(event1,subj) & for(Y) & organization(Y) & large(Y)).
relation(work(event1,Y) & for(event1,subj) & employee(Y)).
relation(work(event1,subj) & for(event1,Y) & salary(Y)).
relation(employee).
relation(employer).
internaltrait(shy).
internaltrait(mathematical).
internaltrait(intelligent).
internaltrait(organized).
internaltrait(self-contained).
internaltrait(kind).
appearance(wear(subj,Y) & glasses(Y)).
appearance(pretty).
appearance(clean_cut).
function(program(subj,Y) & computer(Y)).
function(supervise).
education(trained).
status(high).
tool(computer).
tool(tractor).

Because of the feature typing, KT can answer queries about feature types such as COLOR, SIZE, FUNCTION, and so on.

(59)   Q: What color is the paper?
              A: Typically white.
              Q: What function does the company have?
              A: Inherently business.
              Q: What internal traits does the programmer have?
              A: The text says not intelligent.

With respect to the last question, KT looks first at the translation of the text to see whether it contains an assertion which states an internal trait for the programmer. It must distinguish the facts in the text which

are relevant to the feature type queried. In order for KT to answer
"What internal traits does a programmer have?," KT must know that
"not intelligent" is an INTERNAL TRAIT. Without feature types, KT
would not contrast "intelligent" with "unintelligent," or "white" with
"pink."

KT deduces sets of facts, as well as individual facts. When queried
for a type of feature, such as RELATION, KT responds with all relations listed, as in (60). When KT lists parts, bare plurals mean an
unspecified number greater than one.

(60)   Q: What relations does a programmer have?
            A: A programmer works for a manager in
               a large organization,
               works for a salary, and is an employee.
            Q: What structure does a company have?
            A: Typically, a company has a hierarchy of
               board-head-management-staff
               and roles of president for head, manager for
               management, and worker for staff.
            Q: What structure does a fish have?
            A: Inherently, these parts---fins, 1 tail, 1 head,
               2 eyes, scales.

The theory of kind types predicts that as a ROLE, PROGRAMMER
will have certain types of features. Inherited from the SENTIENT
kind type is the feature type INTERNAL TRAIT ("mathematical").
Inherited from the SOCIAL kind type is the feature type FUNCTION
("program(subj,Y) & computer(Y)"), In addition, RELATION type
feature ("employee") and INCOME type features ("high") are predicted
with a ROLE.

The encoding of the verb representations described in Chapter 4 is
illustrated with the verb *program*. Generic information for verbs is
encoded in two lists, a list of typical features and a list of inherent
features. These are arguments of a ground clause which has the same
name as the verb.

(61)   program({what_enables(trained(subj)),
          cause(want(X,Y) & manager(X) & program(Y)),
          where(in(subj,Y) & office(Y)),
          what_happened_next(run(subj,Y) & program(Y)),"
          {goal(solve(subj,Y) & problem(Y)),
          consequence_of_event(exist(Y) & program(Y)),
          selectional_restriction(human(subj)),
          implies(machine(obj)),
          how(with(X) & computer(X))}).

The following illustrates how generic knowledge for verbs may be queried.

Text: John programmed for three years.
Q: Why did John program?
A: Typically, a manager wanted a program.

Q: If John programs, what is the goal?
A: Typically, John wants to solve a problem.

Q: If John programs, what enables it?
A: Inherently, John is trained.

Q: Where did John program?
A: Typically, in an office.

Q: How did John program?
A: Inherently, with a computer.

Q: If John programmed, what happened next?
A: Typically, John ran the program.

Q: If John programmed, what resulted?
A: Inherently, a program existed.

Q: If John programmed a computer, what is implied?
A: Typically, John is human, the computer is a machine.

5.3. Anaphors

NS representations of generic and ontological knowledge is used by all of the reasoning modules. The present implementation of anaphor resolution keeps a stack of head nouns, and uses generic and commonsense knowledge to guess antecedents of anaphors. The algorithm understands three principles: recency, gender agreement, and antecedent stability (once an antecedent has been found for a pronoun, keep using it if possible). In the anaphor resolution module, the referents of *she* and *woman*, and the referents of *it* and *cow* are identified for the text in (62). For (63), the algorithm identifies the referents of *she* and *cow*, because a commonsense rule permits gender pronouns for animals, or neuter pronouns.

(62)   The man loves a woman. She owns a cow. It is in the
        barn.

(63)   The man owns a cow. She is in the barn.

This rudimentary anaphor resolution module is under development. The goal is to use commonsense reasoning to correctly assign referents to anaphors in the complex ways illustrated in "The Programmer" text, as below:

Q: Who was sitting at the desk?
A: The manager.
Q: Who wanted to buy a computer?
A: John.

In order to do this the algorithm must reason that in (54), the manager is *he* because the manager owns the office, as stated in the text, because offices typically contain desks, and because people typically use things they own for their functions. In the second inference, the module must reason that buying is typically done with money, and John has asked for money (because managers give salary raises, and raises are money), therefore the *he* in (55) is John. These inferences require an interaction of word-level CK and discourse reasoning (to be described in Chapter 8).

5.4. PP Attachment

The prepositional phrase disambiguation module, to be described in Chapter 6, works on the first parse of a sentence, and selects a reading for post-verbal prepositional phrases. In "The Programmer" text, this results in attaching the PP in (52) to the object of the verb. This is done using knowledge of the generic relation between WORK and CORPORATION, that is, that working typically takes place in an organization, and ontological knowledge that a corporation is an IN-STITUTION. In (54), the PP is attached to the VP because of a rule which attaches the PP under the VP if the V is STATIVE and there is no direct object. In (55) the PP is attached to the VP because of the syntactic rule which handles VERB-PARTICLE constructions. In (56) KT attaches both PP's to the VP by generic knowledge of BUY, namely that BUY selects a SENTIENT oblique argument, and that buying is typically done with money.

Q: Where does John work?
A: In a large corporation.
Q: How will John buy the computer?
A: With the money.
Q: For whom does John want to buy the computer?
A: For his child.

Without the PP disambiguation module, these questions could not be answered. For example, a syntactically possible, but CK implausible, response by the system with no such algorithm would be:

Q: With whom does John want to buy the computer?
A: With the money.

5.5. Word Sense Disambiguation

Word sense disambiguation in KT selects from among word senses. Chapter 7 details the algorithm with a number of examples. In "The Programmer," KT selects the PLACE sense of office in (53) because *enter* is a MOTION verb, driving the following response.

Q: What is an office?
A: An office is a social place.
Q: What parts does an office have?
A: Typically an office has desks, telephones, typewriters
   and filing cabinets.

On the INSTITUTION reading of *office*, the responses would be more
like those above in (59) for *company*.

5.6. Discourse Reasoning

A theory of how to use Naive Semantics to recover discourse coherence is explored in Chapter 8. An algorithm based upon this theory
is under development. Eventually, KT will be able to recover the
coherence relations among the sentences in a text. Suppose that to each
sentence there is given an event number as below:

The Programmer
event1 John is a programmer who works for a large
    corporation.
event2 John entered his manager's office.
event3 He was sitting at his desk.
event4 John asked for a raise.
event5 He wanted to buy a home computer for his
       child with the money.
event6 John and his manager reviewed his accomplishments.

Our theory suggests that the following coherence relations among the
events should be assigned:

goal(event2,event4).
situation(activity(event3,event4)).
cause(event5,event4).
cause(event4,event6).

Chapter 8 describes the way NS representations, especially of verbs,and
other information including syntactic structure, tense and aspect and

discourse clue words, jointly determine discourse relation assignment. These assignments will make it possible for KT to respond as follows:

Q: Why did John ask for a raise?
A: Because he wanted to buy a home computer.
Q: What was John's manager doing
   when John asked for the raise?
A: Sitting at his desk.
Q: What was John's goal in entering his manager's office?
A: To ask for a raise.
Q: Why did John and his manager review his accomplishments?
A: Because John asked for a raise.

5.7. Kind Types Reasoning

The kind types constrain the generic knowledge. These constraints are used in several ways. One use is in encoding the generic knowledge. The KT lexical augmentation facility checks the ontological attachment node of a new word being encoded and brings up the set of feature types expected for that particular node, based upon kind type inheritance. For a ROLE term, it asks the encoder for FUNCTION, RELATION and INCOME features (among others, as described for that kind type in Chapter 3), while for a MINERAL term the facility would not ask for such features.

In the reasoning, kind types prune the search for answers. For example, to answer a question such as (64), the KT inference mechanism would ordinarily search for generic knowledge about WATER. But since WATER is INANIMATE, and has no BEHAVIOR features, KT can prune that search and answer based upon kind types alone. Similarly, since LOSE is NONGOAL, the answer to (65) can be derived from relational types.

(64)   Q: What does water do?
            A: Nothing.

(65)   Q: What goal did John have when he lost his watch?
              A: None.

Another use of kind types is to signal a switch from literal to metaphoric interpretation. If the text says something which violates kind type constraints, then the text intends a nonliteral interpretation. For example, if the text says "The mountains surrounded the lake," since mountains are nonselfmoving, they can't be subject of a motion verb. Or if the text says "the chicken's motor whirred," since animates don't have mechanical parts, the system needs to look for a metaphorical interpretation. At this point KT does not find the interpretation, but simply switches to a logic which fails to interpret at all.

Relational types, as discussed in Chapter 4, are used in discourse inferences. For example, relational types ensure that the discourse relation algorithm searches only for enablement, cause, situation, evaluation or prediction relations between clauses with non-goal verbs and other clauses.

5.8. Summary of Inference Mechanism

At present queries drive inferences in the KT system. After a text such as the "The Programmer" has been read, KT can respond to queries and seem to understand the text in a more human-like way using the various aspects of knowledge indicated above. Below are listed some queries and responses.

Q: Who is John?
A: The man who is a programmer.
   ---Programmers are people.
   ---He was referred to by he.
   ---Typical male person is a man (not a boy).
Q: Was the office built?
A: Yes.
   ---By ontology of artifacts
Q: Who built the office?
A: People.

   ---By ontology of artifacts
Q: Does John wear pants?
A: Probably so.
   ---By generic database.
Q: Does John eat eggs?
A: Probably so.
   ---Because eggs are food.
Q: What does an office think?
A: An office doesn't think.
   ---By kind types.
Q: Does John look like a computer?
A: No.
   ---By ontology database.
Q: Does John live in a tent?
A: Probably not.
   ---By generic knowledge of programmer as citydweller and
      of cities as having buildings.
Q: Does John have a function?
A: Yes.
   ---By kind types

6. PREPOSITIONAL PHRASE DISAMBIGUATION

Syntactic ambiguity is a notoriously difficult problem. In this chapter we show that lexical level commonsense knowledge can be used, in conjunction with syntactic and preposition-specific knowledge, to handle 99% of the post-verbal prepositional phrase ambiguity in a corpus of geography text.[8] The method discards spurious syntactic ambiguities introduced by post-verbal prepositional phrase attachment during parsing. A completely naive parser will generate three parses for sentences of the form NP-V-NP-PP. The prepositions alone are insufficiently precise in meaning to guide selection among competing parses. The method employs commonsense knowledge of concepts in preference strategies which appeal to the meaning of the preposition combined with information about the verbs and nouns associated with it drawn from the text and from the generic and ontological databases. These determine which syntactic structures generated by a semantically naive parser are commonsensically plausible. The method was successful in 93% of cases tested.

6.1. Semantically Implausible Syntactic Ambiguities

A problem for text understanding systems is that syntactic rules alone produce numerous ambiguities, many of which are not semantically possible (or likely) interpretations. Consider sentence (66), for which any standard parser would produce three distinct syntactic structures. Figure 13 on page 125 is a syntactic tree showing the parse for (66) in which the key belongs to the lock. The *with*-phrase is a constituent of the noun phrase headed by *lock* (NP constituency). Figure 14 on page 126 is a syntactic tree showing the *with*-phrase as a constituent of the verb phrase (VP constituency). Figure 15 on page 127 shows the parse in which the *with*-phrase modifies the sentence (S-

---

8   This research was originally published as Dahlgren and McDowell, 1986b.

modification), so that the event of buying the lock takes place with the key. Only one of these syntactic possibilities is semantically possible for (66), namely the one in which the prepositional phrase is a complement of the NP whose head is *lock*. Similarly, only VP constituency is semantically possible for (67), and only S-modification for (68).

(66)   John bought the lock with the key.

(67)   John bought the lock with five dollars.

(68)   John bought the lock in the afternoon.

(69)   John took the key to the lock.

Clearly, the semantically implausible syntactic ambiguities generated for (66) - (68) are spurious. On the other hand, some syntactic ambiguities correspond to possible semantic ambiguities. In sentence (69), both the VP constituency and NP constituency parses are semantically possible. It is easy to imagine a situation in which John physically carries the key over to the lock. However, in this case the preferred reading maps to NP constituency because the head of the *to*-phrase is typically 'a part of' or 'used for' the head of the direct object NP. A text understanding system that can guess NP constituency in this case is not only practical and workable, it is also superior to one which chooses randomly. The commonsense disambiguation method to be described in this chapter assigns constituency for prepositional phrases according to commonsense preference, and the only ambiguities which remain after the preference strategy has been invoked are the semantically and commonsensically possible ambiguities, such as those below. In (70) either the seeing event or the man might have been in the park, and in (71) either the building event or the houses might have been by the sea.

(70)   John saw the man in the park.

(71)   John built the houses by the sea.

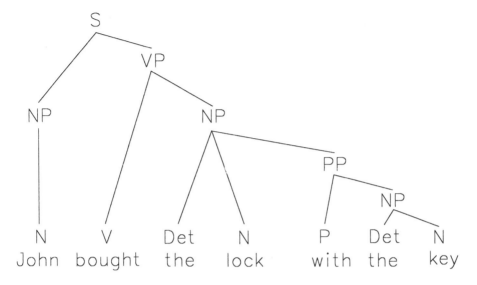

Figure 13: NP-Constituency

(66) - (69) are all of the form NP-V-NP-PP. The same considerations apply when there are multiple PPs. Consider sentence (72), which has eight parses, of which only one is semantically possible (*to the pasture* is a VP constituent, and *in the afternoon* modifies the S).

(72)   The boy took the cow to the pasture in the afternoon.

6.2. Using Commonsense Knowledge to Disambiguate

One solution to the problem of spurious ambiguities is semantically-driven parsing, which forces you to give up the speed and parsimony of autonomous parsing (Arens, 1981, Wilks, 1985). Another solution is to ask the user to disambiguate, as in Tomita (1985). This works well in the database querying environment, but not for text understanding, where human intervention is not feasible. Another approach uses syntactic information alone (Frazier and Fodor, 1978). This approach is inadequate in many of cases. A more successful method uses selection restrictions on the verb to disambiguate post-verbal prepositional

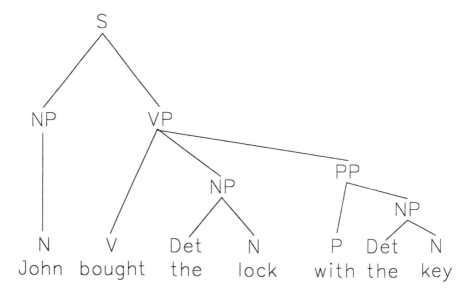

Figure 14: VP-Constituency

phrases (Ford, Bresnan and Kaplan, 1985). While selection restrictions
succeed in many cases, in others they are insufficient, and commonsense
knowledge is required in order to disambiguate. The KT system uses
a mixed method which includes syntactic, semantic and commonsense
knowledge, including knowledge of the specific behavior of each preposition. Exemplifying the method with sentences (66) - (68), in (66),
the *with*-phrase must be a NP constituent because locks typically have
keys. English speakers know this, and that is why (66) is unambiguous.
In (67), the *with*-phrase is a VP constituent because *buy* is a verb of
exchange. In (68), the fact that *afternoon* is a temporal noun forces
the interpretation in which the PP modifies the S because only events
have a temporal argument. (We will describe two related computational
methods, those of Crain and Steedman, 1985, and Hirst, 1987, after
presenting our method).

The KT method uses commonsense knowledge associated with concepts to choose among possible parses for a sentence with a prepositional
phrase to the right of the verb. (Prepositional phrases in the subject of

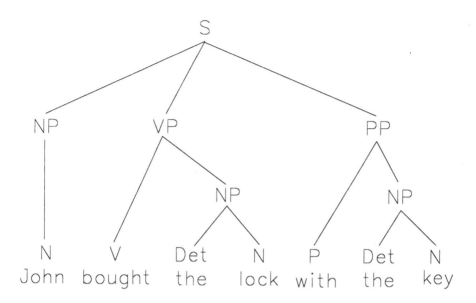

Figure 15: S-Constituency

the sentence are not ambiguous in the same way, because PPs after the
head of the subject noun must be NP constituents. We assume that
preposed PPs as in "In the spring, we go dancing" show up at the end
of the S after parsing.) A text understanding system can eliminate
spurious parses by employing preference strategies in the spirit of Warren (1981). The disambiguation method is independent of the type of
parser and grammar. After each parse is generated, and before semantic
interpretation, word-level commonsense knowledge is employed to decide whether the parse is preferred. The CK required for these PP
attachments is exactly the same CK needed for word sense
disambiguation and discourse coherence, so the only additional spe-
cialized elements of CK needed for PP attachment are several
preposition-specific PP attachment rules. We found that in limited text
understanding, where the grammaticality of the text can be assumed,
the level of detail called for in (Waltz, 1981, Gawron, 1983, Herskovits,
1985) is not necessary.

This chapter will first describe how CK is used in preference strategies for prepositional ambiguities. We then explain the discovery of the preference strategies in an empirical study of prepositional phrase attachment in a corpus. Then we list the preference strategy rules and discuss their implementation.

6.3. Commonsense Knowledge used in the Preference Strategy

Our preference strategy assigns PP constituency according to information from several sources: syntactic information about the preposition (PREP) and the verb (V); information from the Ontology about the V, direct object (DO), and object of the preposition (POBJ); and information from the Generic Database about the V, DO and POBJ. Table 6.1 lists the preference rules, preposition by preposition.

Ontological Class of Object of the Preposition. Frequently the PP is disambiguated by the ontological attachment of the POBJ. This is often preposition-dependent. For example,

- If the POBJ is temporal, the PP modifies the S.

    in the morning, for six days

- If the Prep is *by*, and the POBJ is sentient and the DO is propositional, the PP modifies the NP.

    the book by Chomsky

- If the Prep is *at* or *in* and the POBJ is abstract, the PP modifies the S.

    at once, in detail

- If the Prep is *on*, and the POBJ is propositional, the PP modifies the NP.

    the book on love

Sometimes it is necessary to consider not only the ontological class of the POBJ, but also the ontological class of the DO. For example, in *the report by the committee* it is necessary to know not only that *report* is PROPOSITIONAL, but that *committee* is SENTIENT. Other ontological classes which play a role in the preference strategies are PLACE, EMOTION, ROUTE, MEASURE, RELATION, and DIRECTION. A global rule assigns locative and directional PPs to the VP as in (73), S modifiers if the global rule fails as in (74). though later preposition-specific rules may assign them as

(73)   John put the book in the living room.

(74)   John read the book in the living room.

PLACEs can be social places (*factory*, hospital) or natural places (*valley*, *mountain*). EMOTIONS enter into PPs in such phrases as *under duress*, *in fear, from hatred, with courage,* etc. ROUTES are terms like *way, road, path*. MEASUREs appear in PPs with *to* (*to a degree, to a point*). DIRECTIONS figure prominently in physical descriptions (*to the North, on the South*). PPs headed by *with* and *without* are NP constituents if the DO is a RELATION (*connection with, contact with*).

Ontological Class of The Direct Object. Much less crucial is information about the ontological class of the DO. As described above, the fact that a DO is PROPOSITIONAL is important only in the case of two classes of prepositional objects and then only for certain prepositions. If the DO is a MEASURE, then the PP is an NP constituent (*enough food for their needs, much about the world*).

Ontological Class of Verb. The nature of the verb itself can sometimes induce a preference for a PP assignment without reference to any other information. For instance, the verbs *be* and *stand* and other intransitive STATIVES like them automatically take any PP but a temporal one as a VP constituent (*run in the park, stand in the rain*). Mental verbs force VP constituency for PPs headed by *of, for,* and *about* (Gawron, 1983). as illustrated by (75) as opposed to (76).

(75)   John thought of his sweetheart while he waited.

(76)   John repaired the roof of the house.

Verbs of exchange, such as *buy*, typically take three arguments, the object exchanged, the source, and the goal. In addition, the medium of exchange and the benefactee of the exchange can be expressed. With such verbs, PPs headed by *for, from,* and *with,* are VP constituents.

Generic Information. So far just the ontological classification of the verb and the NPs to its right have been considered. Now we consider the commonsense knowledge associated with nouns, generic information, and the effect it has on PP attachment. Generally, a relationship in the generic representation of the DO and the POBJ can result in NP-attachment, and the unlikelihood of such a relationship can indicate another attachment. In the case of *with* and *on* it is sufficient that the POBJ is mentioned in the typical features for the DO (*car with a wheel, birds with feathers, hair on the head*).

A locative relationship can also be part of generic information. A stove is typically in the kitchen, a book on a shelf, etc. The typical MATERIAL from which an object is made is included in the generic information for physical objects. A house is made from wood, a window from glass. We call SOLVERS the nouns which are typically associated with other nouns by means of *to* (*the key to the lock, the answer to the problem*). SIZE is a generic feature and is encoded in terms of 13 reality-related size ranges which have mnemonic names such as microscopic, person-sized, etc. An object must be of the order of at least two sizes larger than the subject of a sentence in order for it to be a suitable location for an action by the subject. That is, a PP headed by a locative preposition will be a S modifier if the prepositional object is a suitable location for the action of the subject as in (77) and otherwise it will be a VP or NP constituent as in (78).

(77)   John mixed the salad in the kitchen.

(78)   John mixed the salad in the salad bowl.

The relation between a verb and the generic INSTRUMENT with which the verbal action is carried out is encoded in the Generic Database for verbs along with other information, such as selectional restrictions on verb arguments. In (79), because *knife* is a typical INSTRUMENT for the verb *cut*, the PP is assigned to the VP, but it is assigned to the S in (80).

(79)   John cut the loaf with a knife.

(80)   John cut the loaf with glee.

Syntax. Certain syntactic constructions can also force PP interpretation. There is a large class of intransitive verbs which are ill-formed unless accompanied by certain prepositions (*depend on, look for, make up, get along with, revolve about, cooperate with, turn to, divide into, provide for*). These are conventional co-occurrence requirements, and they force the PP to be interpreted as a VP constituent. Adjectives + PP require attachment to the phrase (XP) containing the adjective (*suitable for a child, useful for parsing*). On the other hand, the comparative construction forces NP constituency (*the largest book in the library, uglier than the man at the desk*).

We showed above that the ontological class of the POBJ can determine correct PP constituency. Generics and names are syntactic classes and also guide PP parsing.

(81)   John read the book on Peter the Great.

(82)   John read the book on dogs.

For each preposition there is a general rule which takes effect when all the specific rules fail. This is a kind of Elsewhere Condition for the syntax of prepositions. Generalizing the results of the study, locative PPs are NP constituents; directional PPs are VP constituents; and time/manner/place PPs are S modifiers. However, whether or not a PP falls into one of these classes is a function of the prepositional head in combination with the verb and the prepositional object and not of the preposition alone.

6.4. Success Rate of the Preference Strategy

The PP rules were developed intuitively by considering the interaction of each preposition with one, two and three-place verbs. Then the PP rules were hand-tested on 4100 words of schoolbook geography texts, the original corpus upon which the lexicon and ontology in the KT system were built. The PP-attachment rules were developed independently of these texts, but the success rate was a surprising 100%. Then, as a check against these results, the rules were hand-tested on a second group of three short sample texts. These were (1) a 481-word excerpt from a novel, (2) a 415-word excerpt from a work on the history of science, and (3) a 409-word excerpt from a technical article. We assumed parser translation of the texts into strings of the form NP-V-NP-PP for submission to our rules. We also ignored passive *by*-phrases because the parser recognizes them as distinct from ordinary PPs. On the latter three texts, the rules, which are listed in full at the end of the chapter, were tested by seeing whether the PP attachments assigned by the rules matched our intuitions of the PP attachments. The overall success rate for the second group is 93%. The failures in these tests are of two types. The first type of failure was in idiomatic phrases, most of which have the function of asides or sentence qualifiers (*at all, in effect, in every case, under my eyes, in particular, according to*). We do not view this as a defect in our system since any system must be able eventually to deal with idiomatic phrases. The second type of failure was outright failure of the rules. If we ignore the failures due to idiomatic phrases then the average success rate for the second group is much higher, 98%. One reason why the success rate is so high is the high occurrence rate of *of*-phrases. These constitute 32% of the second group. In every case we have seen so far, they attach to the NP immediately to the left.

6.5. Implementation

Preference rules for thirteen English prepositions are listed in Table 6.1. First, seven global rules are attempted. If none of these rules applies, the procedure relevant to the preposition is called upon. Although there is no single, general algorithm for PP attachment, three points compensate for this lack of generality: (1) the set of prepositions in English is a closed and small set, (2) some rules are used for several prepositions, and (3) for each preposition, the list of rules is short (usually three). The phrase structures which are input to the rules are: VP(V-DO-Prep-POBJ), VP(V-Prep-POBJ), VP(V-comparative) VP(V-Adj-Prep-POBJ) and VP(V-Prep-NP).

The seven global rules are listed below. Lexical(V + Prep) means that the relationship between the verb and the preposition is lexical, as described in "Syntax." on page 131. Stative(V) means the verb is stative, measure(DO) that the direct object is a measure. *Adj* and *comparative* mean that such a construction occurs in the sentence.

1. lexical(V + Prep) → vp_attach(PP)
2. time(POBJ) → s_attach(PP)
3. stative(V)→ vp_attach(PP)
4. xp(...Adj-PP...) → xp_attach
5. measure(DO) → np_attach(PP)
6. motion(V) & DO & endofclause → vp_attach(PP)
7. comparative → np_attach

To illustrate the application of the rules, consider the rule for *of* applied to the sentence "John buys the book of poems." The global rules are tried, and they fail. Then the first *of*-rule consults the Ontological Database to see whether the verb is mental. This fails, so the solution is NP constituency.

The *with*-rule illustrates more complex reasoning. Consider the sentence "Sam bought the car with the wheel." The first *with*-rule consults the entry for *car* in the Generic Lexicon, looking for mention of *wheel* there, and finds it, as cars inherently have wheels. The rule succeeds and the PP is assigned NP constituency. In contrast, consider the sentence "Sam fixed the car with a wrench." The global rules fail, and the first *with*-rule tests whether a generic relationship exists between the DO and the POBJ, in the Generic Lexicon, and whether the DO is a relation in the Ontological Database, and fails. The next *with*-rule checks whether *wrench* is a typical instrument of the verb *fix* in the Generic Lexicon. This succeeds, so the PP is assigned VP constituency. Finally, consider the sentence "Sam fixed the car with Mary." No generic relation can be found between *car* and Mary or *fix* and Mary, so the elsewhere rule applies, and the PP modifies the S.

These generic relationships exist for a number of prepositions but are not mentioned in the rules because they are subsumed by the elsewhere condition. For example, such relationships exist for uses of *for*, as in *the wheel for the car* and *the cap for the jar*, but since the rules are written so that NP-attachment is the elsewhere rule, this kind of relationship does not show up directly.

In the *in*-rules, notice that first the generic relation of location (a place the DO is typically found) is checked for in the Generic Lexicon. If that fails, and VP constituency fails, a check is carried out in the Ontological Database for whether the POBJ is a place. This order captures the difference between (83) and (84). Our system chooses S modification for (85), but it is actually ambiguous.

(83)   John saw the horse in the barn.

(84)   John walked the horse in the city.

(85)   John saw the horse in the city.

The rules work for constructions which have no DO. There are several types of these. One is the type where the verb must always co-occur with a certain preposition (*depend on*). These are covered by the first global rule, which checks for such constraints in the Syntactic Lexicon. Another type is STATIVE verbs, as in "John lives in the house," which are covered by the second global rule. Notice that intransitive constructions are excluded from the sixth global rule which assigns VP constituency for sentences such as "John put the book on the table." This means that the rules will prefer S-attachment in some cases where sentences are commonsensically ambiguous, as in (86).

(86)   John ran at the woman.
         John ran by the park.

6.6. Other Approaches

Psycholinguistic research of Frazier and Fodor (1978) suggests that people employ two principles in attaching ambiguous constituents:

Right Association - attach as low and as far to the right as possible.
Minimal Attachment - use as few non-terminal nodes as possible.

Minimal Attachment explains the preference subjects have for VP-attachment in (87).

(87)   John bought the book for Susan.

In (88), where a long complement intervenes between the main verb and *yesterday*, right association explains the preference for attaching *yesterday* to the lower sentence.

(88)   Tom said that Bill had taken the cleaning out yesterday.

As Hirst (1987) points out, these two principles are not particularly helpful in explaining post-verbal PP attachment, because in that context, right association prefers NP attachment, and minimal attachment prefers VP attachment.

Ford, Bresnan and Kaplan (1982) propose to use the case roles of the verb to disambiguate prepositional phrase modifiers. For example, in (89), the verb *position* prefers VP-attachment for *on the rack*, while in (90), the verb *want* does not.

(89)   The woman positioned the dress on that rack.

(90)   The woman wanted the dress on that rack.

Our method uses the selection restrictions on the verb as only one of several sources of information for PP attachment. Their method cannot handle cases which require commonsense reasoning to NP attach, rather than S attach, as in (92)

(91)   Mary made the salad in the refrigerator.

(92)   Mary made the salad in the kitchen.

Also, the method does not take advantage of preposition-specific rules, so that the whole burden of PP attachment falls to the verb representations in the lexicon.

Crain and Steedman (1985) reject Frazier and Fodor's principles, and propose the following alternative principles which take into account discourse context.

The Principle of Referential Success - If there is a reading which succeeds in referring to an entity already established in the hearer's mental model of the domain of discourse, then it is favored oven one that is not.

The Principle of Parsimony: If there is a reading which carries fewer unsatisfied by consistent presuppositions or entailments than any other, then other criteria of plausibility being equal,that reading will be adopted as the most plausible by the hearer, and the presuppositions in question will be incorporated in his or her model.

The Principle of Plausibility. If a reading is more plausible in terms of either general knowledge about the world, or of specific knowledge about the universe of discourse, then, other things being equal, it will be favored over one that is not.

The Principle of Referential Success prefers and NP attachment if an entity satisfying such a description has already been mentioned in the discourse. For example, instead of having to reason about the plausibility of a lock with a key in (93), if a lock with a key has already been mentioned in the discourse, NP attachment can be assumed. The definite determiner suggests looking in the previous discourse for such an entity.

(93)   John bought the lock with the key.

This principle has been implemented as a global rule in our preference strategy. The Principle of Plausibility is reflected in our system in the preposition-specific rules which consider generic relationships between NPs. The rules which test for plausibility are: the *on*-rule ("the handle on the door," "the cover on book"), the *in*-rule ("the horse in the barn," the pill in the bottle"), the *under*-rule ("the worm under the rock"), the *to*-rule ("the solution to the problem"), and the *with*-rule ("a car with a wheel," "a key with a lock").

Our rules do not take into account the principle of parsimony, but Hirst (1987) argues that the Principle of Referential success handles presupposition anyway.

> *First, a definite NP presupposes that the thing it describes exists and that it is available in the focus or knowledge base for felicitous (unique) reference; an indefinite NP presupposes only the plausibility of what it describes...Second, the attachment of a PP to an NP results in new presuppositions for the new NP thus created, but cancels any uniqueness aspect of the referential presuppositions of both its constituent NPs. Thus, the ocelot with the blue chipmunk presupposes that there is just one such ocelot available for reference (and that such a thing is plausible) the plausibility and existence of an **ocelot** and a **blue chipmunk** continue to be presupposed, but their uniqueness is no longer required. Third, the attachment of a PP to a VP creates no new presupposition, but rather always indicates new (unpresupposed) information.*

Hirst's approach combines the verb-guided preference of Ford, Bresnan and Kaplan (1982) and the preference principles of Crain and Steedman (1985). In "1.6. Computational Approaches to Word Meaning" on page 23 we briefly described Hirst's frame representations. Hirst proposes a Semantic Enquiry Desk (SED) function, which is invoked by the parser whenever it detects a post-verbal PP. The SED first checks for a previously mentioned entity which would satisfy a description defined by the NP-PP combination, as in our global rule. Then it tries verb- guided preference by looking at the case slots in the representation of the verb. Next it tests for plausibility, by inspecting the slot-filler pairs in descriptions, such as (color-red). If the head of the NP or POBJ occurs as a slot- filler for the other, NP attachment is preferred. The effect of this is the same our tests for generic information in the preposition-specific rules. The difference between our tests for generic relationships and the SED's depends upon the amount of detail in the semantic representations. Since Naive Semantics represents more information, the tests will succeed more of the time. Overall, Hirst's approach is like ours in using semantic information, not just structural information, for disambiguation, and in using both verb representations and generic relations hips between nouns. It differs in not using preposition specific information. Our approach, by using them, in effect denies Hirst's across-the-board preference for NP-attachment if it can be established, and followed by preference for VP-attachment.

6.7. Conclusion

The preference strategy presented here can be applied to the output of any type of parser, and the commonsense knowledge can be represented in any language desired. The content of the knowledge derives from available empirical studies. Thus the method is broadly applicable. The method interfaces autonomous syntactic and semantic components of a natural language understanding system, discarding implausible syntactic trees before they are fully interpreted semantically. It is also possible to apply the preference strategy during the parse, if the parser has a lookahead or hold capability, by first generating all the possible places to attach a PP, and looking ahead to parse the object of the PP. At this point all of the information needed by the preference strategy is available, and the rules can be applied, thus eliminating the expense of generating parses only to discard them later.

Table 6.1 Preposition-Specific Preference Rules

of-rules
  mental(V) → vp_attach(PP)
  Elsewhere → np_attach(PP)

on-rules
  (location(DO,POBJ) OR generic(POBJ) OR name(POBJ)
    OR (propositional(DO) & abstract(POBJ))) → np_attach(PP)
  Elsewhere → s_attach(PP)

for-rules
  place(POBJ) OR sentient(POBJ) OR mental(V)
    OR exchange(V) → vp_attach(PP)
  distance(POBJ) → s_attach(PP)
  Elsewhere → np_attach(PP)

at-rules
  abstract(POBJ) OR place(POBJ) → s_attach(PP)
  Elsewhere → np_attach(PP)

in-rules
  (NOT (generic(DO,POBJ))) AND
    (abstract(POBJ) OR emotion(POBJ) OR place(POBJ))
        → s_attach(PP)
  Elsewhere → np_attach(PP)

by-rules
  location(DO,POBJ) → np_attach(PP)
  propositional(DO) & sentient(POBJ) → np_attach(PP)
  Elsewhere → s_attach(PP)

under-rules

twosizeslarger(POBJ,SUBJ) OR propositional(POBJ)
   → s_attach(PP)
Elsewhere → np_attach(PP)

about-rules
  mental(V) OR motion(V) → vp_attach(PP)
  Elsewhere → np_attach(PP)

to-rules
  solver(DO, POBJ) OR route(DO) → np_attach
  geometric(V) & direction(POBJ) → s_attach(PP)
  place(DO) & direction(POBJ) → np_attach(PP)
  measurement(POBJ) → s_attach
  Elsewhere → vp_attach(PP)

with and *without*-rules
  partof(DO,POBJ) OR relation(DO) → np_attach(PP)
  instrument(POBJ,V) → vp_attach(PP)
  Elsewhere → s_attach(PP)

from-rules
  material(POBJ) OR emotion(POBJ) → s_attach(PP)
  exchange(V) → vp_attach(PP)
  Elsewhere → np_attach(PP)

through-rules
  Elsewhere → s_attach(PP)

7. WORD SENSE DISAMBIGUATION

7.1. Approaches to Word Sense Disambiguation

Computational lexical approaches to disambiguation divide into syntactic category assignment such as whether *farm* is a noun or a verb (Milne, 1986) and word sense disambiguation within syntactic category.[9] The latter problem is the subject of this chapter. Assuming that word senses are listed together under one lexical entry in a given syntactic category, the problem is to select the correct one. One computational method of disambiguation is pattern matching where the surrounding words frequently associated with a sense are used to disambiguate a word. Such methods are powerful and can be used to eliminate 70% of the ambiguity (Black, 1986). A second method employs a rich syntactic lexicon which includes selectional restrictions (Gross, 1985). A third method uses a combination of structural and conceptual analysis for disambiguation (Black, 1986). In the present work a method is proposed which combines three types of information to disambiguate: fixed and frequent phrases, syntactic information and commonsense reasoning. It is similar to Black's approach, but it differs in using a psycholinguistically motivated word meaning representations as the basis of a generalized disambiguation procedure. The advantage of the method is that it employs computationally expensive commonsense reasoning only for the difficult cases, and not for simpler cases. In the data examined, half the cases were simple, and the other half required commonsense reasoning.

Two approaches to simplifying disambiguation were considered and rejected as the starting points (though they are important aspects of the process). One was the idea that domain-specificity could be used to reduce ambiguity. In particular domains certain senses of words become more salient and others recede. For example, in a military

---

9 This research was originally published as Dahlgren (1988a).

domain the noun *company* has a salient sense meaning *a unit of soldiers*. In other domains, such as business, this sense is irrelevant, and may be suppressed altogether. Unfortunately, domain-specificity does not eliminate all ambiguity. Firstly, some text is very general, and readers are unsure what terminology will be used. Secondly, even in domain-specific texts, many words remain highly ambiguous. For example, the noun *hand* has sixteen senses and retains ten of them in almost any text. We decided to ignore domain-specific senses for the present research and concentrate upon disambiguating widely-used senses. Similar to domain-specificity is the idea of using paragraph topic to disambiguate. For example, if the paragraph is military, then the sense of *company* in "call the company," which means "military unit," can be selected without any further reasoning. This proposal is attractive because it is computationally efficient, once paragraph topic is determined. However, paragraph topic only partially disambiguates. Other information must be added to paragraph topic information. Furthermore, paragraph topic is difficult to determine. Thus the method must be rejected for the time being.

7.2. Local Combined Ambiguity Reduction

In the present research, the hypothesis was tested that a combined method employing fixed and frequent phrases, syntactic properties and complex commonsense reasoning could be used to progressively reduce ambiguity. A computational disambiguation algorithm should take advantage of whatever relatively simple methods exist, especially in light of the exponentially large number of possible interpretations of a text. The hypothesis is that superficial word associations and syntactic structures take less cognitive processing than does commonsense reasoning. Wouldn't it be bewildering if each time the word *hand* was encountered, all sixteen senses were potential candidates in the interpretation? We can speculate that frequently-used combinations of words are stored in memory, and accessed similarly to the way compounds are. Perhaps natural language is redundant in providing a number of different clues for semantic interpretation, one of which is just that certain sequences of words can have only one interpretation. If this is true, natural language is not as generative as has been believed, in that some complex phrases are memorized rather than generated. On the other hand, in the more difficult cases where fixed phrases and syntactic tests fail, people disambiguate by using a broad level of conceptual and encyclopedic knowledge. Fortunately, in a psycholinguistically based natural language understanding system, a great deal of the information needed for the difficult cases is already encoded for independent reasons. This research began with the prejudice that paragraph topic would do the lion's share of disambiguating. It turned out that half is done by fixed phrases and syntax, and half by local commonsense reasoning.

The combined disambiguation method is local, in that it first attempts to employ the directly adjacent words as fixed phrases, then tries syntactic information in the same sentence, then tries commonsense reasoning concerning elements of the same sentence. Only after all of these have failed does it attempt to disambiguate using information in surrounding sentences. During the parse of a sentence, ambiguous words are flagged. Resolved ambiguity information is passed from sentence to sentence. Anaphora rules identify referents of nouns and pronouns to the extent possible. The algorithm applies cyclically, to the most deeply embedded sentence within a sentence and upward to the topmost sentence. Since fixed and frequent phrases are computationally simple, and reduce ambiguity substantially, they are tried first. Then syntactic tests are attempted. Finally, more complex commonsense reasoning is invoked, in which ontological and generic knowledge is accessed. The algorithm starts with a list of numbers, the sense list, which contains one integer for each sense of a word. At each stage, the progressive reduction of the Sense List is checked to see whether the word has been fully disambiguated, in which case the Sense List is reduced to one member and the algorithm is exited. The algorithm is as follows:

Assume all senses are relevant--set Sense List to all senses
Try all fixed phrases
    Conclusive? Return
    Reductive? Reduce Sense List accordingly.

Try syntactic tests
    Conclusive? Return
    Reductive? Reduce Sense List accordingly.
Use CK reasoning
    Conclusive? Return
    Reductive? Reduce Sense List accordingly.

7.3. Test of Hypothesis

The local ambiguity reduction method described above was tested in the following way. Seven nouns and four verbs were chosen to be tested against concordances drawn from the Hansard parliamentary corpus, which were generously supplied by Ezra Black. Highly ambiguous words were chosen because it is with these difficult cases that commonsense knowledge is most needed. These were the nouns *office, hand, company, idea, crop, people,* and *school,* and the verbs *work, support, use* and *move.* Psycholinguistically based generic representations of these in the Kind Types system (KT) were expanded to account for all senses, and syntactic and fixed phrase rules were written. Employing these, the algorithm fully disambiguates 96% of the 2193 instances of the nouns in the concordances, even though the concordances do not always include the entire sentence in which the word occurred. Of the 91 concordances for which the method failed, only one occurred in a full sentence. It might have been 100% successful if entire sentences had been available. The algorithm was 99% successful for 1789 concordances of the verbs.

7.4. Noun Disambiguation

This section describes the environments in which the algorithm applies, and the effects it has. Fixed and frequent phrases, syntactic tests and commonsense reasoning will be considered in turn. In each description, the name of the rule will be listed in boldface. This may be used as a guide to "7.10. Disambiguation Rules" on page 158, which describes the encoding of the rules. The discussion will turn upon the representation of *office* in (94).

(94)   office({1,INSTITUTION,{hierarchy({management,staff}),
          roles({management(manager), staff(secretary),staff(clerk)})},
          {function(business)}},

          {2,PLACE,{haspart(*,chairs),haspart(*,desks),
          haspart(*,telephones),haspart(*,typewriters),
          location(downtown)},{haspart(*,doors),
          haspart(*,windows),location(building)}},

          {3,ROLEINITSELF,{function(legislative),

          function(executive),function(judicial),
          status(high)},{relation(elected),
          function(government)}},
          {4,TEMPORAL,{},{function(service)}},

          {5,INSTITUTION,{hierarchy({head,staff}),
          roles({head(official),staff(researcher),
          staff(clerk)})},{function(government),
          rank(executive)}}).

Fixed and Frequent Phrases. Using known computational methods, it is possible to identify sequences of words which are always used with the same sense of an ambiguous noun (Black, 1986). Once encoded, they can be compared with an incoming text using fast methods. In order to be worth encoding, such phrases should be frequent. Fixed phrases vary in length from long (*on the one hand, on the other hand, in good company, in good hands*) to short (*iron hand, office space, office hours, by hand, to hand, in hand, in office*). Many of the fixed phrases and verb-noun combinations are idiomatic expressions, that is, phrases in which the meaning is not compositional.[10] However, the method of testing for idioms is identical to that of testing for frequent compositional phrases, so that they are lumped into the same part of the algorithm.

---

10 I am indebted to Eric Wehrli for pointing this out.

Syntactic Tests. Syntactic tests inspect a simplified version of the parse to disambiguate. In *Fred ruled the famous detective agency with a free hand*, *rule* disambiguates *hand* in oblique position, and the simplified parse indicates that the two words have the required syntactic relationship. There is a fixed set of types of tests, to be described here, and for each ambiguous noun, the test consists of a PROLOG rule (predicate name in boldface) associated with the noun which says, in effect, if a particular syntactic context exists, select a certain sense or sublist of senses.

The nature of the determiner in a noun phrase is powerful in disambiguating. The presence or absence of a definite article, the choice of definite article, and the presence or absence of personal pronouns are all clues to disambiguation which may partially or fully reduce the ambiguity of a noun. This relates to the fact that the generic use of a noun is often the clue which disambiguates it. No semantic generalizations have emerged here, simply the fact that these syntactic structures select senses. In some cases the absence of a determiner (**nodet**). disambiguates The phrase *aspire to high office* must use the electoral sense (3) of *office*. When the determiner is present, but is not a definite article (**nodef**), ambiguity can be reduced or eliminated. *hands* with an indefinite article has only seven senses (1,2,5,8,11,12,13). The definite article (**defart**) can disambiguate. *people* with the definite article has three of six senses. The indefinite article (**indefart**) disambiguates. *office* with the indefinite article reduces ambiguity from five senses to three (senses 1,2 or 3). An even more detailed rule is the one which distinguishes *the office of the Senator* from *the office of Senator*. The former is ambiguous between the INSTITUTION and PLACE senses, while the latter can only have the electoral sense (3). The difference is the definite article used with the ROLE term. This difference was frequent in the concordances (n = 203). When the determiner is a personal pronoun (**perspron**), certain senses are selected. The phrase "her hand," has five readings for *hand* (senses 1,2,6,9,12). Add the preposition *in* and the ambiguity is reduced again so that the only possibilities are the bodily part sense (1,2) or the power sense (5). Similarly, "with her hands" can only have the bodily part sense, the INSTRUMENT sense (4) or the ROLE sense (12). Quantifiers (**quant**) can disambiguate.

When *idea* occurs with the quantifiers *some, any* and *no*, the sense which means "vague notion" must be selected.

When nouns take complements (**comp**), the presence of the complement can disambiguate. *idea* with a complement can have only two of four senses. Much of the commonsense reasoning concerns prepositions and verbs. However, word-specific tests for specific prepositions or verbs are also frequent. Being the object of certain prepositions (**prep**) is enough to disambiguate some ambiguous nouns. The preposition *by* selects the INSTRUMENT sense (4) of *hand* as in *Fred made the chair by hand.* The preposition *with* in combination with a personal pronoun reduces the ambiguity of *hand* from sixteen to four senses (1,2,4,12). Ambiguity can be resolved when the noun is in subject, object or oblique position (**verbsubj verbobj verbobliq**) relative to a particular verb. With *hand*, the verb *tremble* selects the bodily part sense (1) in subject position. The verb *shake* selects its bodily part sense in object position.

If some specific noun disambiguates an ambiguous noun in a frequent pair, this fact will be reflected in the list of fixed phrases for the ambiguous noun. If a noun disambiguates another through more complex commonsense reasoning, this fact will be discovered by the commonsense rules. Therefore, no syntactic tests for noun-noun disambiguation exist.

Figure 3 summarizes the effect of the syntactic rules with the noun *office*. After each rule has been tried, if the rule succeeds it either reduces the senselist to one member, resulting in an exit from the algorithm, or it reduces it to more than one member and the algorithm continues. If the rule fails, the senselist remains unchanged, and the algorithm continues. At the end, if the senselist has more than one member, the commonsense rules are tried. The rules in PROLOG form are listed in "7.10. Disambiguation Rules" on page 158.

Commonsense Knowledge. The power of the commonsense knowledge representations in the KT system is demonstrated by the fact that of 2193 concordances, 1068 (49%) were disambiguated using KT commonsense knowledge. Difficult cases of ambiguity can be resolved by

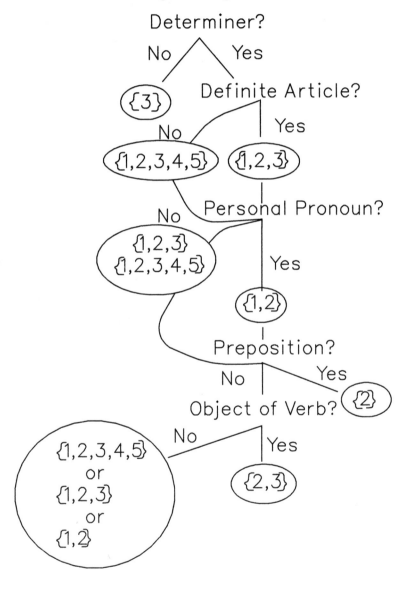

Figure 16

determining ontological similarity or generic relationships. Ontological similarity is defined as the attachment or inheritance of the same ontological node by two nouns. For example, in *the senator or his office* the INSTITUTION sense (1) of *office* is selected because senator is SENTIENT and so is INSTITUTION. (This is not to claim that ontologically dissimilar nouns cannot be conjoined, only that the algorithm prefers ontological similarity.) Where both nouns are ambiguous, the sense of each which matches the other ontologically is chosen. If ontological tests fail, the algorithm looks for information about an ambiguous noun in the generic representation of another verb or noun. In *John patted the dog with his hand*, the personal pronoun in combination with the preposition *with* reduces the ambiguity of *hand* from sixteen senses to two, the bodily part (1) and the laborer sense (12), as in "farm hands." In order to select the bodily part sense, generic knowledge of the typical instruments of the verb *pat* must be accessed.

When the ambiguous noun is in a conjunction with another noun (**conj**), ontological similarity disambiguates, as in the above example of *the senator or his office.* In contrast, in *the office and furniture* only the PLACE sense (2) of *office* is possible because *furniture* is PHYSICAL, and PLACE is under PHYSICAL in the ontology. Where both nouns are ambiguous, the sense of each which matches the other ontologically is chosen, as in *the company and the school* which selects the INSTITUTION sense of both.

An ambiguous noun can be disambiguated by Frequently a noun immediately preceding an ambiguous noun (**prevnoun**) disambiguates because the pair names a subordinate of the head noun. For example, *oil company, coal company* and *manufacturing company* are all ontologically subordinate to *company.* In another type, the ambiguity can be resolved by matching ontological attachments, as in *parent company* where both nouns are attached to SOCIAL. When a noun immediately follows (**subseqnoun**) the ambiguous noun, ontological matching is usually sufficient, as in *company official* and *office worker.* The pairs share a SOCIAL attachment, so the INSTITUTIONAL senses (1) of *office* and *company* are chosen. In *store window* and *office door*, the pairs share the PHYSICAL node, so the PLACE senses (2) of *store* and *office* are chosen. a prepositional phrase (**ppmod**) which modifies it. In the phrase "take a hand in government" the indefinite article reduces the ambiguity of *hand* from sixteen to six senses, and the head of the prepositional phrase modifier selects the power sense (5). In *the office in New York*, the fact that New York is a PLACE selects the PLACE sense (2) of *office*. When the ambiguous noun is inside a prepositional phrase (**nounpp**) which modifies another noun, which preposition is used is irrelevant. Commonsense reasoning concerning the relationship between the modified noun and the ambiguous noun is enough to disambiguate. This was tested on the concordances with 100% success. An example is *a secretary in the office*, where matching the SOCIAL attachments only partially disambiguates from five senses to three, the INSTITUTION (1), PLACE (2) and ELECTORAL (3) senses. The rest of the disambiguation frequently results from commonsense reasoning about the verb, as in *The secretary in the office decided to buy more paper*, *The secretary in the office sits near the door*, and *The secretary in the office of President would be unusual*. When the noun modified by the PP containing the ambiguous noun is a nominalized verb, the selectional restrictions of the underlying verb are used to disambiguate. For example, the verb *establish* selects SOCIAL objects, so that the phrase *establishment of the office* can only have the INSTITUTIONAL (1) or ELECTORAL (3) senses for *office*.

Commonsense reasoning with verbs accounts for a substantial proportion (24%) of the commonsense disambiguations. The reasoning depends upon the relationship between the ambiguous noun and the verb. Disambiguations were evenly distributed across subject, object or oblique argument positions (**verbsubj_cs, verbobj_cs, verbobliq_cs**) for the ambiguous noun. Verb selectional restrictions are very important in determining which sense of a noun is used in the verb's argument positions.

When the ambiguous noun is in subject position, and the verb selects for a certain ontological class in that argument, the verb disambiguates. In subject position, frequently the SENTIENT sense of nouns is chosen corresponding to the agentive role SENTIENTs play in actions. For example, in *The office solved the problem*, because *solve* selects for a SENTIENT in subject position, the INSTITUTIONAL sense (1) of *office* is selected. In contrast, with *The office looks nice,* the verb *look* with no object selects a PHYSICAL OBJECT in subject position, so the PLACE sense (2) of *office* is selected. In object position, selectional restrictions of the main verb disambiguate as well. MOTION verbs select for PLACE in object position, so in the phrases *move the office* and *locate the office* the PLACE sense (2) of *office* is chosen. Verbs select for certain ontological classes in oblique argument position as well. Examples are *send to the office* where *send* selects for PHYS-ICAL in the oblique argument, as opposed to *speak to the office* where speak selects for a SENTIENT in the oblique argument. In the first case the PLACE sense (2) of *office* is selected, and in the second case the INSTITUTION sense (1). Similarly, in *build the ship with his hands*, *build* selects for an INSTRUMENT in oblique argument (sense 4). MOTION verbs select for PLACE in oblique position, so *go across the office* and *arrive at the office* select the PLACE sense (2) of *office*.

Adjectives (**adj**) like verbs, select for certain types of arguments. The phrase "pretty office" selects the PLACE sense (2) for office because *pretty* selects physical objects as arguments. The adjectives *regional* and *local* are ambiguous, and can select either the INSTITUTION sense (1) of *office* selecting a SOCIAL argument, or the PLACE sense (2) which locates physical objects. These choices are reflected in the difference between *The district office is in charge of immigrants* and *The district office has four cubicles*. When the adjective is derived from a verb as in "elective office" and "appointed office," the relevant verb test is used.

7.5. Verb Sense Disambiguation

The disambiguation of verbs can be accomplished using the same local combined algorithm as for nouns. To test the usefulness of the algorithm for verbs, four highly ambiguous verbs were studied---*move, use, support* and *work*. Generic representations and ontological attachments for each were encoded, and these were used to test the disambiguation algorithm against a total of 1789 (1225 transitive, 549 intransitive) instances in the Hansard corpus supplied by Ezra Black. The algorithm succeeded in 99% of the cases. The other 1% (N = 99) ddid not contain full sentences.

As the disambiguation rules for verbs look very similar to those for nouns, this section will only describe and illustrate the types of information used in the rules. Intransitive *work* and transitive *move* will be used as detailed examples. Their senses are summarized in Table 7.1 by synonymous phrases rather than the full formal implicational representation which is actually used in KT. Alongside these are selectional restrictions included in the generic representations of the verbs.

Although there is some overlap, the content of the syntactic rules for verbs differs from the rules for nouns. The syntactic rules for verbs inspect the verb phrase specifier (particularly the auxiliary), adverbs and complement clauses. Commonsense rules for verbs and nouns are very similar, but they apply in opposite directions. They appeal to ontological and generic knowledge. As applied to verbs, the rules use the selectional restrictions of verbs, as shown in Table 7.1, to inspect the ontological attachments of the verb's arguments. For example, the sense of *move* (5) which has to do with proposing motions in legislative bodies requires an object which is PROPOSITIONAL. The ontological attachments of surrounding nouns disambiguate verbs. Sometimes, different senses of a verb all have the same or very similar ontological attachments, as can be observed in the example of *work* in Table 7.1. What differs between senses are the selectional restrictions. The arguments of the verb which are most important in disambiguating are those which occur inside the verb phrase. For transitive verbs, the object of the verb disambiguates in 60% of the cases (n = 737). A number of other elements contribute as well, such as prepositional phrases, adverbs and complements. For intransitive verbs, the most effective disambiguators are adverbs (31%, n = 171) and prepositional phrases (29%, n = 161). Surprisingly, the grammatical subject was not particularly important for either transitive or intransitive verbs (2% and 17% respectively).

Table 7.1. Representation of Two Verbs Summarized		
Verb # Paraphrase of Sense		Selection Restrictions
work	1 to labor	human(subject)
	2 to be employed	human(subject)
	3 to perform its function	social(subject)
	4 to operate effectively	machine(subject)
	5 to influence	human(subject)
	6 to be kneaded	dough(subject)
	7 to move with difficulty	selfmoving(subject)
	8 to change into a specified condition	
move	1 change the position of	selfmoving(subject), physical(object)
	2 set in motion	selfmoving(subject), physical(object)
	3 persuade to do something	sentient(subject), sentient(object)
	4 stir the emotions of	sentient(subject), human(object)
	5 formally propose	sentient(subject), propositional(object)

Frequent Phrases in Verb Disambiguation. Fixed and frequent phrases which fully disambiguate are found in the data. For example, particles with the verb select senses, as in *work on, work against, move ahead.*

Syntactic Tests in Verb Disambiguation. There are fewer syntactic tests for verb senses than there are for nouns. The most clear cut one is the presence of a reflexive object (**reflex**), as in *move himself*, which selects the first sense of transitive *move*. Elements of the specifier of the VP disambiguate, such as aspectuals (**aspectual, modal**). For intransitive *work* the auxiliaries *get to, start, get down to* select the first sense, the modals *can, want, must* select the second sense, and the modals *might, could, would, should* select the fourth sense. Particular adverbs (**adv**) select senses (McDowell, 1987). For intransitive *work* the adverbs *closely, satisfactorily, diligently* select the first sense, *part time, full time* select the second sense, *automatically* selects the third sense, and *effectively, well, successfully* select the fourth sense. The presence of a complement of the verb (**comp**) can disambiguate. With intransitive *work* the presence of a complement clause narrows the ambiguity to senses one or two only, as in *work to expand the economy* (sense one) and *work to support one's family* (sense two). Particular prepositions (**vprep**) select senses. The phrase *work together* can only have the first sense of transitive *work*.

Commonsense in Verb Disambiguation. Commonsense reasoning for verb disambiguation deals most often with selectional restrictions, although generic information is used as well. Most striking are selectional restrictions for objects of the verb. Transitive *move* has five senses, and for each sense, a particular ontological attachment of its object is selected, as indicated in Table 7.1. A SENTIENT or PHYSICAL object reduces the number of senses from five to two, as in *John moved the girl to tears* (sense four) or *John moved his friend to take a stand* (sense three). If *move* has a quantifier as object, sense one is selected, as in *We moved four today*. When transitive *move* has a PROPOSITIONAL object, as in *The congressman moved the previous motion*, sense five is selected. Although this construction may seem less familiar to the reader than one with a complement, as in *The congressman moved that the previous motion be adopted*, the construction with a PROPOSITIONAL direct object accounted for 30% of the occurrences of *move* in the Hansard Corpus of Canadian Parliament proceedings.

Another important selectional restriction concerns oblique arguments. For example, with intransitive *work*, sense two selects for a relational phrase with the prepositions *for, in, at* as in *work for the company*, where the oblique argument is an INSTITUTION. The arguments *to the advantage, to the disadvantage* select sense three. Subject selectional restrictions are less important, but do disambiguate. For example, if the subject of intransitive *work* is a SOCIAL ROLE such as *employee, secretary, mother*, sense two is selected, if ARTIFACT, sense three is selected, and if INSTITUTION, such as *party, system, democracy* sense four is selected. Similarly, a PHYSICAL subject selects the physical sense of *support*, as in *The sandbags support the bank*.

Just as with nouns, verb disambiguation rules are applied to the most deeply embedded sentence first and upwards through the parse. This is how phrases such as *the will to work* and *ready to work* are

disambiguated. At the embedded level in these cases, there is no reduction of ambiguity. At the level of the next higher S, the noun or
adjective disambiguates the embedded verb.

7.6. Interaction of Ambiguous Verb and Noun

How will this algorithm fare with sentences containing more than
one ambiguous element, such as a verb and object which are both
ambiguous? Clearly there will be cases it cannot handle. On the other
hand, it will be able to handle many such cases, as will be illustrated
here. Consider the pair of sentences below:

The sandbags supported the bank.
The investments supported the bank.

Assume that *bank* has two readings, one, "edge of a river" which is a
NATURAL PLACE and two, "financial house" which is an INSTITU-
TION. As we saw above, the verb *support* in the sense which means
"hold up physically" requires a PHYSICAL subject, and the other
senses require SENTIENT subjects, so the verb is disambiguated by
the subject in *The sandbags supported the bank.* In the second case, the
sense of *support* which means "supply funds for" is selected because the
subject is a means of exchange. In order to further disambiguate, the
object rule which inspects generic information in the representation
must be used. It will discover that both the sense of *support* which
means "supply funds for" and the sense of *bank* which means "financial
house" have to do with money, and in this way disambiguate bank.
What about the case where the sentence subject can attach to the
ontology in two places? Consider *John supported the bank.* *John* can
attach either as a HUMAN, in which case he is PHYSICAL and can
be viewed as holding up the bank bodily, or he can attach as a PER-
SON, in which case he is SENTIENT and can be viewed as supporting
the bank financially or furthering the cause of the bank. In the latter
case, after considering all selectional restrictions, the sentence remains
ambiguous. In the former case, the question of choosing between
PHYSICAL and SENTIENT John must be resolved by the wider con-

text of preceding or following sentences or by knowing that a person is not strong enough to physically hold up a bank.

In summary, the disambiguation of nouns and verbs uses information from several sources in the KT system:

1. A lexicon of fixed phrases
2. A set of word-specific rules for each word which relate syntactic structure to word senses
3. The output of the parse of a sentence
4. The ontology
5. Generic information about nouns and verbs, such as selectional restrictions

7.7. Feasibility of the Method

Superficially this method looks too difficult to implement computationally, because of the word-particular rules. However, the commonsense rules are universal, and use CK in representations required for all aspects of text understanding. The feasibility of the word-sense disambiguation algorithm thus rests only on whether fixed phrases and word-particular syntactic rules can be extracted automatically or semi-automatically. One proposal[11] involves employing a relatively large corpus, with several instances of each sense of each ambiguous word. A corpus containing samples from a variety of genres and domains would help ensure a wide spread of senses. Word sense integers would be inserted manually next to each ambiguous word. Once the sense numbers are indicated, a computer program could extract fixed and frequent phrases by statistical methods. Another program could discover syntactic tests for less frequent phrases by parsing the corpus and noticing recurrent syntactic environments. The remaining cases would not be mentioned in word-specific rules, and would require commonsense reasoning.

---

11 I am indebted to Susan Mordechay for this suggestion.

7.8. Syntactic and Lexical Ambiguity

The KT system rules for attaching post-verbal prepositional phrase modifiers to the sentence, the verb phrase or the object noun phrase are described in Chapter 6 (Dahlgren and McDowell, 1986b). These rules apply before the disambiguation rules. The algorithm uses syntactic, ontological and generic information. Consider the sentence *Fred spoke of that in his office today*. No global prepositional phrase attachment rules apply, and so the *in*-rule applies. It checks whether the object of the preposition is a PLACE. The rule scans all the senses of *office* to see whether any is a PLACE ontologically. For *office* there is such a sense, and so the rule disambiguates *office* and selects the PLACE sense (2). It also attaches the prepositional phrase to the sentence. Thus the disambiguation rules never apply to this instance of *office*. It comes into those rules with the sense already selected.

7.9. Intersentential Reasoning

Obviously not all disambiguation can take place within a single sentence. *John argues with his hands* is ambiguous between a reading in which hands are John's body parts, and hands are workers who work for John. A following sentence will usually disambiguate as in the following texts:

Jones argues with his hands. He gestures constantly.
Jones argues with his hands. He listens to their complaints.

Three other senses of *hand* are the promise sense (7), the applause sense (10) and the assistance sense, as illustrated in the following sentences:

She gave him her hand in marriage.
The audience gave him a hand.
She gave him her hand to help him into the boat.

The disambiguation algorithm can use other elements of the above sentences to disambiguate, specifically the PP *in marriage*, the subject noun *audience* and the embedded sentence "to help him." There are cases, however, when the indefinite article is used and other elements do not help, leaving all three senses as possibilities.

She gave him a hand.
   She promised to repay the loan promptly.
She gave him a hand.
   His singing was wonderful.
She gave him a hand.
   He was drowning.

Here we need to look at other sentences to disambiguate. For example, in the first one, the promise sense has a typical function of promising in the generic information. The occurrence of *promise* in the second sentence could be used to reduce the senselist from three to one. In the next case, generic information associated with the applause sense indicates that it is typically located at performances, and the generic information for singing says that it typically takes place at performances, and thus the noun *hand* can be disambiguated. In order to implement intrasentential disambiguations, the fact that a word had been ambiguous, and not that a sense had been assigned, must be recorded in the system and new sentences must be used to re-evaluate the assignments. A similar problem affects PP-attachment and coherence relation assignment. One factor which alleviates the computational complexity of re-evaluating assignments which are preferences, is that the effect of other sentences does not extend beyond the discourse segment (See Chapter 8).

7.10. Disambiguation Rules

The algorithm is independent of the programming language used. Its implementation in VM/PROLOG (International Business Machines, 1985) is described here in terms of a subset of the rule types outlined in "7.4. Noun Disambiguation" on page 144 and "7.5. Verb Sense Disambiguation" on page 151. The top-level disambiguation rule gets the senselist (Senselistin) for the ambiguous word (Word) and finds the index of the appropriate sense (Senselistout) by invoking fixed-phrases, syntactic and commonsense tests. A parse in the form of a labelled bracketing of the entire sentence in which the ambiguous noun occurs (Parse) is passed to this rule.[12]

disambig(Word,String,Parse,Index) ←
    senselist(Word,Senselistin)
    & fixedphrase(Word,String,Senselistin,Senselist1).
    & get_struc(Word,Parse,Struc,Senselist1)
    & syntactic_test(Word,Struc,Senselist1,Senselistout)
    & commonsense(Word,Struc,Senselistout,Index).

The fixed phrases logic attempts to match the ambiguous word and surrounding words to a list of disambiguated or partially disambiguated fixed phrases involving the ambiguous word. For example, the following ground clause says that *Printing Office* selects sense 5 of *office*.

fixedphrase(office,{Printing,Office},{1,2,3,4,5},5).

Since the disambiguation algorithm is local, only one S-node is considered at a time (no higher or lower S-nodes). This makes possible a simplification of the parse. The procedure **get_struc** takes Parse and simplifies it into a fixed-position list of the verb and its arguments in the sentence, followed by a fixed-position sublist. The sublist differs for ambiguous nouns and verbs. For ambiguous nouns, the sublist has elements of the NP in which the ambiguous noun occurs, such as determiner, quantifier, and adjective, that is, the specifier of the NP. For verbs the sublist has the VP specifier and structures such as reflexive and complement. The elements returned by **get_struc** in the variable

---

12 The algorithm is shown as VM/PROLOG code. For readers unfamiliar with PROLOG, the rule has inputs Word, String, and Parse. Word is used to look up the Senselist for the word, which is passed first to the fixed phrase clause. It outputs a possibly reduced Senselist1. Then the get_struc clause makes elements of the parse readily available to the syntactic tests in Struc. Then Senselist1 is passed to the syntactic tests clause, which returns a possibly reduced Senselist2. It is passed to the commonsense rules which output the final list, Senselistout.

Struc are employed by syntactic and CK tests. Both their presence and their content are significant information in the algorithm. In what follows, Struc is not given in detail. Irrelevant positions are indicated by (...).

There is a fixed set of types of syntactic tests. The logic of the syntactic test algorithm assumes that the rules for any given ambiguous word draw upon this fixed set of types. Each type of rule is attempted for each ambiguous word. If the rule type is irrelevant to that word, it trivially succeeds. If the senselist has already been reduced to one member (a solution), the test trivially succeeds. Otherwise, the test is relevant, and the rule type is attempted. Because PROLOG can represent rules as data, the content of the rule can differ for each noun. The test is carried out by interpreting PROLOG clauses listed in the lexical entry for the word, and applying them in the same way regardless of the word. This makes the programming very simple. The order of the types is fixed, and for any given word a variable number of the types of rules is actually applied.

The top-level syntactic test rules for nouns follow. Notice that the names of the predicates are the same as those listed next to the rule type descriptions in "7.4. Noun Disambiguation" on page 144 The first rule is for the case where fixed phrases fully disambiguate, and the disambiguated senselist is simply passed through the rule.

```
syntactic_test(Noun,Struc,Senselistin,Senselistin) ←
        atomic(Senselistin).
syntactic_test(Noun,Struc,Senselistin,Senselistout) ←
        nodet(Noun,Struc,Senselistin,Senselist1)
    & nodefsing(Noun,Struc,Senselist1,Senselist2)
    & nodefplu(Noun,Struc,Senselist2,Senselist3)
    & defart(Noun,Struc,Senselist3,Senselist4)
    & indefart(Noun,Struc,Senselist4,Senselist5)
    & perspron(Noun,Struc,Senselist5,Senselist6)
    & quant(Noun,Struc,Senselist6,Senselist7)  .
    & propappos(Noun,Struc,Senselist7,Senselist8)
    & prep(Noun,Struc,Senselist8,Senselist9)
    & verbsubj(Noun,Struc,Senselist9,Senselist10)
```

& verbobj(Noun,Struc,Senselist10,Senselist11)
& verbobliq(Noun,Struc,Senselist11,Senselist12)
& bepp(Noun,Struc,Senselist12,Senselist13)
& comp(Noun,Struc,Senselist13,Senselistout).

A subset of the word-particular syntactic rules for *office* appears below. The **nodet** rule succeeds if there is no determiner and returns sense 3, the electoral sense. **defart** succeeds if there is a definite article and reduces the senselist to three senses. **perspron** reduces it to two. The **prep** rules look for specific prepositions, and the *verb* rules for specific verbs and argument positions. Notice that some rules have bodies, and others are ground clauses.

nodet(office,Struc,Senselist,3) ← nodet(Struc).
defart(office,Struc,Senselist3,{1,2,3}) ← defart(office,Struc).
indefart(office,Struc,Senselist3,{1,2,3}) ← indefart(office,Struc).
perspron(office,Struc,Senselist,{1,2}) ← perspron(office,Struc).
prep(office,{...at...},Senselist,2).
prep(office,{...against...},Senselist,1).
prep(office,{...through...},Senselist,{1,2}).
prep(office,{...to...},Senselist,{1,2}).
verbobj(office ,{...occupy...},Senselist,{2,3}).
verbobliq(office ,{...elect...},Senselist,3).
verbobliq(office ,{...appoint...},Senselist,3).

The top-level syntactic test rules for verbs are listed below. The names of the predicates are the same as those used in the descriptions in "7.5. Verb Sense Disambiguation" on page 151.

syntactic_test(Verb,Struc,Senselistin,Senselistin) ←
        atomic(Senselistin).
syntactic_test(Verb,Struc,Senselistin,Senselistout) ←
        reflex(Verb,Struc,Senselistin,Senselist1)
    & aspectual(Verb,Struc,Senselist1,Senselist2)
    & modal(Verb,Struc,Senselist2,Senselist3)
    & adv(Verb,Struc,Senselist3,Senselist4)
    & comp(Verb,Struc,Senselist4,Senselist5)
    & vprep(Verb,Struc,Senselist5,Senselistout).

Some of the word-specific rules for intransitive *work* are given below. As with nouns, some word-specific verb rules are ground clauses, and others have bodies. The **aspectual** rule succeeds if the auxiliary is *get* or *start* In either case the senselist is returned as 1. The **modal** rule succeeds if there is a modal, and it is *can* or *might*. The cases select different senses. The other rules work similarly. Irrelevant elements of Struc are elided with (...)

```
aspectual(work,{...get...},Senselist,1).
aspectual(work,{...start...},Senselist,1).
modal(work,{...can...},Senselist,2).
modal(work,{..might...},Senselist,4).
adv(work,{...diligently...},"Senselist,1).
adv(work,{...part,time...},Senselist,2).
adv(work,{...automatically...},Senselist,3).
prep(work,{..to...},Senselist,{1,2}).
```

The commonsense rules operate similarly to the syntactic rules in that a fixed set of types of rules is attempted for every ambiguous noun, if the senselist has not yet been reduced to one member when the commonsense test is invoked. Below is the top-level commonsense rule, which applies to both nouns and verbs. Those tests irrelevant to a particular word trivially succeed.

```
commonsense(Word,Struc,Senselistout,Senselistout) ←
    atomic(Senselistout).
commonsense(Word,Struc,Senselistin,Senselistout) ←
    conj(Word,Struc,Senselistin,Senselist1)
    & prevnoun(Word,Struc,Senselist2,Senselist3)
    & subseqnoun(Word,Struc,Senselist3,Senselist4)
    & ppmod(Word,Struc,Senselist4,Senselist5)
    & nounpp(Word,Struc,Senselist5,Senselist6)
    & verbsubj_cs(Word,Struc,Senselist6,Senselist7)
    & verbobj_cs(Word,Struc,Senselist7,Senselist8)
    & verbobliq(Word,Struc,Senselist8,Senselist9)
    & subj_cs(Word,Struc,Senselist9,Senselist10)
    & obj_cs(Word,Struc,Senselist10,Senselistout).
```

The commonsense rules are more general than are the syntactic rules, in that rather than accessing lexical rules specific to each word, they compare ontological and generic information in ways which apply to any noun or verb. For example, in the conjunction rule **conj_cs** the ontological attachment of an ambiguous word (Word) is compared with the ontological attachment of a word it is conjoined with, and if they match for some sense of the ambiguous word, that sense is chosen. This reflects the fact that sentences like *The office and the office door solved the problem*, which would conjoin the INSTITUTION and PLACE senses of *office* are semantically anomalous. Rules which look at generic information, such as the second **ppmod** rule, access elements of the commonsense knowledge representations of typical and inherent features of objects named by nouns and actions named by verbs. **adjselect** and **verbselect** extract selectional restrictions for adjectives and verbs in the form of nodes in the ontology.

```
conj_cs(Word,{...Word...Conjunct...},S1,S2) ←
        ontattach(Conjunct,Node)
        & ontattach(Word,Node,S1,S2).
prevnoun(Word,{...Prevnoun...Word...},S1,S2) ←
        isa(Prevnoun,Word).
prevnoun(Word,{...Prevnoun...Word...},S1,S2) ←
        ontattach(Prevnoun,Node)
        & ontattach(Word,Node,S1,S2).
subseqnoun(Word,{...Word...Subseqnoun...},S1,S2) ←
        ontattach(Subseqnoun,Node)
        & ontattach(Word,Node,S1,S2).
adj(Word,{...Adj,Word...},S1,S2) ←
        adjselect(Adj,Node)
        & ontattach(Word,Node,S1,S2).
ppmod(Word,{...Word...Prep,Noun...},S1,S2) ←
        ontattach(Noun,Node)
        & ontattach(Word,Node,S1,S2).
ppmod(Word,{...Word...Prep,Noun...},S1,S2) ←
        generic_relation(Noun,Word).
nounpp(Word,{...Prep,Noun...Word...},S1,S2) ←
        ontattach(Noun,Node)
        & ontattach(Word,Node,S1,S2).
```

nounpp(Word,{...Prep,Noun...Word...},S1,S2) ←
     generic_relation(Noun,Word).
verbsubj_cs(Word,{...Word,Verb...},S1,S2) ←
     verbselect(Verb,subj,Node)
     & ontattach(Word,Node,S1,S2).
verbobj_cs(Word,{...Verb,Word...},S1,S2) ←
     verbselect(Verb,obj,Node)
     & ontattach(Word,Node,S1,S2).
verbobliq_cs(Word,{...Verb...Word...},S1,S2) ←
     verbselect(Verb,obliq,Node)
     & ontattach(Word,Node,S1,S2).

7.11. Efficiency and Timing

The efficiency of the algorithm depends upon a number of factors. Fixed phrases account for 70% of lexical ambiguities, and finding them is a simple matter of a table lookup. If these fail, then for each term the 14 syntactic rules, and the 10 commonsense rules are tried in turn until they succeed. A maximum of 22 rules is applied for any ambiguous word. Rules try to unify with a word-specific rule, but not all words have all rule types. For example, *office* has only eleven word-specific syntactic rules.

The fixed phrases portion of the algorithm is linear because it matches the input string to a database of fixed phrases. The length of time it takes is $O(n)$ where n is the number of fixed phrases. The syntactic tests are also linear. Syntactic complexity of the sentence is simplified by applying to only one S-node at a time, and by converting the parse into a fixed-position list in **get_struc**. The logic then employs PROLOG unification in applying syntactic tests. PROLOG unification is at best linear (Paterson and Wegman, 1978). The commonsense reasoning has two levels of efficiency. Generically-based tests search a database of generic information which consists of PROLOG ground clauses, which again can be accomplished in linear time relative to the number of entries in the generic database. Ontologically-based tests are non-linear. The KT ontology is an acyclic, directed, connected graph which can be searched in $O(\log n)$ time. Another source of non-linearity would be long-distance dependencies. Since the algorithm applies locally, to only one S-node at a time, the above description of efficiency does not include the case where an embedded sentence contains a trace, and cannot be disambiguated until the NP which belongs in the trace has been located in a higher S. Such long-distance dependencies can result in non-linear processing time.

The relative timing of the elements of the algorithm have been tested in relation to the noun *office*. The algorithm was coded in VM/PROLOG (International Business Machines, 1985) using the output of the parser as input. Ten sample sentences were chosen to test timing, as shown in Table 7.2. For purposes of the test, it is assumed that *office* is the only ambiguous word in the sentences, and that no sentence is syntactically ambiguous. There were 11 fixed phrases in the VM/PROLOG workspace. The first sentence is disambiguated by fixed phrases, the second through fifth by syntactic tests, and the six through tenth by commonsense reasoning. In order to factor out the effect of trying fixed phrases first, then all syntactic tests, then commonsense reasoning, the timing for each aspect of the algorithm for each sentence was measured, as shown in Table 7.2. The program was run on an IBM 3081 with no other users. The algorithm is very fast, and takes an insignificant amount of time in comparison with parsing. As predicted, commonsense reasoning takes the most time. The differences among sentences disambiguated by commonsense reasoning is due to the fact that it is faster to look up generic knowledge than it is to search the ontology (which is a lattice). This test was based upon simple sentences, because the algorithm works to disambiguate each sentence as it is parsed, including embedded sentences.

The timing test shows that speed could be improved by an implementation using parallel processing. Since fixed phrases, syntactic tests and generic commonsense reasoning are linear, all three processes could be started at once. The reduced sense lists from the three disambiguation methods could then be intersected. Parallel processing is not indicated for ontologically-based commonsense reasoning, as in Sentence 10, because, as described above, it is nonlinear. Therefore a version of the algorithm using parallel processing should start up only the generically-based commonsense rules in parallel with the fixed phrases and syntactic tests, and if these do not fully disambiguate, then try ontologically-based commonsense reasoning. Such an implementation would bear no relation to cognitive modelling.

Table 7.2. Timing of Test Sentences in Milliseconds				
Test Sentence	*Fixed Phrases*	*Syntax*	*CK*	*Total Disambiguation*
1. John called the patent office.	2.1	-	-	2.2
2. John walked through his office.	2.5	2.7	-	2.7
3. John ran for office.	2.5	2.5	-	2.7
4. John arranged for it through his office.	2.8	3.0	-	3.0
5. John ran the office.	2.0	2.1	-	2.2
6. The office desk is pretty.	2.4	2.5	3.4	3.4
7. John saw the desk in the office.	2.7	2.8	4.0	4.3
8. John moved his office to Chicago.	2.6	2.9	5.6	6.0
9. John called his office.	2.1	2.3	4.4	4.7
10. The office clerk called John.	2.5	2.4	6.1	6.5

7.12. Problems for the Method

The disambiguation algorithm is a preference strategy which sometimes fails, as in the text

Jones reached the office he had been seeking.
He served with distinction.

The present disambiguation rules will use the verb *reach* to guess the PLACE sense for *office*, which is incorrect. The way to solve this problem would be to keep a trace of the reasoning rules used to disambiguate for possible later revision. The verb *serve* in the second sentence selects the INSTITUTION sense of *office* in subject position, and the electoral sense in object position. This fact could be used to overturn the original guess of the PLACE sense and replace it with the electoral sense.

Certain nouns are ambiguous within the same ontological attachment and the disambiguation occurs situationally. The commonsense reasoning involved may go way beyond lexical level representations. An example is the noun *mat* which has four senses, one for floor mats, under vase mats, exercise mats and matted objects (such as a mat of vines):

mat({1,artifact,{size(2x3),   shape(rectangular),   material(woven hemp)}, {function(protect a floor)}},
{2,artifact,{size(5″   diameter),   shape(circular),   material(lace)}, {function(protect a table)}},
{3,artifact, {size(3′ by 8′), shape(rectangular), material(foam rubber)}, {function(cushion a person)}},
{4,natural, {form(matted)},{}}).

The first three are all artifacts, and all quite similar, except that generic information differs in values. Some disambiguation rules apply, but frequently the senses cannot be distinguished. The only solution would be more sophisticated commonsense reasoning, which would employ naive physics to reason that the agent in a paragraph is exercising, and needs the protection of the mat. Such reasoning is possible, and would connect this work with other work in commonsense reasoning (Hobbs, et al, 1985, Hobbs, et al, 1986).

7.13. Other Approaches

Alternative approaches to word sense disambiguation in general use word meaning representations to disambiguate. Almost all approaches, including ours, employs selectional restrictions on verbs to disambiguate (Wilks, 1975, Hayes, 1978, Hirst, 1987). Hayes (1978) and Hirst (1987) use word associations as well. Hirst has a *marker-passing* mechanism, which associates elements of meaning representations for one concept with many related concepts. For example, the representation of airplane is as follows:

```
[ frame:  airplane
isa:    vehicle
        slots: (owner (airline))
               (type (airplane-type))
  ...]
```

The marker passing mechanism can relate *airplane* to *corporation* via the following associations:

```
(airplane
    (restriction (owner (airplane)) (airline))
 airline
    (isa airline corporation)
 corporation)
```

Consider (95)

(95)   Nadia's plane taxied to the terminal.

In disambiguating the sentence (95) the marker passing mechanism associates *plane* with *airplane* and **terminal** with *airport building*. Since there is a path between *airplane* and *airport-building*, and between *air-plane* and *aircraft-ground-travel*, the appropriate senses of *plane, taxi* and *terminal* are selected. Since the Hirst's semantics is a net with frames superimposed, in effect all concepts ultimately have paths between them, so the reasoner considers only very short paths in the disambiguation. The commonsense rules in our approach have much the same effect as these marker passing rules. The difference between the approaches is that we try fixed and frequent phrases and syntactic environment first, and only then then use commonsense. Another difference is that our semantic representations contain more information than is encoded in Absity, so that we should be able to handle more cases. In addition, our rules are simpler, because we have no net representation. The features to be used for disambiguation are in the generic entry for a word. On the other hand, Absity will correctly disambiguate cases where an association chain is the only source of information which can disambiguate, a situation we cannot handle.

7.14. Conclusion

In summary, the KT system disambiguates word senses by trying fixed and frequent phrases first, then syntactic clues, and only when these fail, commonsense knowledge. The databases for fixed and frequent phrases are relatively easy to generate computationally. Commonsense rules do not vary across vocabulary. The computational problem is building in the commonsense knowledge for every word, but this problem affects the whole approach in KT, which uses one naive semantic lexicon for all the commonsense reasoning. We have suggested a way to generate word-specific syntactic rules with combined hand and computational methods. The KT method for word sense disambiguation is powerful and effective, as indicated by its success with the Hansard Corpus. The next step is to try it on other texts, and in relationship to other aspects of disambiguation and to discourse reasoning.

8. DISCOURSE COHERENCE

The naive semantic representations in the KT system contain enough information to recover much of the discourse structure of a text. The first part of this chapter describes coherence and segmentation phenomena in text understanding, and defends a set of genre-relative coherence relations. The next part places discourse coherence in an overall theory of grammar and relates coherence theory to the formal semantics of discourse as expressed in Discourse Representation Theory (DRT) (Kamp, 1981, Heim, 1982, Asher, 1987). The broad theory in place, we demonstrate that just the syntax and logical form of the sentences in the discourse do not provide sufficient information to assign coherence. In order to recover the discourse structure of the text, the recipient must often appeal to commonsense knowledge (Lockman and Klappholz, 1980, Hobbs, 1985). Given that syntactic and semantic information alone does not suffice to assign discourse coherence, the next section analyzes the contribution of each level of grammar in parallel to this task. Next we illustrate the parallel use of all levels of grammar in recovering the structure of a text taken from the newspaper. Finally, the processing implications of the parallel model of discourse is explored.

8.1. Background

A discourse is unintelligible unless the recipient is able to find some meaningful structure among its sentences. Only by understanding how a new sentence relates to the information introduced by the previous discourse can the new sentence be interpreted. In this way the speaker's intention is recovered (Grosz, 1981). The recipient of a narrative discourse with two goal-oriented past events, as in (96), assumes that the speaker reported just these two events because they were causally related in some way.

(96)   John opened the door. He went out.

(97)   John ate fish. Mary ate beef.

In (96), the recipient infers that John's opening of the door probably had as goal his going out. The report of two goal-oriented past events does not always have this discourse structure. In (97), the speaker may be referring to two events which were parallel parts of some broader meal event. Coherence relations have events, states, propositions and segments of discourse as arguments. In (98) the recipient infers that the event of eating fish caused John's state of feeling full.

(98)   John ate fish. He felt full.

Coherence relations are sometimes directly indicated by the speaker, as in (99), and at other times they must be inferred by the recipient as in (96) and (97).

(99)   John opened the door so that he could go out.

The recipient recovers at least some of the causal structure intended by the speaker whether the speaker explicitly structures the discourse or not.   The recipient has the same interpretation of (100) and (101).

(100)   John was indicted. He broke the law.

(101)   John was indicted because he broke the law.

Coherence Relations. Studies of discourse structure have proposed a variety of coherence relations with each investigator having a different set. There appears to be an open-ended list of these relations--**cause, goal, sequence, elaboration** and so on. Fundamental theoretical questions about coherence relations arise. What is the nature of the relationships? What does it mean for one event to cause another? What are the arguments of the relationships? What is an event? Are events mental constructions or real? How many coherence relations are there? Because of these foundational problems, Grosz and Sidner (1986), in their recent work on discourse structure, emphasize structural properties of discourses, such as which clauses dominate which others, and reject coherence relations as the basis of computational discourse research.

An alternative approach, one which will be adopted here, is to view the theory of coherence relations as in an exploratory phase and to investigate within a clear, but limited, theoretical framework whatever coherence relations have been tentatively established. In this way pioneering research can begin to incorporate coherence relations into linguistic theory, and to account for the coherence and segmentation intuitions which have been reported in a large number of studies (Grosz and Sidner, 1986, Mann and Thompson, 1987, Fox, 1984, Hobbs, 1985, Lockman and Klappholtz, 1983, to name just a few). This is more likely to produce results which contribute to the explanation of the psychology of language, because the coherence relations which have been proposed are clearly based in part upon beliefs about the causal structure of the world.

It is tempting to speculate that these coherence relations are instantiations in discourse comprehension of more general principles of coherence that we apply in attempting to make sense out of the world we find ourselves in, principles that rest ultimately on some notion of cognitive economy. (Hobbs, 1985)

The explanation of coherence facts will lie in natural language metaphysics, that is, in the beliefs built into language concerning the nature of time, events, and the causal relations among events (Bach 1981). The speaker typically structures a discourse in order to convey a certain understanding and belief about the causal relations among the events, facts or opinions the discourse is about. The choice of events to report, the choice of tense, and the choice of order of sentences are to some extent determined by the speaker's intention to convey such relationships. To ignore coherence relations because they raise difficult foundational issues is an unfortunate impoverishment of the theory, because in them we expect to find the main explanatory factor in discourse structure. Furthermore, it is unnecessary to exclude them, because in the development of any science there is a stage at which the theoretical terms reflect hypotheses and only partially cover the known phenomena.

Discourse Segments. Discourse coherence is defined over sets of sentences (segments) as well as over clauses. It is intuitively clear that the recipient segments the discourse. Consider text (102).

(102)   a. John went to the park.
             b. He ate lunch.
             c. The park was at a lovely lake with ducks and row-
             boats.
             d. The weather was balmy.
             e. John dove into the lake and swam across it.

             Later, John told Mary that

             f. it_i had been a nice day_i.
             g. it_j had been a nice $park_j$.
             h. it_k had been a nice $picnic_k$.

Intuitively, the text has three segments, a narrative segment consisting
of sentences (102a), (102b) and (102e), a **description** segment consisting
of sentences (102c) and (102d) which "interrupts" the narrative segment
(Reichman, 1985), and a subsequent narrative segment, consisting of
(102f), (102g), or (102h). As pointed out by Asher (1988), the notion
of discourse segment is needed to explain anaphoric reference to chunks
of text, as with it_k, which has as antecedent the collection of events[13]
constituting a picnic which are reported in the entire narrative segment.
The truth conditions of (102h) require as antecedent the collection of
all of the events in the sequence (102a), (102b) and (102e). With $picnic_k$
the recipient is forced to segment because *picnic* is a temporal noun
which denotes collections of events. With (102f), *day* is ambiguous.
One of its readings denotes weather conditions, and another the set of
events experienced by a person during a day-long interval. On the
latter reading, it_i has both the **narrative** and **description** segments as
antecedent, that is, all of the previous discourse, as with it_k, while on
the former it has just the **description** segment as antecedent. Such forced
segmentation is not in evidence in the case where the text concludes
with (102g), where it_j has a noun phrase as antecedent. However, even

---

13 When we talk of a pronoun having as antecedent a collection of
   events, it is not the real events which are in the collection, but
   discourse events, a term which will be defined below.

in this case, the recipient will tend to segment the text (Rumelhart, 1977, Thorndyke, 1977).

In addition to truth-conditional justifications for the notion of discourse segment, there are also cognitive processing considerations. Discourse segmentation cuts the search space in anaphora resolution, because anaphoric pronouns have antecedents only in certain segments. In terms of statistical frequency, pronouns most often have their antecedents in the same segment. Grosz and Sidner (1986) show the relationship between discourse segmentation and accessibility of antecedents for referring expressions in a rhetoric text and a task-oriented dialogue. In order to test the robustness of that relationship, we analyzed 10,000 words of commentary text (from the *Wall Street Journal*) and found that anaphoric relations tend not to extend beyond the discourse segment. In our corpus, there were 121 pronouns. The antecedents of 76 of these were in the same sentence, and of 42 others in the same segment. In general, except when referring back to highly salient segments of text, to highly salient events, or to important agents, pronouns refer within the discourse segment. Thus discourse segmentation provides some of the explanation for the ability to reason quickly with pronouns.

Another factor justifying the notion of discourse segment is speaker-directed discourse segmentation, as opposed to non-directed segmentation. In (102) the speaker does not directly guide the recipient and make clear the intended discourse structure. But frequently the speaker does directly structure the text, as in (103).

(103)   Because it was a balmy day, John cycled to a park on a lovely lake. He ate lunch, then swam across the lake. In sum, the outing was delightful.

Genre-Relativity of Discourse Structure. Early work on discourse treated the narrative genre. Labov (1972) noticed that narrative is structured around a backbone of narrative clauses which have temporal sequence, and free clauses, which do not. Labov's analyses of narratives revealed that discourse functions such as orientation and evaluation are concentrated in free clauses. Thus the clauses which form the action tend to be in the simple past tense, and orientation and evaluation

clauses in the simple present or the past progressive. Evaluatives tend
to be in the future, the negative, or to contain modals.

Hopper and Thompson (1980) correlate the foreground (main
points) of a discourse with temporally sequenced clauses, as well. They
define *background* and *foreground* as follows:

> *That part of a discourse which does not immediately and crucially
> contribute to the speaker's goal, but which merely assists, amplifies,
> or comments on it, is referred to as BACKGROUND. By contrast,
> the material which supplies the main points of the discourse is known
> as FOREGROUND.*

They identify foregrounded material with material which has temporal
structure. (They also found a correlation between foregroundedness
and *transitivity*, to be discussed in "Transitivity Test." on page 202.)
Later work of both Thompson and Reinhart showed that temporally
ordered clauses and those which carry the "important" material in a
narrative are not always the same clauses. (Thompson, 1984, Reinhart,
1982).

Reichman (1985) elucidates the question of genre-relativity. Genre
is the structure dictated by content and purpose. Narrative, argument,
news article, conversation, and scientific report each have their own
content structure, that is, their own set of relations between clauses.

> *"Setting," for instance, is part of a "narrative genre," but not part
> of an argument structure; "support" is part of an "argument genre"
> but not of a narrative. Where one's goal is to account for differences
> in thematic developments, the idea that different genres have differ-
> ent structures allows us to set up specific predictions of what is to
> come next in a given discourse form.*

But she points out that there is also an abstract underlying structure
to discourse, consisting of trees, lists and tables, which is genre-
independent.

What is foregrounded in a discourse depends upon the genre. While in narrative, the structure tends to revolve around past events in a real or fictional world, in other genres the structure revolves around other types of events. Grosz and Sidner (1986) describe task-oriented dialogue as structured around the task and rhetorical discourse as structured around arguments. Conversation has been analyzed in terms of conversational moves (Reichman, 1985) and adjacency pairs such as question-answer and invitation-acceptance (Fox, 1984). Cohen (1984) shows that arguments take their structure from the logic of the argument.

The Commentary Genre. This chapter reports an extensive empirical study of text in the *commentary* genre, which is found in newspapers and magazines. Unlike narrative, in which a foregrounded event is one of a sequence of actions which form the backbone of the story, commentary foregrounds a single event (or set of related but not necessarily temporally sequenced events) and is structured around comments by various persons about that event. The foregrounded event is typically a policy statement, product announcement, agreement which have been reached, sentence in court cases or other social event. It may be an announcement of what an institution has decided to do. The verb may be a performative verb (such as *pledge*) and the complement may contain a modal (McDowell, 1987). Thus in commentary, the events around which the discourse is structured are not necessarily claimed to be real world events which have taken place. Despite their unreality, future and hypothetical events can be important in commentary. The announcement of a business decision to do X can have causal efficacy in the world of business, even though the event X has not yet occurred. An announcement of a plan or decision can be a significant event in itself. For example, after reading the report that the Federal Reserve has decided to raise interest rates, home buyers and investors behave differently. While in commentary hypothetical and future events can be foregrounded, in narrative the foreground events tend already to have taken place (in reality or fiction). Similarly, in task-oriented dialogue, the foregrounded events and salient objects are those which are physically present and presently occurring (Grosz and Sidner, 1986). The implication is that each genre requires a different definition of foregrounded event.

Although what is foregrounded in discourse is genre-relative, and
the types of coherence relations which structure a text are genre-relative,
there are also formal discourse properties, such as hierarchy structure,
and methods for conveying these properties which can be found in all
genres. These general discourse structure phenomena are described in
Hobbs (1985), Reichman (1985), Grosz and Sidner (1986), and Mann
and Thompson (1987).

Compendium of Discourse Relations. In this section we discuss a
number of the coherence relations which have been suggested in the
extensive literature on discourse (Cohen, 1984, Fox, 1984, Grosz and
Sidner, 1986, Hirst, 1981, Hobbs, 1978, Hobbs, 1985, Lockman and
Klappholz, 1983, Litman and Allen, 1984, Mann and Thompson, 1984,
Mann and Thompson, 1987, Polanyi, 1985, Polanyi and Scha, 1984,
Reichman, 1985, Thompson and Matthiesen, 1987). The literature was
reviewed and the proposed definitions of coherence relations examined
from the two points of view: their logical basis and their usefulness in
the analysis of commentary text. 6,000 words of commentary text
taken from six articles in the *Wall Street Journal* were analyzed clause
by clause for coherence relations.[14] The set of relations which accounted
for intuitions concerning the coherence of the sample text was selected.
Actually a relation such as **cause** can be broken down into a number
of related types of causes (Mann and Thompson, 1987). In this research
the most general relations are considered in the interest of focusing on
how to extract the relations, but the ultimate complete theory would
have to take into account such complexities. Also, Mann and Thompson
point out that coherence involves the intended effect on the recipient
in the discourse, another factor we ignored. As the set of coherence
relations differs from author to author both in terminology and definition, our choice from among them is listed here, along with the names
of the authors whose definition and terminology roughly agree with
the stated one. All are found under some formulation in the literature.

---

14 All were taken from *Wall Street Journal* of February 23, 1987, here-
after cited as WSJ.

Sequence   The event or state in one clause follows the other in time, but is not otherwise causally related (Mann and Thompson, 1987).

(104)   Levine was indicted and convicted.

Reported Event   The **sequence** relation is relevant to narrative, which is structured around a temporal sequence of events, and not to commentary, which is structured around a single event, or set of related events, which may not be temporally sequenced. A **reported** event is one of the events around which a commentary is structured, and upon which comments are made. These can either be real or hypothetical events. They frequently consist of attitudes (mental states) such as *expect, plan* and mental achievements such as *say, decide, announce* which have as arguments hypothetical events. This relation is somewhat similar to Fox's (1984) **issue** relation.

(105)   The judge has decided to jail Levine.

Enablement   The event or state in one clause enables the other if the former does not cause, but makes possible the latter. It provides a situation in which the latter can take place. The first event in (106) enables the second (Hobbs, 1985, Mann and Thompson, 1987).

(106)   John got off the subway and walked up the street. (Hobbs, 1978)

Cause   The event or state in one clause causes the other if the latter occurs as a result of the former, as in (107) and (108). Note that the same relation would hold if the two clauses had reverse order in the discourse (Hirst, 1981, Mann and Thompson, 1987).

(107)   Levine engaged in insider trading.

(108)   He was indicted.

Goal   The event or state in one clause is the goal of the event
                 or state in another clause if the former was done in
                 order to achieve the latter. **goal** is like **cause**, except
                 that it involves agency.

(109)   Levine invested heavily.

(110)   He made a huge profit.

Parallel   The event or state in one clause parallels that in another
                 clause if the two involve the same or similar actions or
                 states, or the same or similar participants (Hirst, 1981).
                 Other definitions of this relation are too narrow, as in
                 Hobbs (1985). In (111) the actions are the same, and
                 the participants differ. The events in (112) are parallel
                 but this time the participant is the same and the actions
                 are similar (they are attached closely in the ontology).
                 (113) exhibits no such parallelism.

(111)   Levine and Boesky paid for their crimes.

(112)   The judge examined and investigated the ev-
         idence in the case.

(113)   The judge investigated the case and wrote a
         report.

Contrast   The event or state in one clause contrasts with the
                 event or state in another clause if the two involve con-
                 trasting actions or states, or contrasting participants
                 (Fox, 1984, Hirst, 1981, Hobbs, 1985). Contrast here
                 is loosely defined to include both pairs of events which
                 are negations of each other, as in (114), and pairs of
                 events in which some parallel elements are seen as mu-

tually exclusive in some way, as in the verbs of (115).

(114)   Analysts supported the light sentence, and Giuliani opposed it.

(115)   Argentina's economy prospered while Chile's faltered.

Evidence   One clause can provide evidence for another in the sense that the truth of the first is supported by the second. (Fox, 1984, Mann and Thompson, 1987).

(116)   The lawyer must have made a statement.

(117) - He took a speech into the courtroom with him.

Generalization   A clause functions as a **generalization** in a discourse if subsequent clauses or previous clauses exemplify or elaborate upon it (Hobbs, 1985). Thus a discourse summary is a generalization: so is as an introductory clause which is elaborated by subsequent discourse. Some view this relation as holding only for narrative clauses, but it also holds among evaluative clauses, as below. The clauses in (119) are generalized by (118).

(118)   The scandal has hurt the economy.

(119)   Stock prices are down and confidence has been undermined.

Elaboration   One clause gives details about or describes a part of a larger event reported in another clause. The clauses in (119) are elaborations of (118) (Fox, 1984, Hirst, 1981, Hobbs, 1985, Mann and Thompson, 1987).

Restatement   One clause reports the same event or state as another (Mann and Thompson, 1987). The sentence in (120) describes a portrayal which is quoted in (121).

> (120)   Levine's lawyer tried to portray his client as ruined by the scandal.

> (121)   He said, "Mr. Levine is suffering a form of banishment."

Qualification   A qualification denies one of the implications of the event or state expressed by another clause. The main clause in (122) qualifies the *though*-clause.

> (122)   Though Levine pleaded for sympathy, the judge was unmoved.

Evaluation   An **evaluation** is a clause which expresses a moral or value judgment about an event or state expressed by another clause (Hobbs, 1985, Mann and Thompson, 1987). Examples are in (118) and (119).

Description   Entities or actions introduced into a discourse may be identified or explained by the speaker. Sometimes this takes the form of a definition. The relative clause in (123) identifies the entity Levine.

> (123)   Mr. Levine, who was an investment banker until his arrest, was sentenced Friday.

Situation   Three **situation** relations describe the activities, place and time for events or states expressed in other clauses.

Situation - Activity   Activities can be part of the situation when an event occurs, as in the main clause of (124) which describes the activities of Levine during the event reported in the *as*-clause.

> (124)   As he was sentenced, Mr. Levine showed no emotion.

Situation - Time

One clause can identify the time when an event or state described in another clause occurs, as in the *when*-clause of (125).

(125)   When Levine had finished speaking, the judge turned to his lawyer.

Situation - Place

One clause can identify the place where an event or state described in another clause occurs, as in (126)

(126)   Levine engaged in insider trading while he was working on Wall Street.

Import

An **import** clause expresses the significance of another clause, in the opinion of the author. In commentaries, **import** clauses explain why the commentary was published. (128) expresses the import of (127).

(127)   The judge gave Levine a light sentence.

(128)   This was meant to reward cooperation with the government investigation.

Unbiased Comment

Similar to **import** is **unbiased comment**, which expresses an opinion concerning an event or state in the discourse, by a disinterested party who is not the author of the article. The clauses in (129) express unbiased opinion of (127).

(129)   Economic analysts doubt that insider trading will be stopped soon.

Biased Comment

A **biased comment** is defined as attributed to a participant in an event in the discourse, especially a conflict. The clauses in (130) express biased opinion of (127).

(130)   Giuliani complained that the sentence was too light.

justifications (Mann and Thompson, 1987) are **biased comments** which are **import** clauses as in (131).

(131)   The judge said that the light sentence will reward cooperation with the government investigation.

8.2. Modularity and Discourse

Given the existence of genre-relative coherence relations, which relate not only entities and discourse events, but also segments, the question is how to fit these relations into linguistic theory. This question can be divided into several subparts. Is the theory to account for the speaker's intended structure for the discourse or the recipient's recovery of the structure? What entities are the arguments of coherence relations? Is coherence a structural property which can be derived just from the several levels of sentence structure? Is discourse structure a cognitive representation less tied to the form of words in the discourse than other levels of representation? If so, how does the form of words affect the discourse structure?

Modelling the Recipient. Consider now the question of whether the goal should be to represent the speaker's intended structure or the recipient's recovery of that structure. In syntax the tradition has been to model the ideal speaker/hearer's knowledge of grammar. Since questions of processing are set aside, the speaker's grammar and the hearer's grammar are the same. In formal semantics, syntactic deep structure is mapped to intensional logic, based directly upon the results of semantic rule application. Here again, no distinction need be drawn between the representations produced by the speaker and hearer. But in the case of discourse structure, except in cases where the speaker directly controls the structure with cue phrases, the structure recovered by the recipient is partially based upon the recipient's inferences concerning the relationships among the events in the discourse. In (132) the recipient infers a **goal** relationship between the two events, even though the speaker does not directly state it. Thus for a given discourse, there are two structures, the one intended by the speaker, and the one actually inferred by the recipient, which may be equivalent.

(132)   John invested heavily. He made a huge profit.

Further, in a case where the context differs for the recipient because of background knowledge, the structure of the discourse can differ from the one intended by the speaker (Barwise and Perry, 1983). Suppose the recipient B knows that John wanted to take losses on his investments, and speaker A doesn't know it. When B hears A say (132), the interpretation B constructs of the discourse will differ from that which A intended, in that A might have intended a **goal** relation between the two events of investing and making a huge profit, while B will know that the outcome contradicted John's goals. Clearly for computational text understanding, research should be directed towards the recipient's interpretation, as that is the one to be constructed by the computer.

Discourse Events. Consider next what sorts of entities are coherence related. There are three possible positions. One would place coherence relations as relations between pieces of discourse. This is the position of Mann and Thompson (1987). The problem is that it doesn't account for the relationships between discourse and states of affairs, included the relations among events. The opposite extreme would be a Russellian view in which coherence relations operate over real events and the real relations between them. The problem with this approach is that it fails to account for the speaker's view of events. Part of the task of a discourse theory is to account for the semantic effects of the speaker's choice of certain events to report, and certain relations between them (either stated or implied). A third position is that coherence relations operate over discourse events, which are the events mentioned in the discourse, and which have a truth-conditional mapping to a model. There is a mapping from discourse events to real events, and therefore the possibility of ultimately explaining discourse coherence in terms of a theory of causality (as it affects human discourse and reasoning). Asher (1988) argues persuasively that the representations of events, or *discourse events*, introduced during the semantic interpretation of sentences, are the entities over which coherence relations are predicated. The notion of discourse event is defined within Discourse Representation Theory (DRT). DRT accounts for the fact that the search for antecedents of pronouns begins with the entities and events previously introduced into a discourse. The interpretation of a pronoun or definite description employs a saliency stack of objects and events which have already been mentioned in the discourse. DRT proposes to account for truth in a model at a separate level from the semantic representation of the discourse, which is a discourse representation structure (DRS). A DRS has reference markers for the entities and events introduced in the interpretation of the discourse. These have privileged status as targets of anaphora resolution. DRT, then, separates real entities and events from discourse entities and events. In addition, as a result of the embedding of discourse representations into a model, the theory accounts for reference of both the pronoun and its antecedent to entities and events in the world. The theory handles both the mediation of coreference via real objects (Sidner, 1983), and previous mention in anaphoric uses of pronouns.

Bauerle (1987) and Asher (1988) extend DRT to handle event anaphora and propose that discourse structure should be defined over discourse events. Asher (1988) argues that different types of objects in natural language metaphysics, such as events, states, facts and propositions are reflected in the conceptual representation of reality. He proposes that these types of objects have a range of causal efficacy, and that there is a spectrum of world-immanence from highly abstract type objects (mental states) to very real type objects such as events and states. This spectrum is reflected in a range of reference markers from highly abstract, such as mental state (propositional) reference markers, to world-immanent reference markers such as events and states which are located in space-time and have causal efficacy in the actual (or fictional) world. Facts are in between. All of these are entities in the discourse representation. Coherence relations tend to involve world-immanent reference markers, that is, event or state reference markers. Coherence relates these entities of naive metaphysics, which map systematically to real events and real states, not pieces of text. This property of DRT makes it an attractive theoretical framework for a realist theory of coherence.

Another factor is that the form of DRT proposed by Asher (1988) is many-sorted. There are individuals, events, states, mental states, discourses, and so on, in the theory. This makes it possible to state relations between events, such as goal(e_1,e_2) as first-order expressions. There is no need for a higher-order logic to state coherence relations. They are predicates like any others in the theory.

A DRS $< U_k, Con_k >$ consists of a set of reference markers U_k (the universe of the discourse) which stand for the entities mentioned in the discourse, and a set of conditions Con_k, which are the properties ascribed to the entities. The types of reference markers are: individual ($x, y, z...$), event(e_1, e_2,...), mental state(p_1, p_2,...), DRS(K_1, K_2,...), and delineated DRS (K_1, K_2,...). The DRT notation is illustrated in (134), which represents the text in (133). The discourse entities x, which stands for the woman, and e_1, which stands for the event of skiing, are available for anaphora resolution to the pronouns in the second sentence. The reference markers y (for *she*) and e_3 (for *it*) are equated with x and e_1 in the course of DRS construction. When entities are introduced in other contexts, such opaque contexts and inside the scope of certain quantifiers, they are not accessible for anaphora resolution.

Although coherence relations must be assigned to event and state reference markers introduced into the DRS by the clauses of the text, the theory cannot rely upon these alone. Coherence relations must also be assigned relating stated to implicit events. In building a cognitive picture of the meaning of the text, the recipient often included events implied by but not stated in the text. The phenomenon of bridging is well-known (Clark, 1975). In the following text, the definite description *the courtroom* forces the recipient to form the bridging implication that the Levines entered the courtroom. The existence of this implied event is confirmed in subsequent text which reports Levine making a statement to the court. Although events and entities mentioned in the discourse should be the first ones considered in coherence, some discourses cannot be made intelligible without hypothesizing events which are not directly mentioned, as in bridging.

Coherence as Compositional Semantics? If coherence relations have discourse events and implied events as arguments, then coherence would

appear to be part of the theory of formal semantics. First we will
outline what such a theory would look like, and then argue against it
and in favor of a separate cognitive theory of coherence.

(133)   The woman skied. She said it was fun.

(134)

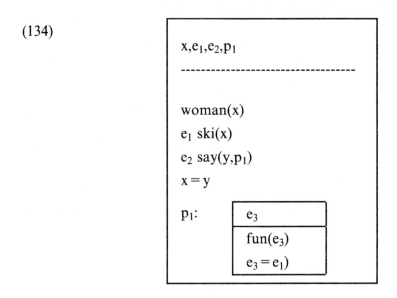

(135)   When Mr. Levine arrived with his wife in a rented limou-
         sine, the crush of onlookers was dispersed by police, so the
         Levines could emerge. *The courtroom* was packed with a
         crowd...(WSJ)

A theory of coherence must account for the fact that recipients extract
the same information from texts (136) and (137).

(136)   John invested heavily. He made a huge profit...

(137)   John invested heavily in order to make a huge profit.

If coherence is part of compositional semantics, and we adopt DRT as
the compositional semantics, the relation between the investing event
(e_1) and the making profit event (e_2) can be represented as an implication
realized in a predicate goal(e_1,e_2) added to the DRS as in (138).

(138)

$$
\begin{array}{|l|}
\hline
x,y,e_1,e_2 \\
\text{-----------------------------} \\
John(x) \\
e_1 \; invest(x) \\
heavily(e_1) \\
profit(y) \\
huge(y) \\
e_2 \; make(x,y) \\
goal(e_1,e_2) \\
\hline
\end{array}
$$

In DRT, such an analysis would imply that $goal(e_1,e_2)$ is true if there is a proper embedding of (138) such that there are real events e_1 and e_2 and the goal of e_1 was e_2. The central difficulty with attempting to account for coherence relations in compositional semantics is not built up directly from structure of the sentences. In contrast, compositional semantic interpretation can be built up from elements in the sentences. Compositional semantics inspects syntactic structure and interprets the semantics of articles, quantifiers, tense markers, pronouns and so forth. Although naive semantics is required to disambiguate the set of interpretations produced, the process of compositional semantic interpretation is relatively algorithmic. Coherence relation assignment, on the other hand, takes into account knowledge which frequently is not directly expressed in the sentences, but rather is associated with the objects and relations mentioned. Speaker and recipient must have enough common knowledge and agreement concerning the causal connections of real-world events, so that it is possible for the recipient to recover the speaker's intention. For example, in (136) the recipient assigns a relation $goal(e_1,e_2)$ based not only upon the compositional semantics of the text, but also upon knowledge that usually when people invest, their goal is profit. Graesser and Clark's (1985b) studies of story comprehension amply demonstrate the use of world knowledge in generating such inferences.

Most of the inferences that individuals generate during comprehension are plausible knowledge-based inferences which are based on mundane knowledge about the world. This mundane knowledge includes (a) the motives, goals, and plans of characters, (b) events and states in causal chains, and (c) static properties of characters, objects and spatial regions. These knowledge-based inferences are needed to establish conceptual connectivity between/among the explicit passage statements.

Furthermore, coherence relation assignment is probabilistic and retractable, especially when the speaker does not directly guide the discourse structure. In cases such as (136), the hearer has to guess at the speaker's intention. Coherence relation assignment is retractable, because subsequent discourse can force the recipient to revise the guess, as when (136) continues as (139). In this case, the initial guess that $goal(e_1,e_2)$ must be revised by the recipient.

(139)   despite his intention to take losses as write-offs.

Although coherence relations are retractable and probabilistic, once grasped by the recipient they have truth-conditional force. In (138), the inference $goal(e_1,e_2)$ is believed by the recipient to have been believed true by the speaker.

Another important difference between coherence relations and the logical semantic properties of discourses, has to do with ambiguity. Compositional semantic representations are the result of the application of construction rules to syntactic structures. These rules result in whole classes of interpretations for each discourse. Coherence relations reflect the recipient's guess as to the single intended structure of the discourse, choosing from among the many logically possible structures of the discourse the most plausible one, given the possible causal structure of the discourse events. The psycholinguistic justification that the recipient chooses a single model is amply supplied in Johnson-Laird (1983). This suggests that coherence belongs in the cognitive module, so that recipient's choice of discourse structure is accounted for in the same theory which explains word sense and syntactic disambiguation. A parallel model accords with the fact that syntactic information fades rapidly, while content representation persists (Sachs, 1967).

In summary, coherence relations are probabilistic and retractable, the information used to build them comes not only from knowledge of syntax and compositional semantics, but from conceptual knowledge, and the reasoning involved selects from among the many possible logical structures of the discourse the single most plausible one. This conceptual knowledge belongs at a different level of grammar, connected with memory and cognition, shown as the module "Naive Inference" in Figure 17 on page 192. In the figure, the module "Compositional Semantics" is the one which translates a single sentence into a truth conditional semantic representation. The module "Compositional Augmentation of the Discourse" adds the semantic representation of a single sentence to the semantic representation of the whole previous discourse, resolving anaphoric pronouns. In the DRT framework, the former builds the DRS for a single sentence, and the latter augments the DRS for the previous discourse with this new DRS.

Coherence as Naive Inference. Coherence belongs in the same module of grammar as lexical commonsense knowledge, because both draw upon vague, possibly inaccurate, and probabilistic knowledge. Lexical knowledge probabilistically assigns objects to the extensions of concepts, and properties to objects assigned to concepts. Similarly, coherence probabilistically assigns causal relations among discourse events and states based upon typical situations (verb generic knowledge), and typical objects. In contrast, compositional semantics reads the translation directly off of the structure of the sentence (and discourse) and certain morphemes more or less algorithmically. It produces sets of possible interpretations, while naive inference selects the most plausible one. Coherence relations and discourse segmentation cannot be read directly off of the syntactic and semantic structure of the sentences in the discourse. Instead the recipient must use commonsense knowledge, memory and conceptual generalization to build the picture. Thus the theory of coherence must take into account the links between cognition in general, and language (Partee, 1982). Nevertheless, once the CDRS is built, it has truth conditions, just as a category assignment shirt(X) has truth conditions.

Discourse Cues. But if coherence relations are to be explained in a Naive Inference module, where is speaker-directed discourse structure

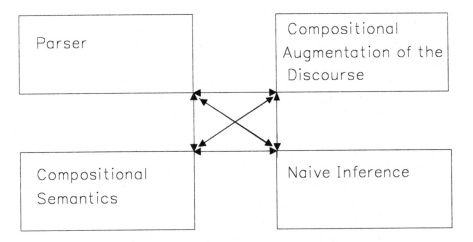

Figure 17: Parallelism in Text Understanding

to be explained? The effect of discourse cues on coherence relations and discourse segmentation has been thoroughly studied (Reichman, 1985, Cohen, 1984, Grosz and Sidner, 1986, Schiffren, 1987). Grosz and Sidner point out that discourse cues do not affect the propositional content of the clauses which contain them. Rather, they are meant to guide the recipient in recovering the discourse structure. Further, discourse structure is not governed by inviolable rules, as syntax and compositional semantic structure are. Discourse structure, whether implicit or guided by cue phrases, is probabilistic and revisable. Moens and Steedman (1987) use the following example to show that *when* introduces not only a temporal adverbial, but a sentence which is related causally to the matrix sentence. Their example also illustrates the varying effects of discourse cues. In (140a) and (140b), the matrix clause is a **situation** clause for the *when*-clause. In (140c), the matrix clause is a **cause** clause relative to the **when**-clause. Thus interpretation of the *when*-clause the depends upon naive semantics.

(140)   When they built the 39th Street bridge,
         a) ...a local architect drew up the plans.
         b) ...they used the best materials.
         c) ...they solved most of their traffic problems.

Not only are the effects of discourse cues variable, but they do not have to be expressed. Their effects on the cognitive picture of the recipient is often achieved by naive implication. Would representation of coherence be produced by the compositional semantic component for (137) and by the naive semantic component for (136)? Comparing intuition for the two sentences, in (137) the recipient is sure that the speaker intends a **goal** relation between the two events, while in (136) the recipient guesses that the relation is intended, but is less sure. If the speaker says (141), the recipient is sure of the intent, but doubtful of the validity.

(141)   John invested in real estate in order to make it rain.

The solution is to account for the effect of discourse cues in the same module which guesses coherence relations, the Naive Inference module. The recipient's assignment could be strengthened in some way (with ordering, or weighting) in cases where a discourse cue is present.

Parallelism. Further, if discourse structure and relations are expressed in a cognitive picture, how do we take into account the contributions of syntactic and compositional semantic information in the building of that structure? A plausible model separates these components of grammar. Each component generates representations empirically justified at its level and each employs special types of rules required at its level. But the model should not require that all aspects of the parse be determined by the parser, and all of the discourse structure be determined by the Naive Inference module. Instead, all modules should have access to all others at any point in the generation of the cognitive representation (CDRS). This assumes that the separate modules operate in parallel, and denies a serial model in which first words are recognized, then syntactic structure is generated, then semantically interpreted and finally pragmatically interpreted. Such a model can account for many of the facts already described in previous chapters and for the complexity of discourse coherence. Here is a sample of the kinds of facts such a model could explain, since any level of representation has access to any other during the construction of the interpretation of a sentence and discourse.

Facts Explained by the Parallel, Modular Model.

- Cue words and phrases, which are the function words of discourse structure, can have the same effects on discourse as conceptually-based inference as in (136) and (137).

- A relative clause is usually descriptive, not a sequenced event, and the discourse coherence assignment algorithm needs access to the parse, not just to the semantic translation of the sentence, in order to know that a clause was relative.

- Events which have been temporally ordered in the semantics are probably sequence related in the cognitive picture.

- In order to assign temporal order as in (96) and to assign temporal overlap in (97), naive semantics is required.

- In order to choose a parse, naive semantics is required, as in PP attachment and quantifier scoping.

- Anaphora resolution, which results in compositional semantic level representations, requires naive semantics.

- Anaphora resolution requires discourse structure, because there is a strong bias against anaphora outside the discourse segment.

In the proposed model, separate theories explain the contributions of syntax, compositional semantics, and naive semantics to the interpretation of text. Although the nature and interaction of these modules in human language comprehension is unknown, there is evidence from psycholinguistic research that a parallel modular model may be correct. Marslen-Wilson and Tyler (1980) test the hypothesis that a serial model is incorrect, and that an alternative "on-line interactive model" could better explain timing phenomena in text processing. They gave subjects semantically meaningful sentences, syntactically correct but semantically unmeaningful sentences, and random order sentences with target words embedded at all the points from the first to the 9th word in the sentences. Examples of their materials follow:

Semantically meaningful: The church was broken into last night
Some thieves stole most of the *lead* off the roof.
Syntactically well-formed: The power was located into great water.
No buns puzzle some in the *lead* off the text.
Random word order : Into was power water the great located. Some
the no puzzle buns in *lead*. text the off.

They found that semantic effects on word recognition are apparent
within the first 200 ms. of hearing a word (within the first two
phonemes), before the whole word, and way before the whole sentence
has been heard. Furthermore, they found that semantic effects began
with the first word of a sentence, and that syntactic effects were weaker
and later. One of their experiment put sentences in meaningful context,
as in the meaningful example above. They find that prior discourse
affected word recognition from the first word of the sentence, so that
clearly the level of word recognition (a relatively low, early level in the
serial model), is affected by the "highest" level of processing from the
very beginning of processing the sentence. Their study also provides
evidence that syntax and semantics/pragmatics are separate knowledge
sources, but that a semantics/world knowledge modular distinction has
no basis (buttressing the NS position). They argue for massive interaction between modules of grammar in a bottom-up model in which
"the input is will always be represented at the maximal level of representation to which its analysis can be taken." If discourse context
disambiguates a word, then word recognition's job is done more quickly.
Otherwise, the word recognition module proposes all of the English
words consistent with the first two phonemes of the word (which av-
erages 29 words), and the syntactic and semantic components immediately begin attempting to build a a possible interpretation of the sentence based upon the proposed "cohort" of words.

Our parallel modular model (like Marslen-Wilson and Tyler's) implies that instead of generating all possible parses, given syntactic information alone, the parses are pruned early based upon naive semantic
information (as described in Chapters 6 and 7). For example, in our
example (142) of post-verbal prepositional phrase attachment ambiguity, the model predicts that naive semantic knowledge of the relation
between locks and keys is used to attach the PP as it is interpreted, and

that only one syntactic structure is generated for the sentence, rather than the three a serial model would generate.

(142)   John bought the lock with the key.

Similarly, the choice of word senses is informed by semantic and syntactic context, so that multiple word senses are not carried along to a later stage of processing. Instead, lexical choice uses all levels of grammar at once and selects early. Similarly, rather than generating all possible semantic interpretations (such as quantifier scope ambiguities), naive inference guesses the most plausible one. And instead of building all the discourse structures given discourse cues and naive semantics alone, discourse structure is guided by syntactic and semantic information as well. It is well known that syntactic and semantic ambiguities can lead to huge numbers of different representations for a single sentence. A distinct advantage of a highly parallel model is that it does not predict the generation of all of the possible interpretations in discourse understanding.

In summary, the proposed model posits a finite (though open-ended), empirically-based set of genre-relative coherence relations. Coherence relations are conceptual relations (CRels) between reported events, states, and other abstract type reference markers, including discourse segments. CRels appear in the representation of the recipient's cognitive picture of the discourse (CDRS) as predications such as cause(e_1,e_2), goal(e_1,e_2), or situation(s_1,e_1). These predications represent implied (or asserted) beliefs of the speaker concerning the structure of events and states in the actual (or fictional) world, such as that one event caused another, that an agent had certain intentions when engaging in an act, or that a sequence of events or states had a particular importance or salience ordering. The CDRS is like the delineated DRS's described in Asher (1987), which represent the cognitive states of the agents of mental state verbs, such as *believe*. The CDRS represents beliefs of the recipient, the objects of which are the events and entities mentioned or implied by the discourse. The implication is that though the representation in (138) is incorrect as a DRS representing the truth conditional semantics of (136), it is a fine example of a CDRS representing the recipient's beliefs concerning what the text said, and its implied coherence. A fuller theory will eventually add a probability to the coherence relation, making it $goal(e_1,e_2,G)$. G should reflect the strength of the guess that the speaker intended a **goal** relation. The fuller theory would assign a value to G and incorporate a non-monotonic logic to decide when subsequent discourse increases G, or alternatively, lowers it to 0, retracting the coherence guess.

Similarly, discourse segments(DSegs) are (possibly disjoint) sequences of reference markers which the recipient takes to be both structurally and functionally related in the discourse. DSegs can figure in CRels. A DSeg is represented as a sequence of reference markers and conditions $<u_1,Con_1,u_2,Con_2...>$ where $u_i \subseteq U_k$, $Con_i \subseteq Con_k$. u_i is a sequence of reference markers which is *dense* with respect to U_k and Con_i are the conditions affecting u_i. *dense* means that reference markers are not widely spread out in the discourse. Denseness accounts

(143)

$$u_1,u_2,e_1,u_5,e_3,e_4,u_6, u_7,u_8,e_5, p_1$$

$john(u_1)$
$park(u_2)$
$e_1 go(u_1)$
$to(e_1,u_2)$
...

...
$lake(u_5)$
$e_3 dive(u_6)$
$into(e_3,u_5)$
$e_4 swim(u_6)$
$across(e_4,u_5)$
$u_6 = u_1$
$mary(u_8)$
$e_5 tell(u_7,u_8,p_1)$
$e_7 = e_1$
$p_1:$

$$u_9,e_6,dseg_1$$

$day(u_9)$
$nice(u_9)$
$e_6 = u_9$
$e_6 = dseg_1$
$dseg_1 = <\{u_1,u_2...,p_1\},$
$\{john(u_1,...e_7 = e_1\}>$

for flashbacks or interruptions, but not for the cognitively implausible case of choosing reference markers from arbitrary positions in the discourse. The segmentation of the text is revisable.

The CDRS for the narrative portion of the picnic discourse in (102) with completion sentence (102f) is shown in (143). It looks just like the DRS, except that in the sub-DRS which contains the representation of the complement of *tell*, the DSeg for the narrative is represented (the remaining conditions affecting the reference markers are indicated by the "..."). That segment is equated with the reference marker for *it$_i$* in the equation $e_6 = dseg_1$.

8.3. Syntactic and Semantic Tests for Discourse Relations

A number of writers have argued that certain syntactic structures always (or almost always) signal particular discourse functions. Labov's (1972) definition of narrative clauses in the simple past tense is one such claim. Other researchers have suggested correlations between semantics and discourse functions, such as the transitivity hypothesis of (Hopper and Thompson, 1980). We tested these claims in an empirical study of our WSJ sample of commentary text, and found that syntactic and semantic information is insufficient, though contributive, to coherence relation assignment. This section reports the results of the empirical examination of these claims. The next section summarizes the contributions that syntax, compositional semantics and naive semantics each make to the interpretation of discourse coherence.

Decker (1985) makes the strongest claims for syntactic tests for coherence relations. Her computational text understanding system "relies solely on syntactic structure to create summaries of one particular genre of discourse--that of newspaper reports--and to label the kinds of information given in them." Decker (1985) provides a list of syntactic tests for the "important" events in a news story, as below:

Main clause
Not nominalized
Active voice

Past tense
Simple aspect
No modals
Transitive clause (as defined by Hopper and Thompson, 1980)

Backgrounded clauses have opposing or more inclusive tests. Our empirical study of six WSJ articles in the commentary genre shows that these syntactic tests do not predict which clauses are reported events. The analysis shows that syntactic tests alone are insufficient to determine coherence relations, and that semantic and commonsense knowledge are often used to determine them. The remainder of this section is devoted to considering each of the tests in the above list in turn.

Main Clause. Reinhart (1982) and Thompson (1984) have shown that events which update the reference point in narrative can be introduced in subordinate clauses, as in the following examples from the literature:

(144)   *When I let go his arm,* there was a knife on the table, he just picked it up... (Reinhart, 1982).

(145)   *Only after he stopped smiling and shrieking,* did he go to Stephanie and hug her (Thompson, 1984).

In commentary, frequently the **reported** events in the story are presented in embedded clauses, even several deep. Of 51 **reported** events in two WSJ articles almost half were embedded. The text below is the first paragraph of a story reporting the results of a negotiation on foreign exchange trading:

(146)   Finance ministers of the U.S. and its major economic allies declared that the dollar has declined enough and indicated they are prepared *to intervene in the currency markets* to help stabilize exchange rates at "about their current levels."(WSJ)

In this sentence, there are two main clause **reported** events, that of declaring and indicating, but the hypothetical event of intervening is the important one in terms of the discourse. Subsequent commentary in the article describes the reactions to the possibility of intervention.

Not Nominalized. The **reported** event can even occur in a nominalization. In the first sentence of an article on Brazilian debt payments, the **reported** event is introduced by the nominal *suspension* in the subject noun phrase:

(147)   Brazil's unilateral *suspension* of interest payments ... presents
          international banks with one of their biggest
          challenges...(WSJ)

The action is nominalized here because the article presupposes that the reader already knows about the suspension, and the purpose of the article is to comment upon the move, both from an objective and biased viewpoint.

In order to test Decker's remaining claims, the 6,000 words of WSJ commentary were analyzed and one or more coherence relations were assigned to 385 clauses. Clauses in opaque contexts were eliminated from consideration for two reasons. First, opaque contexts introduce discourses of their own, the discourse of the agent of the matrix sentence. The propositional objects of mental verbs such as *say, believe, plan, announce* have coherence among themselves in terms of the belief worlds of the agent of the verb (Asher, 1987). Second, because of this, tense, reference and other features have differing significance in opaque contexts, rendering such clauses incomparable directly with the clauses in the main discourse. Table 8.1 displays the results of an analysis in which the 385 clauses were assigned coherence relations by hand, and then the syntactic properties of the clauses were tabulated with respect to their coherence relations. These data clearly defeat any notion that coherence relations can be read off of syntactic properties of clause. **reported** events are found in subordinate clauses, nominalizations, passives, with modals and in present tense. Furthermore, many other types of clauses pass the syntactic tests but are not **reported** events, nullifying information from the tests which would indicate that the clauses are **reported** events. Syntactic tests are not hard and fast, because the syntactic properties show up in clauses with a variety of

Table 8.1 Syntactic Properties and Coherence Relations					
Coherence Relation	*Reported Event*	*Description*	*Situation*	*Import*	*Comment*
Main	29	22	55	66	70
Relative	2	33	9	7	10
Nominalization	1	2	7	-	1
Participial	-	5	7	5	5
Infinitival	1	4	15	2	4
Appositive	-	3	3	-	-
Conjunction	-	2	-	1	-
Adverbial	1	4	17	5	3
Complement	-	-	8	6	4
Passive	5	16	20	6	1

Table 8.2 Tense, Aspect and Coherence Relations					
Coherence Relation	*Reported Event*	*Description*	*Situation*	*Import*	*Comment*
Pres Simple	1	26	12	24	11
Past Simple	25	22	47	31	60
Pres Perfect	4	4	7	3	2
Past Perfect	-	1	9	4	1
Pres Prog	-	-	3	1	1
Past Prog	-	-	2	1	-
Pres Modal	-	6	2	16	5
Past Modal	-	-	1	2	1
Non-finite	4	16	38	13	16

coherence relations. On the other hand, the data indicate preference for certain coherence relations given certain syntactic properties of clauses, though not decisively, as will be explored in "Weak Predictions of Coherence Relations." on page 204. Reported events in the passive were relatively frequent (19%).

Active voice. Some action clauses were in the passive, as in the timeline forwarding clause of (148).

(148)   Dennis B. Levine, who engaged in massive insider trading...,
         was sentenced to two years in prison and fined $362,000.
         (WSJ)

Tense and Aspect. Table 8.2 shows the results of tabulating the tense/aspect for the same 385 clauses.[15] These data show that **reported** events tend to be in the simple past, but that clauses of all types were predominantly in the simple past (45%), so that simple past is not predictive of any coherence relation.

Transitivity Test. Hopper and Thompson's (1980) work correlating transitivity with foregroundedness in narrative is important because it provides subtle but clear syntactic and semantic correlations with transitivity. Transitivity is defined as a property of the whole clause, not just the verb. A transitive clause is one which is:

Multiparticipant, not nominalized or participial
Kinetic (easy transfer from subject to object)
Telic (achievement, accomplishment)
Volitional (goal)
Punctual (achievement)
Affirmative (not negative)
Realis (events which have occurred)
Agentive, where the agency hierarchy is
1st person > 2nd person > 3rd person >
proper name > human > animate > inanimate

---

15 There were also a few **qualification** and **evaluation** clauses.

Whole objects(the milk, not some milk)

Backgrounded clauses tended to fail these tests, according to Hopper and Thompson. According to the hypothesis, high-transivity verb types will be NONSTATIVE GOAL ACHIEVEMENT, or GOAL ACCOM-PLISHMENT verbs in the verb ontology (Chapter 4).

Is transitivity important for commentary texts? A number of the Hopper-Thompson tests of high transitivity were applied to the 385 non-opaque clauses of WSJ text in order to test the hypothesis that the correlation does hold for commentary. Translated into Naive Semantics terminology, the tests applied were as in column one of Table 8.3. Column 2 gives the number of **reported** events among the 385 which satisfied the test (in accord with the hypothesis). Column 3 shows the number of **reported** event which failed the test (against the hypothesis). Column 4 shows the number of other clause types which satisfied the test (against the hypothesis), and Column 5 the number of other clause types which failed the test (in accord with the hypothesis). A verb passed the telic test by being either an ACHIEVEMENT or ACCOM-PLISHMENT verb. A verb passed the goal test by being a GOAL verb (and NONSTATIVE). The multiparticipant test was inappropriate to the texts because they contained so many abstract complement structures and nominalizations as subjects. In the commentary genre, the foregrounded events are reported in clauses with any of the following types of verbs:

1. SOCIAL EVENT verbs such as *appoint, fire, pay* (ACHIEVE-MENT) or *thwart, build, sue* (ACCOMPLISHMENT).
2. SOCIAL EVENT MENTAL verbs such as *agree, decide, settle, sentence*
3. Performative verbs of saying such as *pledge, promise*
4. Change of state verbs or STATIVE verbs with nouns referring to economic indicators, as in *the stock market rose, GM showed a profit*

To a large extent the 34 **reported** event clauses among the 385 were highly transitive clauses as defined by Hopper and Thompson. However, the other clause types did not correlate negatively, as predicted. While **reported** event clauses were overwhelmingly expressed with GOAL

ACHIEVEMENT verbs, so were events and states of other types. Thus the test cannot be used to identify **reported** events in commentary. Comparing columns 4 and 5 of Table 8.3, among clauses which were not **reported** event, more of them passed the transitivity test (against the hypothesis), than failed it (which would have favored the hypothesis). As for negation, although the prediction that **reported** event clauses are not negative is generally borne out by the data, there were examples of them, as in (149) and (150). In (150), the negation is indicated in the verb meaning, not in the syntax.

(149)   But Judge Goettel, in passing sentence, mentioned no factor that had influenced him in Mr. Levine's favor other than his cooperation in the government's investigation.

(150)   Only the U.S. failed to pledge any policy changes...

The Hopper-Thompson transitivity test does indicate tendencies. Of the 34 **reported** events, 30 (88%) were telic, as compared with 220 (55%) of the other relations. But the test is not useful in identifying **reported** events in the commentary genre. This makes sense because what structures commentary text is not a sequence of actions, as in narrative and procedural text, but the reactions of various participants and observers to an action. The typical commentary text has relatively few **reported** events. Furthermore, many clauses which in a narrative would provide the "backbone" of the discourse, do not have that function in commentary text. Instead they typically provide background for the main event being commented upon in the text. Such clauses may go on in narrative sequence, but the discourse segments of which they are a part are **situation** segments, as will be illustrated in "Using Commonsense Knowledge to Segment Discourse." on page 221.

Weak Predictions of Coherence Relations. Although syntactic and semantic tests are inconclusive in assigning coherence relations, they can be useful heuristics to be combined with other sources of information. One important other source of information is naive semantics.

Table 8.3 Transitivity Test Applied to Commentary				
Test	*Reported Event*		*Other Coherence Relation*	
	Pass	*Fail*	*Pass*	*Fail*
1	2	3	4	5
Telic(achievement, accomplishment)	30	4	220	177
Volitional(goal)	29	5	269	128
Punctual(achievement)	30	4	219	178
Affirmative(not negative)	33	1	381	18
Realis(past or perfect tense)	29	5	191	206

This word-level commonsense knowledge, added to syntactic and structural semantic information, provides enough information to assign coherence relations in a large number of cases. This section will indicate some of the contributions of these three modules to coherence relation assignment, as they emerged both in the empirical study of the WSJ sample, and as suggested in the discourse and tense literature. There remains a residual of cases which require non-lexical domain knowledge or other encyclopedic knowledge in order to recover the discourse structure. The ultimate solution to computational discourse understanding will be to teach the computer most of what a person knows and believes when the person reads the text. Short of that long-term goal, a useful portion of the interpretation can be recovered using just lexical level naive semantics.

Table 8.1 shows that given the syntactic structure of a clause, certain coherence relations for the clause are more likely than others. According to these data, its status as a main clause does not predict that a clause introduces a **reported** event. All types of coherence relations were introduced by main clauses. On the other hand, it might be that NOT being a main clause predicts that a clause does not introduce a **reported** event (a weak main clause test). In order to investigate the efficacy of such a weak main clause test, it is necessary to consider the results of the study "Main Clause." on page 199 which considered all 51 **reported** events in two articles, including those in opaque contexts. That study found that almost half of the **reported** events were embedded. Thus a weak main clause test doesn't work. Other syntactic cues are more powerful. Relative clauses are likely to be **description** clauses. Nominalizations, infinitivals and adverbials tend to be **situation** clauses. Passives and appositives are likely to be **description** or **situation** clauses.

The data in Table 8.3 indicate that clauses which fail the transitivity tests are very probably NOT **reported** event clauses. Among such clauses, the verb ontological attachments are fairly evenly distributed, although statives accounted for a higher percentage of **import** (34%) and **description** (25%) clause verbs. Both GOAL and NON-GOAL verbs were spread across all non-reported-event clauses rather evenly. Negations were concentrated in **import** clauses.

Similarly, looking at Table 8.2, we can consider how much can be learned about the coherence relation of a clause from its tense/aspect. Apparently a weak tense/aspect test holds, namely that a clause which is not in the simple past probably does not introduce a **reported** event. These data also illustrate that a clause in the present tense is probably a **description** or **import** clause, and that a clause with a modal is probably an **import** clause. The above empirical study establishes that although tense and aspect alone do not indicate which coherence relations hold in a text, they are suggestive of certain coherence relations. At this point we can consider exactly how to represent the temporal semantics of a text, and how that information can be used to help predict coherence relations. Recent model theoretic accounts of tense and aspect differ on basic questions, such as the ontological status of states and events, and whether events or time intervals should be taken as the primitive notion (Dowty, 1979, Hinrichs, 1987, Kamp, 1979, Parsons, 1985, Partee, 1984, Moens and Steedman, 1987). However, they all accept Reichenbach's (1947) observation that temporal relations in discourse are interpreted with respect to three times--speech time(now), reference time (r_i) and event time (e_i). Further, they agree that intervals, or intervals defined in terms of instants, are the times over which temporal relations are defined. Reichenbach's insight was that in the present perfect, the reference time is the same as the speech time, while in the simple past, the reference time and the event time are both before the speech time. For example, in (151), the reference time, r_1, is equal to the speech time (now), and the event time, e_1, is before the reference time, as indicated in the equations to the right.[16] In (152), the reference time is before the speech time, and the event time, e_1, is included in the reference time. Similarly, a past perfect in a subordinate clause embedded under a matrix verb in the simple past tense is evaluated with respect to the time of the matrix clause, not with respect to speech time, as illustrated in (153)

(151)   John has gotten up. $r_1 = $ now, $e_1 < r_1$
              e_1

(152)   John got up. $r_1 < $ now, $e_1 \subseteq r_1$
              e_1

(153)   John got up $r_1 < $ now, $e_1 \subseteq r_1$
              e_1
        because Mary had wakened him. $r_2 < r_1, e_2 \subseteq r_2$
                  e_2

As Partee points out, in narrative, events introduced in simple past tense main clauses with telic (ACHIEVEMENT or ACCOMPLISH-MENT) verbs cause the reference time to be updated to just after the event. The whole clause must be interpreted as telic, a topic to be explored in the next section. Non-telic clauses do not cause the reference time to be updated. The generation of tense equations in the DRS accesses the current reference time, which may have been updated as the result of an event. Consider the text in (154).

(154)   John got up because Mary had wakened him. He went out.

The corresponding DRS is as in (155). The current reference time (r_p) is set to some past time at the beginning because of the simple past tense in the matrix clause of the first sentence. Because of the simple

---

16 The notation of Partee (1984) is used in the examples.

past tense, a new reference time, just after it, r_1, is introduced. But in the interpretation of the subordinate clause, the current reference time is not changed to this new reference time, and in general it is not in subordinate clauses. Instead, another new reference time is introduced, r_2, before r_0, because of the past perfect in the subordinate clause. Then in the interpretation of the second sentence, with a simple past tense ACHIEVEMENT, the current reference time is set equal to the new reference time r_1, and another new reference time, r_3, just after it, is introduced.

The decision to update the reference point in augmenting the DRS is not based only upon the tense information in the discourse. Adverbials, clause aspect and world knowledge are also considered. Although in narrative a general rule says update the reference time after a telic main clause past tense, as in (156), this rule can be overridden by world knowledge. In the interpretation of (157), naive semantic knowledge suggests that the reference time should not be updated, so that the fish eating and beef eating overlap in time (Kamp, 1979). that the interpretation of temporal relations in discourse requires access to naive semantic information further justifies

(155)

$$
\begin{array}{l}
r_0, u_1, e_1, r_1, u_2, r_2,\ e_3, r_3 \\
\hline
r_0 < now \\
r_p = r_0 \\
john(u_1) \\
e_1\ get\ up(u_1) \\
e_1 \subseteq r_0 \\
r_1 > r_0 \\
r_1 < now \\
mary(u_2) \\
e_2\ waken(u_2, u_1) \\
r_2 < r_1 \\
e_2 \subseteq r_2 \\
e_3\ go\ out(u_1) \\
r_p = r_1 \\
e_3 \subseteq r_1 \\
r_3 > r_1 \\
r_3 < now
\end{array}
$$

the fully parallel model proposed in "8.2. Modularity and Discourse" on page 184 in which all modules of grammar have access to each other at all stages of interpretation.

If we assume that the discourse augmentation module contains an algorithm which generates reference times and event equations as in (155), we can consider how these representations can be used to predict coherence relations.

(156)   John ate fish and Mary paid the bill.

e_1 e_2

$r_0 < now$

$e_1 \subseteq r_0$

$r_1 < now$

$r_0 < r_1$

$e_2 \subseteq r_1$

(157)   John ate fish and Mary ate beef.

e_1 e_2

$r_0 < now$

$e_1 \subseteq r_0$

$e_2 \subseteq r_0$

Table 8.4 Tense and Coherence Relations

δ_1 and δ_2 - world-immanent reference markers

$r_1 < r_2$ - reference times

1. $\delta_1 \subseteq r_1, \delta_2 \subseteq r_2$	Elaboration(δ_1,δ_2), Cause(δ_1,δ_2), Goal(δ_2,δ_1), Evidence(δ_2,δ_1), Enablement(δ_1,δ_2), Comment(δ_2,δ_1)
2. $\delta_1, \delta_2 \subseteq r_1$	Parallel(δ_1,δ_2), Contrast(δ_1,δ_2), Description(δ_1,δ_2), Qualification(δ_1,δ_2), Evidence(δ_1,δ_2), Generalization(δ_1,δ_2), Import(δ_1,δ_2)
3. $\delta_2 \subseteq now$	Import(δ_2,δ_1), Evaluation(δ_2,δ_1), Description(δ_2,δ_1)

We compared the temporal and coherence relations between pairs of clauses in the WSJ sample. Table 8.4 summarizes this empirical study of the types of coherence relations predicted by various temporal relationships. Temporal relations involve world-immanent reference markers, that is, events and states which are placed in space-time. In the table, δ_i is a world immanent reference marker. The first case of Table 8.4 shows in which ways two world-immanent reference markers are likely to be coherence related if they are sequenced in time. The second case of Table 8.4 shows which coherence relations are likely if two world-immanent reference markers are included in the same reference time. The third case shows the likely relations if one of the markers is included in the speech time.

There are a few weak predictions of coherence relations from clause aspect. *Clause aspect* refers to the aspect of an entire clause. The classic example in (158) through (160) illustrates differing clause aspects with the same verb and tense. (158) is telic, while (159) and (160) are activity clauses.

(158)   John pushed the cart under a shed.

(159)   John pushed the cart under a blue sky.

(160)   John pushed the cart.

Clause-stative means not only the opposition between an inherently stative verb and an eventive verb (as in *be* vs *hit*), but to the various ways in which a whole clause can end up being stative, as with the presence of the progressive, or a number of other factors. *Clause-telic* means that the clause reports a change of state with a terminus. *John built the house* is clause-telic, while *John was building the house* is clause-stative. A telic clause has an ACHIEVEMENT or ACCOMPLISH-MENT verb not in the progressive, not in the simple present (which would be habitual, and with no modal (eg., *John will build the house* is not telic). *Clause-activity* has to do with a clause which reports an event which has no terminus, and which has the sub-interval property, as defined in Chapter 4. *John ran* is clause-activity.

Table 8.5. Clause Aspect and Discourse Relations	
Clause telic	Generalization, Elaboration, Evaluation
Clause stative	Description, Situation, Import, Evaluation, Comment
Clause activity	Description, Situation

The examples in (158) through (160) illustrate the use of naive semantics in the assignment of clause aspect. Knowledge that a shed is a place which is a plausible destination for the cart contributes to the interpretation of (158) as telic, while the other two are activity clauses. The discourse augmentation module should inspect verb ontological information, aspect information and naive semantics in order to assign clause aspect, as in Moens and Steedman (1987). The fact that all of these types of information are required again supports a fully parallel model of grammar.

We studied clause aspect in relation to coherence relations in the WSJ sample. Table 8.5 lists the CRels which the study showed are preferred in the presence of certain clause aspects. The CRels not mentioned (such as **cause**) are not indicated either positively or negatively in relation to clause aspect.

Naive Semantics and Coherence. Clearly coherence relation assignment draws upon syntactic, compositional semantic and naive semantic knowledge. We would like to have a computational algorithm for coherence relation extraction which draws upon all of these sources of knowledge in parallel. Although our research has not progressed to the point of an algorithm, we can show in this section that the naive semantic representations of nouns and verbs contain sufficient information to handle a large number of cases in which world knowledge is required to structure the discourse. Generic representations of the typical implications of verbs such as cause, goal, enablement and consequence are the very same information as coherence relations. Their content means, "If there was an event (or state) of $VERB_1ing$, then it probably had as goal a later event (or state) of $VERB_2ing$." For example, "If there was an event of buying, it probably had as goal a state of owning." The representations contain generalizations about objects and actions which are common to a linguistic community, and thus explain the ability to understand a discourse without resort to particular scripts describing familiar real-world situations. Using generic and ontological representations derived as described in Chapters 2 and 4, the coherence relations indicated in the following examples can be assigned. The examples involve verb representations which were generated without reference to the examples.

(161)   e1 Levine engaged in insider trading.

(162)   e2 The government charged him with violations of the securities laws.

(163)   cause(e1,e2)

(164)   (e3) Levine invested heavily and (e4) profited handsomely.

(165)   goal(e3,e4).

(166)   (e4) Levine profited handsomely. (s1) He was rich.

(167)   cause(e4,s1).

(168)   (e5) The judge examined and (e6) investigated the evidence in the case.

(169)   parallel(e5,e6).

(170)   (e7) Analysts supported the light sentence, and (e8) Giuliani opposed it.

(171)   contrast(e7,e8).

(172)   (e9) Levine was charged and (e10) convicted.

(173)   sequence(e9,e10)

To assing the relation (163), the generic entry for *insider trading* can be used to infer that Levine broke the law. The entry associated with one reading of the verb *charge* includes information that a typical cause of charging someone is that that someone has committed a crime. (See Table 8.6 for generic entries for all verbs in the examples.) Putting these two together, cause(e1,e2) can be inferred. Likewise the consequence feature of a verb can be used to extract a **cause** relation.

Table 8.6 Verb Generic Entries

charge
  ({whnext(tried(obj)),whnext(convicted(obj) acquitted(obj)),
  cause(commit(obj,X) & crime(X)),
  implies(suspect(subj,commit(obj,obliq)))},
  {sel_restrict(sentient(subj)),sel_restrict(sentient(obj)),
  implies(crime(obliq)),paraphrase(indict(subj,obj))}).

invest
  ({implies(lucrative(obliq)),how(with(X) & money(X)),
  implies(money(obj))},
  {sel_restrict(sentient(subj)),goal(profit(subj)),
  paraphrase(gain(subj))}).

profit
  ({what_enables(invest(subj)),implies(lucrative(obliq)),
  how(from(X) & investment(X))},
  {sel_restrict(sentient(subj)),cons_of_event(have(subj,X) &
  money(X)),paraphrase(gain(subj))}).

To assign the relation A consequence of *profit* is having money [17] This can be used to extract the **cause** relation in (167) Using the goal feature of *invest*, (165) can be recovered. The parallelism relation in (169) can be extracted by noting that the entries for *examine* and *investigate* both contain implications that the subject of the verb studies the direct object. Similarly, the contrast of *support* and *oppose* could be inferred

---

17 whnext stands for "what happens next," cons_of_event "consequence of event," sel_restric for "selection restriction."

from the causal implications that the former is caused by approval of the object, while the latter by disapproval of the object. The **sequence** relation between charge (e9) and and convict (e10) can be inferred from the generic lexical entry for *charge*, which states that if a person is charged, typically what happens next is that the person is convicted.

Table 8.6 Verb Generic Entries (continued)

examine
({cause(curious(subj)),how(closely),implies(physical(obj)),
implies(study(subj,obj)),cons_of_event(know(subj,X))},
{sel_restrict(sentient(subj), goal(learn_about(subj,obj)))}).

investigate
({cause(curious(subj)),cause(involved_in(obj,Y) & trial(Y)),
implies(pursuc(subj,Y) & lead(Y)),
implies(study(subj,obj)),cons_of_event(know(subj,X))},
{sel_restrict(sentient(subj), goal(learn_about(subj,obj)))}).

support
({cause(approve(subj,obj)),goal(prevail(obj)),
cons_of_event(encouraged(obj))},
{sel_restrict(sentient(subj)| propositional(subj)),
paraphrase(favor(subj,obj))}).

oppose
({implies(disagree(subj) & with(obj)),implies(dislike(subj,obj)),
cause(disapprove(subj,of(obj))),whnext(work(subj) &
against(obj))},{sel_restrict(sentient(subj)),
paraphrase(against(subj,obj))}).

convict
({cause(commit(obj,X) & crime(X)),implies(crime(obliq)),
whnext(sentenced(obj)),what_enables(arrested(obj) &
charged(obj) & tried(obj)),whnext(punished(obj)),
whnext(imprisoned(obj)),whnext(fined(obj)),
where(in(court)),implies(dishonored(obj)),
whnext(appeal(obj))},{sel_restrict(sentient(subj)),
sel_restrict(sentient(obj)),goal(punished(obj))}).

In a similar way, naive semantic representations can be used to find antecedents for anaphors in cases where a number of discourse entities are potential antecedents by the rules of c-command and agreement. Consider the following text. In (174) either Liman or Levine could be the antecedent of *his*. The information that Levine is the defendant in the case must be used to resolve the ambiguity. In (175) the knowledge that Liman is speaking about Levine must be used to choose Levine as the antecedents of *he*, and that knowledge must be used the other way in (176) to choose Liman.

(174)   Arthur Liman...tried to portray his client as financially and personally ruined by the scandal. (WSJ)

(175)   "Every penny he's ever earned is encumbered," Mr. Liman told the court. (WSJ)

(176)   He said Mr. Levine is suffering "a form of banishment." (WSJ)

These choices would be based on a combination of knowledge from the text itself, and of lexical commonsense knowledge such as "some clients are defendants" and "a speaker tends to continue." In (177) only lexical information about the selection restrictions on *pare back* are needed to choose between *changes* and *imbalances* and *economists* as antecedent of *they* (and subject of the relative clause).

(177)   ... moving toward more serious policy changes designed to reduce the global trade imbalances, which economists say could bring on a world-wide recession if they aren't pared back (WSJ)

In (178) knowledge of government is required to assign *he* to Reagan. Lexical knowledge alone of *resign* and *replace* can be used to choose Volcker as the antecedent of *him*.

(178)   ...Reagan announced that Volcker had resigned as Chairman of the Federal Reserve Board and that he would nominate Greenspan to replace him... (WSJ)

Situation Activity (topic event)

Situation Activity	s_1	At the sentencing, Mr. Levine was besieged by media attention
Description (s_2,x)	s_2	usually reserved for celebrities
Elaboration (s_3,s_1)	s_3	The small federal courthouse in suburban White Plains, N.Y... was surrounded by reporters and television camera crews.

Narrative

Situation Time (e_1,e_2)	e_1	When Mr. Levine arrived with his wife in a rented limousine,
Sequence (e_2,e_1) Goal (e_2,e_3)	e_2	the crush of onlookers was dispersed by police
Sequence (e_3,e_2)	e_3	so the Levines could emerge.
Sequence (e_5,e_3)		
Situation Activity (s_4,e_5)	s_4	The courtroom was packed with a crowd
Description (e_4,y)	e_4	that spilled into the hallway.
Situation Activity (s_5,e_6)	s_5	Mr. Levine,
Description (s_6,z)	s_6	conservatively dressed in a gray suit..., showed no emotion
Sequence (e_6,e_5)	e_6	as he delivered a statement to the court,
Elaboration (e_7,e_6)	e_7	saying in flat tones that he has been sentenced to "a life of disgrace and humiliation..."
Sequence (e_8,e_6)	e_8	Mr. Levine's lawyer tried to portray his client as financially and personally ruined by the scandal...
Restatement (e_9,e_6)	e_9	He said Mr. Levine is suffering "a form of banishment..."
Sequence (e_{10},e_9), Contrast (e_{10},e_{13})	e_{10}	But Judge Goettel,
Sequence (e_{11},e_9)	e_{11}	in passing sentence,

Description (e_{12},e_9)	e_{12}	mentioned no factor that had influenced him in Mr. Levine's favor other than his cooperation in the government's investigation.

Figure 18: A Narrative (WSJ)

8.4. Parallelism in Coherence Exemplified

In this section the interaction of syntax, compositional semantics, cue phrases and naive semantics in the extraction of discourse coherence relations will be illustrated in an analysis of an article from the WSJ, shown in Figure 18 on page 216 and Figure 19 on page 223. The article concerns the sentencing of a stock broker who engaged in insider trading. The article is in the commentary genre, and is structured around comments by various parties upon the wisdom of imposing a light sentence. This structure is interrupted by the **situation** segment in Figure 18 on page 216 which describes publicity at the sentencing. The first two sentences of the **situation** segment are part of the commentary, but the segment continues in the form of a narrative. The recipient interprets the clauses in the narrative as referring to the following events and states (stated and implied):

(179) e_1 The Levines arrive
          e_2 The police disperse the crowd
          e_3 The Levines emerge from their car
          e_4 The crowd spills into the hallway
          e_5 The Levines move into the courtroom
          e_6 Levine delivers statement
          e_7 Levine delivers statement
          e_8 His lawyer delivers statement
          e_9 His lawyer delivers statement
          e_{10} The judge justifies the sentence
          e_{11} The judge passes the sentence
          e_{12} No factors influenced the judge
          e_{13} The judge is influenced by the statements of
                      Levine and his lawyer

A possibly controversial element of this analysis is inclusion of two implied, unstated events, e_5 and e_{13}. e_5, in which the Levines move from their car into the courtroom, is implied by the definite description *the courtroom*. e_{13} is hypothetical. If it had occurred, the judge would have been influenced by Levine and his lawyer. e_{13} is implied by the *but*, which contrasts the hypothetical event of the judge being influenced by the statements in e_6 and e_8, with the judge's claim that he had not been influenced by any factors (other than Levine's cooperation in the investigation).

The recipient assigns the coherence relations in Figure 18 on page 216 incorporating information from cue words, syntax, semantics and commonsense knowledge. How several levels of grammar contribute to the interpretation of coherence will be illustrated here in relation to the example text. Next their effects on discourse segmentation will be exemplified.

First consider the **sequence** clauses. In the Partee tense notation, each of the events e_i is included in a time interval r_i. The text is interpreted as asserting the following relationships among the reference times of the events:

$$r_1 < r_2 < \left\{ {r_3 \atop r_4} \right\} < r_5 < \left\{ {r_6 = r_7 \atop r_8 = r_9} \right\} < \left\{ {r_{12} \atop r_{13}} \right\} < r_{10} = r_{11}$$

As can be seen, the events referred to in the narrative are temporally ordered, except the statements by Levine (e_6, e_7) and his lawyer (e_8, e_9). These seem unordered for reasons to be explained below. The hypothetical event of the judge's being influenced (e_{13}) is unordered relative to the event reported by the judge of being influenced by Levine's cooperation (e_{12}).

The sequencing facts as shown in (179) illustrate the contributions of several levels of grammar to the interpretation of the coherence relations among clauses. At the lexical level, the discourse cue words *when, so,* and *as* affect the sequencing. The contribution of *when* in the clause with e_1 is two-fold. First, it signals a change from commentary to narrative genre. Second, it places the time of the crowd dispersal (e_2) after the arrival(e_1). *so* in the clause with e_3 indicates that the Levines emerged directly after the crowd dispersal. *as* with e_6 places the Levine's statement at the same time as the showing of no emotion.

It is important to notice that these cue words cannot operate independently. Their exact effects on the interpretation of temporal order in Figure 18 on page 216 depend upon tense and clause aspect. Tense can override the interpretation indicated by cue words. In (180), the preferred interpretation has enable(s_1,e_1), along with a less plausible interpretation evidence(s_1,e_1). But if the tense is changed to present in the e_1 clause, as in (181) the preference changes to evidence(s_1,e_1).

(180)   John was in the kitchen, so he made dinner.
             s_1 e_1

(181)   John was in the kitchen, so he makes dinner.
             s_1 e_1

The preferred interpretation of a sequence of simple past tense clauses places the events in temporal sequence. As predicted, all of the clauses in **sequence** relation are in fact in the simple past tense. However, as we saw in "8.3. Syntactic and Semantic Tests for Discourse Relations" on page 198, it is not always the case that two consecutive clauses in the simple past tense report a sequence of narrative events. A counterexample may be found in the text. Events e_8 and e_9 are reported in consecutive clauses in the simple past tense, but they refer to the same event, not to two temporally ordered events. The e_8 clause describes the event as an attempted portrayal, the e_9 clause reports what the lawyer said to achieve the portrayal.

Aspect can also override the effect of cue words. If the clause with e_2 had been in the progressive, then the interpretation would have been one of overlap in the intervals of the arrival and the crowd dispersal as in (182), rather than sequence.

(182)   When they arrived, the crowd was being dispersed.

Modality is another semantic factor which can override cue words. In (183) the preferred relation enable(e_1,e_2) is indicated by the cue word *where*. In (184), with *could*, the effect of the cue word is overridden, and the preferred relation is goal(e_1,e_2).

(183)   The antelope went to the river, where he drank.
          s_1 e_1

(184)   The antelope went to the river, where he could drank.
          s_1 e_1

Cue words and other lexical items, with direct discourse structuring effects, and the semantics of tense and aspect are two levels of grammar which contribute to coherence relations. Another level is pure syntax. Subordinate and relative clauses tend not to give rise to **sequence** interpretations (Hopper and Thompson, 1980). Returning to Figure 18 on page 216, the s_2 clause and e_4 clauses are relative clauses and both are **descriptive**. Passives tend not to be **sequence** clauses, as in the s_1 clause, which is **situation-activity**. Copula sentences tend to be **situation-activity** or **descriptive** as in the s_3 and s_4 clauses. The e_7 clause is an adverbial participial, which is less likely to introduce a sequenced event than it is to introduce an **elaboration** or **restatement**. On the other hand, just as cue words are inconclusive in coherence relation assignment, so are syntactic structures. e_1 and e_3 are sequenced events, even though syntax suggests against the interpretation because they are subordinates. The e_2 clause is in the passive, but nevertheless is sequenced relative to e_1.

Naive semantics is the final level of grammar to be considered in the assignment of coherence relations. Naive semantics is needed to assign the relation of **elaboration** between e_7 and e_6. First, naive semantic knowledge indicates that they are the same event, because delivering a statement is saying something. If the two clauses refer to the same event, a **restatement** relation is indicated. But additional naive semantic knowledge suggests that court statements typically include more than one sentence, so that the e_7 clause is probably only part of the statement. The relation is thus probably one of **elaboration**. In contrast, the recipient assigns the relation **restatement** between e_9 and e_8. because the recipient knows that a portrayal is a characterization of a person, and so that the saying in e_9 might be the same as the portrayal e_8. Also, this is not interpreted as an **elaboration** because the recipient knows that suffering a form of banishment can amount to being personally ruined, so that e_9 might be the very same event as e_8.

Both are instances of naive semantics winning out over tense information.

Two past tense clauses suggest temporal order between them. This preference is overridden by naive semantics, at least for recipients unfamiliar with the details of courtroom procedure, because naive semantics for *courtroom* and *court case* does not provide a typical order for these events. When naive semantics provides a strong preference for ordering events, as in (185), or overlapping them, as in (186), naive semantics wins.

(185)   John ate the meal. Mary paid the bill.

(186)   John ate fish. Mary had veal.

Even more striking examples of the use of naive semantics are to be found in the implied events e_5 and e_{13}. If the analysis is accepted that the recipient does fill in implicit events, which has been amply substantiated in the psycholinguistics literature (Graesser and Clark, 1985a, Rickheit and Strohner, 1985), then the only source for the implied events has to be naive semantics or knowledge in general. It seems to be naive semantics, in that the mention of the courtroom implies a change of place (from the street to inside the building). This knowledge is all at the lexical level. All that we need to posit is some kind of general bridging rule which requires that people move from one place to another, rather than magically appearing. In contrast, the lack of order between Levine's statement and his lawyer's may involve a less lexically-based, more domain knowledge oriented level of knowledge.

Using Commonsense Knowledge to Segment Discourse. Discourse segmentation will be illustrated with the text in Figure 19 on page 223, which consists of two genres, a commentary which contains within it a short narrative (the one in Figure 18 on page 216). This illustrates that in constructing a picture of a discourse, the recipient is not only trying to assign coherence relations to the sentences, but to assign genre

Topic event (e_1)

> Dennis B. Levine, who engaged in massive insider trading but helped the government expose the largest scandal in Wall Street history, was sentenced to two years in prison and fined $362,000.

Unbiased Comment ($dseg_2, e_1$)

> Lawyers and investment bankers said the sentence was surprisingly lenient, given Mr. Levine's breaches of client trust and his efforts to conceal his crimes, including perjury in testimony before the SEC. They suggested that the sentence was meant to encourage any other wrongdoers to cooperate in the government's broadening investigation.

Situation-Activity ($dseg_3, e_1$)

> Mr. Levine, an investment banker and takeover specialist at Drexel Burnham Lambert Inc. at the time of his arrest last May, pleaded guilty to four felony counts and could have been sentenced to as much as 20 years in prison.

Biased Comment ($dseg_4, e_1$)

> U.S. District Judge Gerard L. Goettel said that if Mr. Levine's cooperation hadn't proved so "truly extraordinary," leading to the capture of, among others, takeover speculator Ivan. F. Boesky, he would have sentenced Mr. Levine to five to 10 years in prison. The judge noted that with Mr. Levine's help, the government had "uncovered an entire nest of vipers on Wall Street... In comments from the bench, Judge Goettel acknowledged recent criticism by Rudolph Guiliani, U.S. attorney for New York's southern district, who has charged that lenient sentences are being meted out to persons convicted of insider trading...

Biased Comment ($dseg_5, e_1$)

> Mr. Guiliani, in a telephone interview, said the two-year prison sentence was "entirely appropriate, "given Mr. Levine's "very substantial cooperation" with the government. He said that "it was quite helpful that the judge indicated the range of sentence that he would have imposed had Mr. Levine not cooperated...and that judges are meting out increasingly harsh sentences agains those who don't cooperate. But he said it will take prison terms ranging from four to nine years to deter insider trading.

Situation-Activity ($dseg_6, e_1$)

> At the sentencing, Mr. Levine was besieged by media attention as in...

Figure 19: A Commentary (WSJ)

and segments to the discourse. Segments have the same outermost coherence relation for each clause. The results of segmenting the Levine article are illustrated in Figure 19. A single event, Levine's sentencing, is commented upon by unbiased experts (dseg2), the judge in the case (dseg4), and a lawyer critical of leniency towards insider traders (dseg5). In addition, there are segments which describe the situation before (dseg3) and during (dseg6) the sentencing event. Notice that internal to each segment are clauses which have coherence relations among them, so that each clause may have multiply embedded discourse relations. Not all coherence relations are exclusive, though not all clause types can embed all others, as we will see below. In summary, the CDRS representing a discourse contains genre-attributions for sets of discourse segments, coherence relations among the genre sets and the discourse segments, and coherence relations among the events in the discourse segments. This structure is similar to the hierarchies proposed in many studies of discourse structure (Fox, 1984, Hobbs, 1985, Grosz and Sidner, 1986, Mann and Thompson, 1987, Reichman, 1985). The segmentation portion of the CDRS for the example in Figure 18 on page 216 and Figure 19 reflects the hierarchy shown in Figure 20 on page 224. The tree summarizes the segmentation of the text as comment and situation segments concerning the topic **reported** event, that of Levine's sentencing. The details of the coherence relation assignments in the narrative segment are included to illustrate the way in which they give rise to a hierarchy structure. The CDRS represents the hierarchy structure as predications relating event and state reference markers, and as predications on discourse segments.

How can these segments be assigned? As we established earlier, genre has a lot to do with it. For each genre the recipient expects certain types of relationships among the segments. In this text, since the genre is commentary, the recipient expects to find a topic event as the first sentence or paragraph, and this is indeed the case. Then the recipient expects to see **comment** segments. **comment** segments are ones in which the coherence relation of the clauses is one of **comment**. The comment relation is identified by three factors: the use of a verb of saying (MENTAL- SOCIAL- GOAL- ACHIEVEMENT), a sentient subject, and a reference to an event. All three of these are illustrated in the first sentence of dseg2, with subject *lawyers*, verb *say* and reference

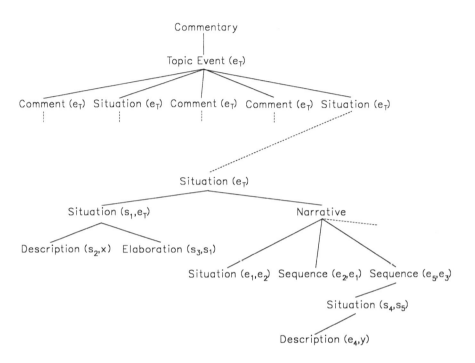

Figure 20: Discourse Hierarchy in the Levine Text

to the sentencing in the complement clause. Whether a **comment** segment is interpreted as biased or unbiased depends upon both convention
and naive semantics. In the WSJ, unbiased comment is conventionally
attributed to reliable social role names such as *lawyer, analyst, sources
close to the situation* and so on. Also, in this text, the judge is biased
concerning the event since he was the agent of the sentencing (by generic
knowledge of sentencing). In the case of Giuliani, his comments are
biased because the text describes him as the judge's critic.

That dseg3 is a new segment which switches from unbiased **comment**
to **situation-activity**, is indicated by a shift of subject from lawyers and
investment bankers to Levine. That the segment is a **situation-activity**
is indicated by the fact that its only sentence is a situation- activity
relative to the topic event. This is identified as a **situation-activity** by
several indicators. Since the main clause is in the simple past tense,

and the main verb is a GOAL ACHIEVEMENT verb, tense and verb suggest a **sequence** clause on the topic event. However, naive semantic knowledge that pleading guilty comes before sentencing suggests that the clause is a **situation-activity** activity relative to the topic event. The shift again from **comment** to **situation-activity** with dseg6 is indicated by the place adverbial, which shifts the context from the propositional world of commentary to the physical setting of the sentencing. The first clause of the segment is assigned the relation **situation-activity** because of the passive.

Empirical Study of Discourse Hierarchy. We studied the hierarchy structure of the sample of 6 WSJ articles and found constraints affecting which coherence relations can dominate which others in the hierarchy. The least constrained relations are **comment, import** and **evaluation**. This is because **comment** clauses simply reflect the shift of speaker from the author to another person, who can then be quoted, employing as many discourse devices as the speaker. Furthermore, **comment** clauses are not dominated by any other types of clauses. They are independent. **import** and **evaluation** clauses can dominate all types of clauses except **comment** because the significance or value of an event can be a whole new situation with as much complexity as the action itself.

reported events and **cause** clauses can dominate only a constrained set of three other clause types, **generalization, contrast**, and **parallel**, which are essentially ways of continuing the same discourse function. **generalization** clauses tend not to dominate other clause types, but rather to summarize a number of clauses as its relation to them. The nature of a generalization is to summarize rather than to elaborate or argue. **situation** and **description** clauses can dominate all of the clause types dominated by **reported** events, and in addition **cause** clauses.

8.5. Other Models

Our goal in this chapter is to establish two things: that naive semantic knowledge is needed in order to recapture the structure of a discourse, and that word level naive semantics is sufficient to assign coherence relations and segment discourse in a large number of cases.

We have a theory of discourse which posits independent modules, explained in different theories, which contribute to discourse structure in parallel. Some approaches to discourse deny the role of syntax and compositional semantics in discourse structure, and place all of the explanation for coherence in world knowledge and causal inference (Schank and Abelson, 1977). Unlike these approaches, we acknowledge that syntax alone serves to signal some of the discourse structure, as does compositional semantics. Our goal here is simply to show that with the naive semantic representations described in Chapters 2 through 4, part of discourse coherence can be recovered.

A number of studies from the computational linguistic point of view propose a variety of ways of representing and capturing the formal relationships among the elements of a discourse. A key result of such studies is that discourse is recursively structured as a hierarchy (Grosz and Sidner, 1986, Hobbs, 1985, Lockman and Klappholz, 1980, Mann and Thompson, 1987, Reichman, 1985). In narrative, a sequence of narrative events can be interrupted by a descriptive segment, which itself contains a subnarrative concerning an element of the descriptive segment. The hierarchy structure implied by our model is exemplified in Figure 20 on page 224. The hierarchy has been shown to affect the use of pronouns, definite descriptions and deictic elements (Grosz, 1977, Reichman, 1985). Furthermore, these studies show that in a given discourse, a variety of genres can be employed at various points (as illustrated in the Levine text in "8.4. Parallelism in Coherence Exemplified" on page 217). Our claim is that, along with cue phrases, domain knowledge (such as task structure), syntax and compositional semantics, naive semantics is one of several levels of linguistic knowledge which contributes to the recovery of this structure.

Grosz and Sidner (1986) break discourse structure into three components: 1) intentional structure, which reflects the purpose of the discourse in dominance and satisfaction-precedence relationships; 2) attentional state, which contains a focus space of entities which are salient at a point in the discourse; and 3) linguistic structure, which reflects the factoring of discourse into segments. The linguistic structure is that aspect of discourse structure explicitly indicated by cue phrases, tense, aspect and intonation. The embedding structure (or hierarchy structure) is found in the linguistic structure. The attentional structure provides a saliency stack of objects, properties, events and relations which are in focus in a particular discourse segments. As the discourse proceeds sequentially, the focus spaces can be opened, closed, pushed and popped in relation to the segmentation. Grosz and Sidner show how focus spaces associated with discourse segments account for uses of pronouns. The main phenomenon, supported by our research ("8.1. Background" on page 171), is that antecedents are sought first in the current focus space (that is, among the entities and events introduced in the current segment). Another phenomenon is found with true interruptions. When segment A is interrupted with segment B, pronouns cannot refer to elements in the focus space of A, because there is an impenetrable boundary between the focus spaces.

Grosz and Sidner choose not to use coherence relations as a basis of analysis because of the exploratory nature of the relations. Instead they define dominance in the intentional structure in general terms as stemming from either a *supports* or *generates* relationship between the purposes of discourse segments. Their theory attempts to account for the structure of the discourse in terms of the intentions of the speaker with regard to the beliefs or actions of the hearer. In the *supports* relation, one proposition supports another with the intention of affecting the speaker's beliefs. In the *generates* relation, the speaker tries to get the hearer to perform a set of actions.

The rhetorical structure theory of Mann and Thompson (1987) posits relations between clauses and spans of text which are similar to the coherence relations in our model (though the content differs in some cases). Their view that coherence relations are unstated propositions in the discourse is similar to our calling them higher-order predicates. They analyze the formal structure of discourse in schemas, which consist of a nucleus and satellite. For example, in the text (187), a *circumstance* relation holds between (187c) (the nucleus) and (187d) (the satellite).

(187)   P.M. has been with KUSC longer than any other staff
         member.
         a. While attending Occidental College,

b. where he majored in philosophy,
c. he volunteered to work at the station as a classical music announcer.
d. That was in 1970.

In our model the satellite is the first argument and the nucleus is the second. If the volunteering is e_1, and the time state is s_1, the corresponding relation would be situation_time(s_1,e_1).

The Mann-Thompson model differs in several respects from ours. First, the goal of the research is to describe how an analyst should structure a given text in a top-down manner. Mann and Thompson provide no theory of how coherence relations are extracted. Secondly, the model takes into account the intended effect on the hearer. Our model ignores this complexity. This means that the Mann-Thompson definitions of causal relations are more refined than ours. Third, the relations are defined over spans of text rather than clauses and segments. This is a notational difference between our approach and theirs. Fourth, they define relations for all genres of exposition text, so that it is more inclusive. The advantages of our approach over Mann and Thompson's are that 1) we attempt to explain how relations are assigned, clause by clause, by the recipient, and 2) we provide a formal connection between discourse coherence and compositional semantics.

Lockman and Klappholz (1980) describe an algorithm for assigning contextual referents in text, where contextual referents are broadly defined as any intended connections among entities and events, mentioned or implicit. Their approach is quiet similar to ours because it sees syntactic information, tense, aspect and world knowledge as independent contributors to discourse coherence. They do not provide, as we do, any method for representing or accessing the world knowledge. On the other hand, they propose an algorithm for inferring coherence relations, which we lack at this stage. In later work, they address the problem of controlling the amount of inferencing in text understanding, which is unmanageable on its face. They suggest text-driven inference, where the system attempts to plausibly connect a new clause to the nearest clause in the text hierarchy (not the nearest on the surface). The inference mechanism quits searching as soon as it finds some plausible connection with the previous text, and assumes that it is the one intended by the speaker.

The approach in Hobbs (1985) is similar to ours because it accounts for coherence in terms of substantive coherence relations which arise from our concepts of the causal structure of the world. Many of our definitions of coherence relations are drawn from Hobbs. Further, Hobbs sees coherence structure as a hierarchy. The differences are three. Hobbs recognizes that CK representations must be employed in extracting coherence reactions, but he does not specify how this can be done. Second, his goal is to describe a procedure for analyzing texts after the fact, while ours is to account for the recipient's extraction of coherence relations as the discourse is interpreted sentence by sentence. Third, Hobbs does not attempt to integrate coherence with a formal theory of syntax or semantics.

8.6. Conclusion

When people communicate they do more than string syntactically well formed sentences together. They try to convey a meaningful picture of the world, to convince by argumentation, to get their interlocutor to act differently. Part of linguistic theory is the description and explanation of the stock of strategies speakers marshal to convey discourse meaning, which is more than the sum total of the interpretations of isolated sentences strung together. This is evident from the fact that people agree that a text with no explicit discourse clues has a certain structure. Our research and that of our predecessors shows that a that a theory of coherence is required for several reasons. Most importantly, it is needed to explain the structure of arguments, instructions, stories, and commentaries. The psycholinguistic literature amply substantiates that people extract such structures in text comprehension. In addition, the phenomenon of event anaphora to segments of text requires a theory of discourse structure. Further, there is a strong tendency to use anaphors with antecedents only inside the discourse segment, indicating that the notion of discourse segment is part of the speaker's linguistic competence. Initial work in discourse theory emphasized narrative, which is only one of a number of genres which have distinct structures and mechanisms for conveying them. It has been instructive to consider the commentary genre, as well as narrative, in our research. We found that in commentary, a special type of event is important, the **reported**, which may consist of a past event, or may not. Some **reported** events are the announcements of future events. We found that the clues in the discourse for **reported** events differed from the clues for narrative events.

Some previous work in discourse has analyzed only structural properties, to the exclusion of coherence relations (Reichman, 1985, Grosz and Sidner, 1986). The work which we follow has hypothesized a set of coherence relations (Hobbs, 1978, Hirst, 1981, Fox, 1984, Hobbs, 1985, Mann and Thompson, 1987). Our contribution has been to begin to integrate the theory of coherence with linguistic theory, particularly with Discourse Representation Theory (Asher, 1988). We have shown that the only model which makes sense given the facts of discourse interpretation, is a parallel model which sanctions unlimited access by each of the components of grammar to interpretations generated by other modules. In addition, we have shown how to use naive semantic representations to extract coherence relations from text. This theory hints at the mechanisms used by human recipients of text in building a coherent cognitive picture of its meaning.

REFERENCES

Abbott, V., B. J. Black and E. Smith. 1985. The Representation of Scripts in Memory. *Journal of Memory and Language* 24.1:179-199.

Addanki, S. and E. Davis. 1985. A Representation for Complex Physical Domains. *Proc. IJCAI* 1:443-446.

Arens, Y. 1981. Using Language and Context in the Analysis of Text. *Proc. IJCAI.*

Ashcraft, M. H. 1976. Property Norms for Typical and Atypical Items from 17 Categories: A Description and Discussion. *Memory and Cognition* 6(3):227-232.

Asher, N. 1984. Non-Monotonic Reasoning and the Conceptual Foundations of Linguistic Understanding. *Proc. AAAI Workshop on Non-Monotonic Reasoning* 1-20.

Asher, N. 1987. A Typology for Attitude Verbs and their Anaphoric Properties. *Linguistics and Philosophy* 10:125-198.

Asher, N. 1988. The Semantics for Proposition-Type Nominals and Proposition-type Anaphora. Paper Presented at the University of Texas Conference on the Structure of Events and Natural Language Metaphysics.

Asher, N. and H. Wada. 1986. BUILDRS: An Implementation of DR Theory and LFG. *Proc. International Conference on Computational Linguistics* 540-545.

Bach, E. 1981. On Time, Tense, and Aspect. An Essay in English Metaphysics. In P. Cole, ed., *Radical Pragmatics*, New York: Academic Press.

232   REFERENCES

Barwise, J. and J. Perry. 1983. *Situations and Attitudes.* Cambridge,
        MA: MIT Press.

Bauerle, R., U. Egli and A. von Stechow. 1979. *Semantics From Dif-
        ferent Points of View.* Berlin: Springer-Verlag.

Bauerle, R. 1987. Ereignisse und Representationen. Habilitationschrift.
        Universitat Konstanz.

Bennett, M. and B. Partee. 1978. *Towards the Logic of Tense and
        Aspect in English.* Bloomington, Indiana: Indiana Uni-
        versity Linguistics Club.

Berlin, B. 1972. Speculations on the Growth of Ethnobotanical No-
        menclature. *Language and Society.* 1:41-86.

Bierwisch, M. 1981. Basic Issues in the Development of Word Meaning.
        In W. Deutsch, ed., *The Child's Construction of Lan-
        guage*, New York: Academic Press, 341-380.

Black, E. W. 1986. *Towards Computational Discrimination of English
        Word Senses.* Dissertation, City University of New
        York.

Boyd, R. 1986. Natural Kinds, Homeostasis and the Limits of
        Essentialism. To appear.

Brachman, R. J. 1979. On the Epistomological Status of Semantic
        Networks. In N. J. Findler, ed., *Associative Networks.*
        New York: Academic Press.

Brachman , R. J. and J. G. Schmolze. 1985. An Overview of the
        KL-ONE Knowledge Representation System. *Cognitive
        Science* 9:171-216.

Brachman, R. J., V. P. Gilbert and H. J. Levesque. 1985. An Essential
        Hybrid Reasoning System. *Proc. IJCAI* 1:532-539.

Bransford, J. and M. K. Johnson. 1972. Contextual Prerequisites for Understanding: Some Investigations of Comprehension and Recall. *J. Verbal Learning and Verbal Behavior* 11:717-726.

Bree, D. S. and R. A. Smit. 1986. Linking Propositions. *COLING* 177-180.

Bobrow, D.G. and T. Winograd. 1977. An Overview of KRL, a Knowledge Representation Language. *Cognitive Science* 1:3-46.

Cantor, N. and W. Mischel. 1979. Prototypes in person perception. *Advances in Experimental Social Psychology* 12:3-52.

Carey, S. 1987. *Conceptual Change in Childhood.* Cambridge, MA: MIT Press.

Carlson, G. 1977. Reference to Kinds in English. University of Massachusetts, Amherst, dissertation.

Chomsky, N. 1965. *Aspects of the Theory of Syntax.* Cambridge, MA: MIT Press.

Clark, H. H. 1975. Bridging. In R. Schank and B.L. Webber, eds., *Theoretical Issues in Natural Language Processing*, Cambridge.

Clocksin and Mellish. 1986. *Programming in Prolog.*

Cohen, C. E. 1976. *Cognitive basis of stereotyping: an information processing approach to social perception.* Dissertation, University of California, San Diego.

Cohen, P. 1984. The Pragmatics of Referring and the Modality of Communication. *CL* 10:97-146.

Cohen, P. and C. R. Perrault. 1981. Elements of a Plan-Based Theory of Speech Acts. In B. L. Webber and N. Nilsson, eds., *Readings in Artificial Intelligence*, Palo Alto, CA: Tioga Publishers.

Cohen, R. 1984. A Computational Theory of the Function of Clue Words in Argument Understanding. *COLING* 251-258.

Cohn, A. G. 1985. On the Solution of Schubert's Steamroller in Many Sorted Logic. *Proc. IJCAI* 2:1169-1174.

Crain, S. and M. Steedman. 1985. On Not Being Led Up the Garden Path: the Use of Context by the Psychological Syntax Processor. In Dowty, et al.

Croft, W. 1986. *Categories and Relations in Syntax: The Clause-Level Organization of Information*. Dissertation, Stanford University.

Dahlgren, K. 1976. *Referential Semantics*. Dissertation, University of California, Los Angeles; University Microfilms.

Dahlgren, K. 1985a. The Cognitive Structure of Social Categories. *Cognitive Science* 9:379-398.

Dahlgren, K. 1985b. Social Terms and Social Reality. *Folia Linguistica Historica* 6:107-126.

Dahlgren, K. 1988a. Using Commonsense Knowledge to Disambiguate Word Senses. In F. St. Dizier and V. Dahl, eds., *Natural Language Understanding and Logic Programming 2*, Amsterdam: North Holland.

Dahlgren, K. 1988b. Origins and Conceptions of Kinds. To appear.

Dahlgren, K. and J. McDowell. 1986a. Kind Types in Knowledge Representation. *Proceedings COLING86*.

Dahlgren, K. and J. McDowell. 1986b. Using Commonsense Knowledge to Disambiguate Prepositional Phrase Modifiers. *Proceedings AAAI 86.*

Davis, T. R. and S. J. Russell. 1986. A Logical Approach to Reasoning by Analogy. *AAAI 86.*

Davis, S. and M. Mithun, eds. 1979. *Linguistics, Philosophy and Montague Grammar.* Austin: University of Texas Press.

Davidson, D. 1967. Casual Relations. *Journal of Philosophy* 64:692-703.

Decker, N. 1985. The Use of Syntactic Clues in Discourse Processing. *Proceedings Association of Computational Linguistics* 315-323.

Dorffman, M. 1986. A Model for Understanding the Points of Stories. *Proceedings, Cognitive Science Society* 262-266.

Dougherty, J. W. D. 1978. Salience and Relativity in Classification. *American Ethnologist* 5:66-80.

Dowty, D. R. 1979. *Word Meaning and Montague Grammar.* Dordrecht, Holland: D. Reidel Publishing Company.

Dowty, D. R., L. Karttunen and A. M. Zwicky. 1985. *Natural Language Parsing: Psychological, Computational and Theoretical Perspectives.* Cambridge, England: Cambridge University Press.

Dowty, D., R. Wall and S. Peters. 1981. *Introduction to Montague Semantics.* Dordrecht, Holland: D. Reidel Publishing Co.

Dunin-Keplicz and W. Lukaszewicz. 1986. Towards Discourse-Oriented Nonmonotonic System. *COLING* 504-506.

Dupre, J. 1981. Natural Kinds and Biological Taxa. *Philosophical Review* 60:66-90.

Fahlman, S. 1979. *NETL: A System for Representing and Using Real-World Knowledge.* Cambridge, MA: MIT Press.

Fehr, B. and J. A. Russell. 1984. Concept of Emotion Viewed From a Prototype Perspective. *Journal of Experimental Psychology: General* 113.3:464-486.

Field, H. 1977. Logic, Meaning and Conceptual Role. *Journal of Philosophy* 74:379-409.

Fillmore, C. 1985. Frames and the Semantics of Understanding. *Quaderni di Semantica* 6.2:222-254.

Fodor, J., M. Garrett, E. Walker and C. Parkes. 1980. Against Definitions. *Cognition* 8:263-367.

Ford, M., J. Bresnan and R. Kaplan. 1981. A Competence-Based Theory of Syntactic Closure. In Joan Bresnan, ed., *The Mental Representation of Grammatical Relations*, Cambridge, MA: MIT Press.

Fox, B. 1984. *Discourse Structure and Anaphora in Written and Conversational English.* Dissertation, University of California, Los Angeles; University Microfilms.

Gawron, J. M. 1983. *Lexical Representations and the Semantics of Complementation.* Dissertation, University of California, Berkeley.

Gelman, R. and Spelke, E. 1981. Thoughts about Animate and Inanimate Objects. In J. H. Flavell and L. Ross, eds., *Social Cognitive Development*, Cambridge, England: Cambridge University Press.

Graesser, A. and Clark, L. 1985a. *Structure and Procedures of Implicit Knowledge.* Norwood, NJ: Ablex. Graesser, A. and L. Clark. 1985b. The Generation of Knowledge-Based Inferences during Narrative Comprehension. In G. Rickheit and H. Strohner, eds., *Inferences in Text Processing*, Amsterdam: North-Holland.

Graesser, A. and P. Hopkinson. 1987. Differences in Interconcept Organization between Nouns and Verbs. *Journal of Memory and Language* 26.

Green, G. 1983. *Some Remarks on How Words Mean.* Bloomington, Indiana: Indiana University Linguistics Club.

Grice, H. P. 1969. Utterer's Meaning and Intentions. *Philosophical Review* 78:147-77.

Gross, M. 1985. Projecting the lexicon-grammar on Texts. Paper presented at the Roman Jakobson Conference, New York University.

Grosz, B. 1977. The Representation and Use of Focus in Dialogue understanding. SRI Technical Note #151.

Grosz, B. 1981. Focusing and Description in Natural Language Dialogues. In Joshi, Webber and Sag.

Grosz, B. and C. Sidner. 1986. Attention, Intensions and the Structure of Discourse. *ACL* 12:175-204.

Gruber, J. S. 1976. *Lexical Structures in Syntax and Semantics.*

Gupta, A. 1980. *The Logic of Common Nouns.* New Haven: Yale University Press.

Hahn, U. 1984. Textual Expertise in Words Experts. *COLING* 402-407.

Halpern, J. 1985. *Theoretical Aspects of Reasoning About Knowledge.* Los Altos, CA: Morgan Kaufmann.

Haugeland, J. 1986. *Artificial Intelligence: The Very Idea.* Cambridge: MIT Press.

Hayes, P.J. 1977. On Semantic Nets, Frames and Associations. *Proc. IJCAI.* 99-107.

Hayes, P. J. 1985. The Second Naive Physics Manifesto. In J. R. Hobbs and R. C. Moore, eds., *Formal Theories of the Commonsense World*, Norwood, NJ: Ablex.

Heeschen, C. 1979. On the Representation of Classificatory and Prepositional Lexical Relations in the Human Brain. In Bauerle, Egli and von Stechow, eds.

Heim, I. 1982. *The Semantics of Definite and Indefinite Noun Phrases.* Dissertation, University of Massachusetts.

Hendrix, G. G. 1979. Encoding Knowledge in Partitioned Networks. In N. J. Findler, ed., *Associative Networks*, New York: Academic Press.

Herskovits, A. 1985. Semantics and Pragmatics of Locative Expressions. *Cognitive Science.* 9:341-378.

Hinrichs, E. W. 1987. A Compositional Semantics of Temporal Expressions in English. *Proc. Assoc. Computational Linguistics* 8-15.

Hirst, G. 1984. A Semantic Process for Syntactic Disambiguation. *AAAI* 341-378.

Hirst, G. 1981. Discourse-Oriented Anaphora Resolution: A Review. *ACL*7:85-98.

Hirst, G. 1987. *Semantic Interpretation and the Resolution of Ambiguity.* Cambridge, England: Cambridge University Press.

Hobbs, J. 1979. Coherence and Coreference. *Cognitive Science* 3: 67-90.

Hobbs, J. 1978. Why is Discourse Coherent? SRI Technical Note #176.

Hobbs, J. R. and R. C. Moore. 1985. *Formal Theories of the Commonsense World.* Norwood, NJ: Ablex.

Hobbs, J. R., T. Blenko, B. Croft, G. Hager, H. A. Kautz, P. Kube and Y. Shoham. 1985. *Commonsense Summer: Final Report.* Stanford, CA: CSLI Report.

Hobbs, J. R., W. Croft, T. Davies, D. Edwards and K. Laws. 1986. Commonsense Metaphysics and Lexical Semantics. *Proceedings ACL86* 231-240.

Hopper, P. and S. Thompson. 1980. Transitivity in Grammar and Discourse. *Language* 56:251-299.

Huttenlocher, J. and F. Lui. 1979. The Semantic Organization of Some Simple Nouns and Verbs. *Journal of Memory and Language* 18:141-162.

IBM. 1985. VM Programming in Logic (VM/PROLOG), Program Description and Operations Manual, IBM Corporation.

Jackendoff, R. 1983. *Semantics and Cognition.* Cambridge, MA: MIT Press.

Johnson-Laird, P. N. 1983. *Mental Models.* Cambridge, MA: Harvard University Press.

Johnson, P. and W. Lehnert. 1986. Beyond Exploratory Programming : A Methodology and Environment for Conceptual Natural Language Processing. *Proceedings AAAI* 594-600.

Joshi, A., B. Webber and I. Sag. 1981. *Elements of Discourse Understanding*. Cambridge, England: Cambridge, England: Cambridge University Press.

Katz, J.J. 1972. *Semantic Theory*. New York: Harper & Row.

Katz, J.J. and J.A. Fodor. 1963. The Structure of Semantic Theory. *Language* 39:170-210.

Kay, P. and C.K. McDaniel. 1978. The Linguistic Significance of the Meanings of Basic Color Terms. *Language* 54:610-646.

Kamp, H. 1981. A Theory of Truth and Semantic Representation. In J. Groenendijk, Th. Janssen, and M. Stokhof, eds., *Formal Methods in the Study of Language*, Amsterdam: Mathematisch Centrum, 277-322.

Kamp, H. 1979. Events, Instants and Temporal Reference. In Bauerle, Egli and Von Stechow, eds.

Keil, F. C. 1979. *Semantic and Conceptual Development*, Cambridge, MA: Harvard University Press.

Kripke, S. 1972. Naming and Necessity. In G. Harmon and D. Davidson, eds., *The Semantics of Natural Language*, Dordrecht, Holland: D. Reidel Publishing Company.

Kroll, J. F. and M. C. Potter. 1984. Recognizing Words, Pictures and Concepts: a Comparison of Lexical, Object and Reality Decisions. *J. Verbal Learning and Verbal Behavior* 23:39-66.

Kusanagi, Y. 1984. Some Linguistic Aspects for Automatic Text Understanding. *COLING* 409-412.

Labov, W. 1972. *Language in the Inner City*, Philadelphia: University of Pennsylvania Press.

Labov, W. 1973. The Boundaries of Words and their Meanings. In C-J. N. Bailey and R. Shuy, eds., *New Ways of Analyzing Variation in English*, Washington: Georgetown University Press.

Lenat, D., M. Prakash, and M. Shepard. 1986. CCY: Using Common Sense Knowledge to Overcome Brittleness and Knowledge Acquistion Bottlenecks. *AI Magazine* 4:65-85.

Levesque, H. 1984. The Logic of Incomplete Knowledge Bases. In M. L. Brodie, J. Mylopoulos and J.W. Schmidt, eds., *On Conceptual Modeling*, New York: Springer-Verlag.

Litman, D. and J. F. Allen. 1984. A Plan Recognition Model for Clarification Subdialogues. *COLING* 302-311.

Lockman, A. and A. D. Klappholz. 1980. Toward a Procedural Model of Contextual Reference Resolution. *Discourse Processes* 3:25-71.

Macnamara, John. 1982. *Names for Things*. Cambridge, MA: MIT Press.

Mann, W. and S. Thompson. 1985. Assertions from Discourse Structure. *Proc. Berkeley Linguistic Society*.

Mann, W. and S. Thompson. 1987. Rhetorical Structure Theory: A Theory of Text Organization. ISI Reprint Series: ISI-RS-87-190.

Marslen-Wilson, W.D. and L.K. Tyler. 1980. The Temporal Structure
    of Spoken Language Understanding. *Cognition*. 8:1-71.

Matthiessen, C. and S. Thompson. To appear. The Structure of Dis-
    course and "Subordination". In J. Haiman and S. A.
    Thompson, eds., *Clause Combining in Discourse and
    Grammar*,

McCarthy, J. and P. J. Hayes. 1969. Some Philosophical Problems
    from the Standpoint of Artificial Intelligence. In B.
    Meltzer and D. Michie, eds., *Machine Intelligence 4*.
    New York: Elsevier.

McCord, M. 1985. *The Lexical Base for Semantic Interpretation in a
    Prolog Parser*. Presented at workshop on the Lexicon,
    Parsing and Semantic Interpretation. City University of
    New York Graduate Center.

McCord, M. 1987. Natural Language Processing in Prolog. In A.
    Walker, ed., *Knowledge Systems and Prolog*. Reading,
    MA: Addison-Wesley.

McCoy, K. 1985. The Role of Perspective in Responding to Property
    Misconceptions. *Proc. of the Ninth Joint Conference on
    Artificial Intelligence*.

McDowell, J. 1981. Anti-Realism and the Epistemology of Under-
    standing. In H. Parret and Y. J. Bouveresse, eds., *Mean-
    ing and Understanding*, Berlin: Walter de Gruyter and
    Company, 225-249.

McDowell, J. 1987. Assertion and Modality. University of Southern
    California dissertation.

McDowell J. and K. Dahlgren. 1987. Commonsense Reasoning with
    Verbs. *Proc. IJCAI*.

Mervis, C. and J. Pani. 1980. Acquisition of Basic Object Categories. *Cognitive Psychology* 12:496-522.

Miller, G. 1978. Practical and Lexical Knowledge. In E. Rosch and B. B. Lloyd, eds., *Cognition and Categorization.* New York: Erlbaum.

Miller, G. and P. N. Johnson-Laird. 1976. *Language and Perception.* Cambridge, MA: Belknap Press of Harvard University Press.

Milne, R. 1986. Resolving Lexical Ambiguity in a Deterministic Parser. *Computational Linguistics* 12:1-12.

Minsky, M. 1975. A Framework for Representing Knowledge. In P. Winston, ed., *The Psychology of Computer Vision,* New York: McGraw-Hill.

Moens, M. and M. Steedman. 1987. Temporal Ontology in Natural Language. *Proc. Assoc. Computational Linguistics* 1-7.

Montague, R. 1974. *Formal Philosophy,* Introduction. R. H. Thomason, ed., New Haven: Yale University Press.

Morgenstern, M. 1984. Constraint Equations: A Concise Compilable Representation for Quantified Constraints in Semantic Networks. *Proc. AAAI.*

Osherson, D. N. and E. E. Smith. 1981. On the Adequacy of Prototype Theory as a Theory of Concepts. *Cognition* 9:35-58.

Parsons, T. 1985. Underlying Events in the Logical Analysis of English. In E. LePore and B. McLaughlin, eds., *Actions and Events: Perspectives on the Philosophy of Donald Davidson.* Oxford: Basil Blackwell.

Partee, B. 1979. Semantics : Mathematics or Psychology? In Bauerle, Egli and Von Stechow, eds., *Semantics from Different Points of View*. Berlin: Springer-Verlag.

Partee, B. 1982. Belief Sentences and the Limits of Semantics. In S. Peters and E. Saarinen, eds., *Processes, Beliefs and Questions*, Dordrecht, Holland: D. Reidel.

Partee, B. 1984. Nominal and Temporal Anaphora. *Linguistics and Philosophy* 7:243-286.

Polanyi, L. 1985. A Theory of Discourse Structure and Discourse Coherence. *Chicago Linguistic Society 21*.

Polanyi, L. and R. Scha. 1984. A Syntactic Approach to Discourse Semantics. *COLING* 413-419.

Putnam, H. 1973. Is Semantics Possible? *Mind, Language and Reality*, Cambridge, England: Cambridge University Press.

Putnam, H. 1975. The Meaning of 'Meaning'. *Mind, Language and Reality*, Cambridge, England: Cambridge University Press.

Quine, W. V. O. 1969. *Ontological Relativity and Other Essays*, Cambridge, England: Cambridge University Press.

Reichman, R. 1985. *Getting Computers to Talk Like You and Me*. Cambridge, MA: MIT Press.

Reichenbach, H. 1937. *Elements of Symbolic Logic*. Berkeley, CA: University of California Press.

Reinhart, T. 1982. Principles of Gestalt Perception in the Temporal Organization of Narrative Texts. Manuscript.

Reiter, R. 1980. A Logic for Default Reasoning. *Artificial Intelligence* 13:81-132.

Rickheit, G. and H. Strohner. 1985. *Inferences in Text Processing.* Amsterdam: North-Holland.

Rifkin, A. 1985. Evidence for a Basic Level in Event Taxonomies. *Memory and Cognition* 13:538-556.

Rosch, E. 1975. Cognitive Representations of Semantic Categories. *Journal of Experimental Psychology-General* 204:192-233.

Rosch, E. 1977. Linguistic Relativity. In P. N. Johnson-Laird and P. C. Wason, eds., *Thinking.* Cambridge, England: Cambridge University Press.

Rosch, E. 1978. Principles of Categorization. In E. Rosch and B. B. Lloyd, eds., *Cognition and Categorization,* New Jersey: L. Erlbaum.

Rosch, E. and C. B. Mervis. 1975. Family Resemblances. *Cognitive Psychology* 7:573-605.

Rosch, E., C. B. Mervis, W. D. Gray, D. M. Johnson, and P. Boyes-Braem. 1976. Basic Objects in Natural Categories. *Cognitive Psychology* 8:382-439.

Rumelhart, D.E. 1977. Understanding and Summarizing Brief Stories. In D. LaBerge and S.J. Samuels, eds., *Basic Processes in Reading.*

Sachs, J. S. 1967. Recognition Memory for Syntactic and Semantic Aspects of Connected Discourse. *Perception and Psychophysics* 2:437-442.

Salter, W. 1983. Tacit Economic Theories. *Proceedings of the Fifth Annual Meeting of the Cognitive Science Society.*

Sanford, J. A. and S. Garrod. 1981. *Understanding Written Language: Explorations of Comprehension.* Wiley Press.

Schank, R. C. and R. P. Abelson. 1977. *Scripts, Plans, Goals and Understanding*. Hillsdale, NJ: Erlbaum.

Schank, R. C. and J. G. Carbonell, Jr. 1979. Re: The Gettysburg Address. Representing Social and Political Acts. In N. Findler, ed., *Associative Networks*, New York: Academic Press.

Schank, R. and C. Riesbeck. 1981. *Inside Computer Understanding*. New Jersey: Lawrence Erlbaum.

Schubert, L. K., R.G. Goebel, and N.J. Cercone. 1979. The Structure and Organization of a Semantic Net for Comprehension and Inference. In N.V. Findler, ed., *Associative Networks*. New York: Academic Press.

Schwartz, S. P. 1979. Natural Kind Terms. *Cognition* 7:301-315.

Schiffren, D. 1987. *Discourse Markers*. Cambridge, England: Cambridge University Press.

Sidner, C. 1985. Focusing in the Comprehension of Definite Anaphora. In R. Berwick and M. Brady, eds., *Computational Models of Discourse*, Cambridge, MA: MIT Press, 267-330.

Smith, E. E. and D. L. Medin. 1981. *Categories and Concepts*, Cambridge, MA: Harvard University Press.

Soames, S. 1985. How Presuppositions are Inherited: A Solution to the Projection Problem. *Linguistic Inquiry* 13:483-545.

Stabler, E. P., Jr., and G. O. Tarnawsky. 1986. NL/Prolog---A Prolog-Based Natural Language Facility. To appear.

Steedman, M. 1977. Verbs, Time, and Modality. *Cognitive Science* 1:216-234.

Steedman, M. J. and P. N. Johnson-Laird. 1976. A Programmatic Theory of Linguistic Performance. In P. Smith and R. Campbell, eds., *Advances in the Psychology of Language: Formal and experimental approaches*, Plenum.

Strawson, P. C. 1953. *Individuals*. London: Methuen.

Swinney, D. A. 1979. Lexical Access During Sentence Comprehension: (re) Consideration of Context Effects. *Journal of Verbal Learning and Verbal Behavior* 15:681-689.

Talmy, L. 1976. Semantics of Causative Types. In M. Shibatani, ed., *Syntax and Semantics 6*, New York: Academic Press.

Talmy, L. 1985. Force Dynamics in Language and Thought. In W. H. Eilfort, P. Kroeber and K. L. Peterson, eds., *Proc. Parasession on Causatives and Agentivity, 21st Chicago Linguistics Society*.

Tarnawsky, G. O. 1982. *Knowledge Semantics*. Dissertation, New York University.

Tenenbaum, J. D. 1985. Taxonomic Reasoning. *Proc. IJCAI* 1:191-193.

Tomita, M. 1985. An Efficient Context-Free Parsing Algorithm for Natural Languages. *Proc. IJCAI*.

Thorndyke, P. W. 1977. Cognitive Structures in Comprehension and Memory of Narrative Discourse. *Cognitive Psychology* 9:77-110.

Thompson, S. 1984. "Subordination" and Narrative Event Structure. Paper presented at Conference on Linguistic Coding of Discourse Relations.

Trabasso, T. and Sperry, L. L. 1985. Causal Relatedness and Importance of Story Events. *Journal of Memory and Language* 24.1:595-611.

Trabasso, T. and P. van den Broek. 1985. Casual Thinking and the Representation of Narrative Events. *Journal of Memory and Language* 24.5:612-630.

Tucker, A., S. Nirenburg and V. Raskin. 1986. Discourse and Cohesion in Expository Text. *COLING* 181-183.

Tversky, B. and K. Hemenway. 1983. Categories of Environmental Scenes. *Cognitive Psychology* 15:121-149.

Vendler, Z. 1967. *Linguistics in Philosophy*. Ithaca, New York: Cornell University Press.

Vlach, F. 1981. The Semantics of the Progressive. In *.Syntax and Semantics 14*, New York: Academic Press.

Waltz, D. L. 1981. Toward a Detailed Model of Processing for Language Describing the Physical World. *Proc. IJCAI*.

Warren, D. H. D. 1981. Efficient Processing of Interactive Relational Database Queries Expressed in Logic. *7th Intl.Conf. on Very Large Databases*, Cannes, France.

Webber, B. L. 1985. Discourse Model Synthesis. In R. Berwick and M. Brady, eds., *Computational Models of Discourse*, Cambridge, MA: MIT Press, 267-330.

Wilks, Y. 1975. Preference Semantics. In E. Keenan, ed., *Formal Semantics of Natural Language*, Cambridge, England, Cambridge University Press.

Wilks, Y., X. Huang and D. Fass. 1985. Syntax, Preference and Right Attachment. *IJCAI*.

Winograd, T. 1972. *Understanding Natural Language*. New York: Academic Press.

Winograd, T. 1976. Towards a Procedural Understanding of Semantics. *Revue Internationale de Philosophie* 117-118:260-303.

Wong, Wing-Kwong C. 1986. A Theory of Argument Coherence. University of Texas AI Laboratory. #AI TR86-29.

Index

Abbott 2
Abelson 26,226
ABSTRACT 45-49, 107
ACCOMPLISHMENT
88-93, 203, 207, 210
ACHIEVEMENT 33, 83-93,
203, 204, 207ff, 223, 225
ACTIVITY 33, 83-94
Agent 24, 90, 91, 150, 167,
175, 196, 200, 202, 224
Algorithm 9, 106, 117-119,
121, 189, 191, 194, 209, 211,
228
  prepositional phrase attachment Chapter 6
  word sense
  disambiguation Chapter 7
Ambiguity 9, 10, 22, 24, 41,
43, 51
  lexical Chapter 7,
  semantic 124
  syntactic 10, 123, 124,
  Chapter 6
Anaphora 8, 105, 143, 175,
186, 187, 194, 229
Arens 125
Arguments Chapter 4, 172,
177, 179, 184, 187, 229
Artificial Intelligence 6,
38-40, 61, 65, 73, 75, 115
Ashcraft 29, 31, 58, 61
Asher 40, 43, 105, 171, 174,
185, 186, 196, 200, 230
Association 135, 142,
168-169

Attentional structure 227

Bach 173
Barwise 82, 185
Belief 6, 14, 32, 36, 41, 45,
173, 196, 200, 227
Bennett 85
Berlin 29
Black 91, 141ff, 151
Boyd 65
Brachman 25, 33
Bransford 5
Bresnan 126, 135, 137

Cantor 58
Categorization 18, 79, 88ff,
95
Causality 38, 91, 96, 185
  and clausal relations 178,
  180, 192, 211, 213, 225
Cause 5, 9, 19, 27, 97, 101,
121, 155, Chapter 8
CAUSE 19, 20, 24
Chomsky 128
Clark 7, 29, 33, 91, 95ff,
187, 189, 221
Cognitive categories 68
Coherence relation Chapter
8
  goal 99, 180
  activity 182
  biased comment 183

cause 178, 180, 192, 211, 213, 225
comment 223ff
contrast 180
description 174, 206, 225
elaboration 220
enablement 179
evaluation 182, 202, 225
evidence 181
generalization 181, 225
goal 180, 184, 185, 193, 197
import 183, 206, 225
parallel 225
qualification 202
situation 182, 192, 204, 206, 217, 225
situation-activity 220, 224, 225
situation-place 183
situation-time 183
unbiased comment 183
Cohn 75
COLLECTIVE 8, 47, 49, 93, 94
Commonsense knowledge
    as lexical semantics Chapter 1
    representation Chapters 2-4
    in disambiguation Chapters 6,7
    in coherence relation assignment 205-221
    in text interpretation 3-9, Chapter 5

Commentary 175, 177-179, 183, 198ff, 217, 218, 221, 223, 225, 230
Communication 29, 35, 65ff
company 93
Competence 13, 229
Compositionality 11
Computational linguistics 39, 43
Concept Chapter 1
Conceptual dependency 24
CONCRETE 55
Conditional 12ff, 36, 43, 66, 68, 175, 185, 190, 191, 196
Conjunction 13, 70, 123, 149, 163
Context 39, 40, 135, 136, 146, 156, 185, 187, 195, 196, 200, 206, 225, 228
    discourse 39, 136, 195
Convention 66, 131, 224
Crain 126, 136, 137
Creativity 16, 17, 71
Culture 3, 5, 28, 29, 31, 66, 67

Database
    generic 108, 165
    ontological 107, 123
    textual 106ff
    typing 113
Decker 198, 200
Definite article 146, 158, 161
Definite description 185, 187, 217, 226
Disambiguation 9, 22, 24, 36, 43, 105, 106, 118, 190

prepositional phrase
Chapter 6
word sense Chapter 7
Discourse Representation
Theory (DRT) 11, 171,
185-189, 191, 230
Discourse segment 158, 174,
175, 194, 196, 197, 221, 223,
227, 229
Dougherty 29
Dowty 80, 86, 88, 206
Dunin-Keplicz 40
Dupre 67

EMOTIONAL 90, 93
ENTITY 47, 49, 59, 74, 75,
110
Event Chapters 4, 8
   discourse 185
EVENT 19, 52, 83, 84, 93,
94, 96, 99, 203
Explanation 83, 173, 175,
226, 229

Fahlman 33
Family resemblance 15, 29,
82
Feature types 34ff, 45, 57,
61, 70ff, 95ff, 114, 115, 120
Fehr 29, 58
Fillmore 26, 69
Focus 83, 137, 178, 226, 227
Fodor 11, 12, 125, 135, 136
Ford 126, 135, 137
Fox 173, 177-181, 223, 230

Frame 11, 24ff, 63, 88ff,
138, 168, 173, 186, 191
Functions 80, 98, 117, 175,
181, 198

Garrod 5
Gawron 127, 129
Gelman 50, 51, 56, 90
GOAL 8, 24, 33, 91ff, 120,
203ff, 223, 225
Graesser 7, 29, 33, 82, 91,
95, 96, 99, 100, 189, 221
Green 69
Grice 41
Gross 141
Grosz 171-173, 175-178, 192,
223, 226, 227, 230

Halpern 40, 41
Haugeland 6
Hayes 6, 40, 168
Heim 11, 171
Hendrix 107
Herskovits 127
Heuristics 42, 204
Hinrichs 206
Hirst 27, 101, 126, 135ff,
168, 178-181, 230
Hobbs 6, 38, 167, 171, 173,
178-182, 223, 226, 229, 230
Hopkinson 82
Hopper 176, 198, 199ff, 220
Huttenlocher 82, 90, 95

Ideal 184

Indefinite article 146, 158
INDIVIDUAL 47, 49, 59,
93, 94, 110
Inference
  naive Chapter 1, Chapter
  5
  heuristics 42, 204
  KT inference mechanism
  110, 111, 120

Jackendoff 13, 18ff, 65, 69,
97, 101
Johnson 5, 13, 17, 18, 26,
69, 95, 101, 190
Johnson-Laird 5, 13, 17, 18,
69, 95, 101, 190

Kamp 11, 36, 171, 206, 208
Kaplan 126, 135, 137
Katz 15
Keil 46, 50, 71
Kind types 35, 45, 70, 71,
76, 105
Kinds 11, 14, 17, 18, 51,
65ff, 80ff, 93, 107, 193, 198
Klappholz 171, 178, 226,
228
Knowledge
  complete 42
  generic 7ff, 29, 33, 45,
  61ff, 76, 79, 101, 108, 111,
  116, 118, 120, 143, 149,
  152
  incomplete 42
  ontological 8, 33, 110,
  117, 118, 191, 224

Kripke 65, 66

Labov 15, 175, 198
Learning 17, 29
Lehnert 26
Lenat 39
Levesque 108
Lexicon 14, 17, 49, 93, 96,
105, 132ff, 141, 156, 169
  representation 23, 40, 43,
  90, 101
  syntactic 141
Liquid 14, 29, 33
Litman 178
Living 15, 52
Location 19, 23, 27, 48, 51,
76, 80, 95, 130, 134
Lockman 171, 173, 178, 226,
228
Logic 39, 40, 41, 105ff, 121,
159, 160, 164, 177, 187, 197
  first-order 37
Lui 82, 90, 95, 100

Manner 93, 131, 228
Marslen-Wilson 18, 69, 194,
195
Mass 39, 49, 93, 94, 195
McDowell 34, 69, 79, 123,
153, 157, 177
Meaning
  extension 11-18, 25, 26,
  35, 39, 66, 77, 80, 83, 191
  intension 11, 12, 17, 184
  necessary and sufficient
  conditions Chapter 1

of nouns Chapter 2
of verbs Chapter 4
of prepositions Chapter 6
reference See Reference
Memory 28, 39, 142, 191
Mervis 15, 29
Metainterpreter 110
Metaphor 24, 34, 40, 60, 70, 96, 121
MENTAL 90, 93, 100, 203, 223
Metasorts 35, 75
Miller 51, 36, 69, 95, 101
Milne 101
Minimal attachment 135
Minsky 26
Mischel 58
Model
cognitive 9, 12, 21, 28, 32, 45, 65, 166
computer 26, 46
mental 136
parallel 184ff
Moens 88, 89, 192, 206, 211
Montague grammar 11, 80
Moore 6
move 154
Naive inference Chapter 1, Chapter 5, Chapter 8

Naive semantics 29ff (defined)
Narrative 41, 95, 171, 174-177, 179, 181, 198ff, 207, 208, 217ff, 226, 229, 230

NATURAL 33, 35, 49, 51, 52, 70, 71, 93, 99, 100, 155
Negation 180, 204, 206
Nominalization 200, 203, 206
NONGOAL 91-95, 120
NONLIVING 46
NONMENTAL 90, 93, 100
NONRELATIONAL 82
NONSELFMOVING 56
NONSTATIONARY 46
Nouns Chapter 2
office 4, 144

Ontological categories 89, 90
Ontology
and disambiguation 128, 147, 154
noun 45
verb 79
and disambiguation
parallel 47, 94
temporal 79
Opaque context 200, 206

Pani 29
Parallel model 171, 190, 196, 209, 211, 230
Parser 105, 123, 127, 123, 127, 132, 128, 165, 193
Parsons 206
Partee 85, 191, 206, 207, 218
Particle 38, 153
Perry 82, 185
PHYSICAL 49ff, 74, 75, 98, 99, 149ff

Pictures 3, 5, 11, 12, 32,34, 62, 70, 187, 191ff, 221, 229, 230
Polanyi 178
PLACE 8, 48, 51, 55, 118, 129, 146-157, 163, 167
Plausibility 136-8
Pragmatics 28, 195
Preference strategy 24, 106, 123-128, 137, 138, 166
Prepositional phrase attachment 43, Chapter 6, 157, 195
Presupposition 136, 137
Principle of A Priori Plausibility 136
Principle of Parsimony 136
Principle of Referential Success 136
Probabilities 43, 112
Projection rules 11
Pronouns 4, 41, 117,143, 146, 147, 149, 174, 175, 185ff, 226, 227
Propositional 128, 186, 192, 200, 225
Prototype 7, 29, 31, 45, 58, 108
Psycholinguistics 7, 9, 28, 32, 34, 37, 45, 58, 59, 75, 82, 90, 91, 141, 143, 190, 194, 221, 229
Psychological reality 29ff
Purpose 89, 176, 200, 226, 227
Putnam 12, 14, 20, 65, 66

Query Chapter 5
Quine 65

Realist theory of semantics 29ff, Chapter 3
REAL 45
Recursion 110
Reference 11, 12, 19, 48, 67, 68, 89, 129, 137, 186, 187, 197ff, 207ff, 218, 223
    anaphoric 4, 8, 10, 41, 105, 106, 117, 143, 174, 175, 186, 187, 191, 194, 215, 229
    causal chain 67, 190
    and semantics Chapter 3
    discourse 188
Reichenbach 206, 207
Reichman 174ff, 192, 223, 226, 230
Reinhart 176, 199
Reiter 40, 107
RELATIONAL 52, 82, 83, 90, 93, 99, 100
Rickheit 11, 221
Riesbeck 95
Right association 135
ROLE 33, 52, 59, 72-75, 93, 111, 115, 120, 146, 154,
Rumelhart 174
Russell 29, 58, 185

Sachs 190
Salter 6
Sanford 5

Schank 10, 23ff, 95, 101, 226
Schiffren 192
Schmolze 25
Schubert 32, 37, 76
Script 24, 26
Selectional restrictions 45, 55, 56, 96, 100, 131, 141, 150ff, 163, 168
SELFMOVING 55, 56
Semantic
   fields 37, 69, 82, 95, 100
   interpretation 127, 142, 185, 189
   networks 25
   primitives 17ff, 69, 97
   translation 106, 194
   component 10, 36, 193, 195
   decompositional 18ff
   model-theoretic 10, 106, 185-189
   naive Chapter 1
SENTIENT 7, 35, 48ff, 70, 74, 90, 110, 115, 118, 129, 150ff
Sidner 172ff, 186, 192, 223, 226, 227, 230
Smith 13, 19, 69, 91
SOCIAL 33, 49ff, 73, 75, 92, 93, 98, 99, 110, 115, 118, 129, 149ff 203, 223
Solid 6
Sowa 24, 101
Space 31, 38, 82, 102, 103, 145, 165 175, 186, 201, 202, 208ff, 216, 222, 226, 227
Spelke 50, 51, 56, 90

Sperry 91, 96
Stabler 105, 110
STATE 84-86, 94, 96
STATIONARY 55
STATIVE 83, 93, 118, 129, 134, 203
Steedman 88, 89, 94, 126, 136, 137, 192, 206, 211
Stereotype 14, 15, 17
Strawson 50, 90
Strohner 11, 221
Syntax 10, 36, 105, 131, 143, 171, 184, 191ff, 204, 217ff, 226, 229
   relation to semantics

Tarnawsky 18, 69, 105, 110
Taxonomy 33, 45, 57, 62
TEMPORAL 49, 79ff
Tenenbaum 107
Tense 80, 83, 119, 173, 175, 189, 198ff, 218ff, 225ff
Thompson 173, 176ff, 198ff, 220, 223, 226ff, 230
Thorndyke 174
Tomita 125
Trabasso 91, 96
Transportability 26
Truth 11-18, 25, 26, 32-36, 66ff, 80,174, 175, 181, 185, 186, 190, 191, 196
Tyler 18, 194, 195
Typicality Chapter 1, 58-62, 79, 82, 96-101, 108, 111-118, 124, 126, 130ff, 149, 158, 163, 173, 177, 191, 204, 211ff, 220, 221

Vagueness 15, 27, 36, 77
Vendler 79, 83, 86, 88, 89, 94
Verbs Chapter 4

Wall Street Journal 57, 175, 178
Words
  definition 15, 25, 26, 38, 62, 66, 108,177ff, 198, 228, 229
  instantiation 37, 48, 173
  learning 17, 29
  meanings 11-40, 68-70, 77, Chapter 7